Teaching with the Internet™

Putting teachers before technology

Douglas R. Steen
Mark R. Roddy, Ph.D.
Derek Sheffield
Michael Bryan Stout

Illustrated by D.J. Hura

Resolution Business Press, Inc.
Bellevue, Wash.

Teaching with the Internet™

Douglas R. Steen, Mark R. Roddy, Ph.D.,
Derek Sheffield and Michael Bryan Stout

Copyright © 1995, Douglas R. Steen *et al.*
Illustrations by D.J. Hura
Illustrations © 1995, Resolution Business Press, Inc.
Cover design by John Fosberg
Cover design © 1995, Resolution Business Press, Inc.
Third printing, 1996

Teaching with the Internet: Putting Teachers Before Technology is a trademark of Resolution Business Press, inc.

In giving information about electronic services and related software and hardware products, this book mentions numerous companies and their products and services by their trade names. In most cases, these designations are claimed as trademark by the respective companies. It is not the publisher's or authors' intent to use any of these names generically, and the reader is cautioned to investigate all claimed trademark rights before using any of these names in any way other than for the company, service or product described.

Every effort has been made to make this book complete and as accurate as possible. But no warranty of suitability, purpose or fitness is implied. The information is provided on an "as is" basis. The authors and the publisher, Resolution Business Press, Inc., shall have neither liability nor responsibility to any person or entity with respect to any loss or damages in connection with, or arising from, the information contained in this book.

Published by
Resolution Business Press, Inc.
11101 N.E. 8th St., Suite 208
Bellevue, WA 98004
Phone: 206-455-4611
Fax: 206-455-9143
E-mail: rbpress@halcyon.com or teaching.with.the.internet@pobox.com
http://www.halcyon.com/ResPress/teacher.htm

Manufactured in Canada

Library of Congress Cataloging in Publication Data

Main entry under title:

Steen, Douglas R.
Teaching with the Internet
ISBN 0-945264-19-4

Praise for Teaching with the Internet

"When I begin [using the Internet], my mouse will be in my right hand and your book will be in my left hand." — **Carol Corrody, elementary teacher, Durant Road Elementary, Raleigh, N.C.**

"This is a people book... [It] offers access to the arcane world of the Internet for we older folk [who] didn't grow up with computers." — **Sally Porter, English teacher, Montgomery Blair High School, Silver Spring, Md.**

"Thank you for sifting, sorting, and organizing a vast amount of information and grounding it [in] territory that is familiar to me. You've broken the image of impossible-to-use computer manuals and utilized sound teaching methods: step-by-step directions, excellent graphics, as well as a strong motivational component." — **Judy Purvis, early elementary teacher, Meyler Street School, Los Angeles, Calif.**

"This book reminds me of a kind explanation: which fork to use for the salad when I arrive at the sit-down Internet meal." — **Kevin Miller, department chair, Gig Harbor High School, Gig Harbor, Wash.**

*This book is dedicated to the teachers,
past and present, who have taught us
to love learning.*

Acknowledgments

We would like to thank all the teachers who read this book in its early stages, who answered our questions in person and over the Internet, and who provided valuable insights into how the Internet is and *should* be used. We are also indebted to Mari Andonian and Debi Wilson for their work on the original version of this project, and Karen Strudwick, John Spilker, and Bob Steen for their contributions to the book as it now stands. Finally, we thank our families for their love and support.

About the authors

Douglas R. Steen is project coordinator in charge of building the Madison Valley Electronic Village Project in Seattle; before joining the teaching profession, he was a software developer. He received a Master's in Teaching degree from Seattle University, and degrees from Brown University in computer science and Russian language and literature.

Mark R. Roddy has taught in grades 6 through 12 and is currently Assistant Professor of Education in the Master's in Teaching Program at Seattle University, where he focuses on integrated mathematics, science and technology education for kindergarten through grade 12 pre-service teachers. He holds a Ph.D. in Mathematics Education from the University of Washington.

Derek Sheffield is a high school language arts teacher in Gig Harbor, Wash., and teaches introductory Internet classes for the Peninsula School District. He received his Master's in Teaching degree from Seattle University.

Michael Bryan Stout is a sixth-grade teacher at the Bush School in Seattle and provides Internet training to professional teachers in the Seattle School District. He holds a Master's in Teaching degree from Seattle University.

D.J. Hura is a freelance artist concentrating on graphic illustration and fine art. He attended the University of Michigan where he received a Bachelor of Fine Arts degree in painting and sculpture.

Preface

Is this book for me?

This book is for teachers who would like to use the Internet. It is based on the assumption that when it comes to K-12 education, teachers know best. The best way to help students is to help you, their teacher, and we want to help you learn about a new, powerful, and possibly indispensable educational tool: the Internet. We want to do more than teach you how to use it, we want to teach you how to use it *effectively*.

Although this book is designed specifically for K-12 classroom teachers, other educators may find it useful as well. If you work outside the classroom as a school librarian, technology specialist, teacher educator, or administrator, you too can benefit from effective use of the Internet, and this book will teach you how. We'll show you around the Internet, drawing from the experience of teachers who have been there before. We'll point out the tourist traps as well as the not-to-be-missed sights as we go, and most of all we'll get you the information you need to decide whether you'd like to make the trip yourself.

What if I know nothing about the Net?

Join the club. For millions of people, all they know about the Internet is that they should know *something* about the Internet. Millions of others know just enough to make it useful. Even those of us who can claim to know more than most cannot possibly know *everything*. This book will teach you some important things about the Internet (what it is, why and how you might use it), but it won't make you an Internet expert.

As it turns out, you don't need to be an Internet expert to use the Internet effectively, any more than you need to be a computer expert to use a computer effectively. At this point, some of you are groaning: "Oh, but you *do* need to be a computer expert to use a computer! I can't figure those darn things out for the life of me—I'm just not a computer person!" Plenty of teachers (and other folk, too) have made exasperated comments like these, and yet those same teachers have very little trouble typing a letter in a word processor or using their electronic gradebook. [1]

To use the Internet (or a computer) all you need is *familiarity*, not expertise. And you don't need to be familiar with the entire Internet; you just need to be familiar with the most useful resources. There are plenty of teachers out there who are using the Internet effectively, and the only thing they know how to do is read and write electronic mail. Of course, there are other teachers—and their students—who are discussing world events in newsgroups, subscribing to educational mailing lists, and surfing the World Wide Web. [2] You will need to determine how the Internet can best serve you and your students, and then learn to use it that way.

Is the Internet really worth my time?

We think so, but that is something you'll have to answer for yourself. Learning and using the Internet can be time-consuming, but you may find that the results are worth the effort: The Internet can be a useful educational tool. Unfortunately, training seminars and descriptions that emphasize the technical aspects omit this point entirely. We'd like to show you how other teachers are using the Internet, so you can decide if it's the right tool for you.

How is this book different?

In the news and on the bookstand, the Internet is the hottest thing going. Any sufficiently large bookstore will carry several shelves full of books about the Internet. But most, if not all, of these books (even the ones aimed specifically at teachers) are not much more than instruction manuals. They may show you how to hold the nail and how to swing the hammer, but they don't tell you why it might be worthwhile

---

1   If you also have trouble with word processors and gradebooks, don't despair. It might take a little more practice, but you can become an effective Internet user, too.

2   We'll explain all of this techno-babble in *What is the Internet?* on page 37.

to learn carpentry or what useful and beautiful projects you can make.

We consider the Internet to be a tool, a means to an end. For us (and for you, too, we hope), that end is better teaching. This book grew out of a project we undertook in order to learn how to make better use of the Internet in our own teaching. After reading articles and books about teaching with the Internet, talking with teachers who have found ways of using the Internet effectively, and using the Internet ourselves, we decided that it was a shame there wasn't more out there for teachers who want to be teachers first, and Internet enthusiasts second.

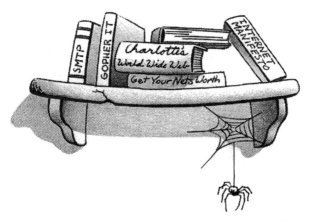

You can imagine the Internet as a huge library: plenty of people to talk to and more information than you'd know what to do with. Of course it's important to know how to use the library once you get there (especially since this one doesn't have much in the way of a friendly librarian), but it's much more important to understand why you'd want to go in the first place. Maybe when libraries first became public, people went because it was all the rage, but they've been going back since because libraries serve their needs. We'd like to show you how the Internet might serve yours.

We'd also like to show you where the Internet falls short. Despite the hype, the Internet is not an educational panacea; there are many things it doesn't do, or doesn't do well. We are teachers, not Internet evangelists, and we've gathered plenty of caveats for teachers new to the Internet. We've also collected tips and strategies for using the Internet to your greatest benefit.

This book will provide you with ideas for using the Internet in your teaching and directions for making these ideas work. It is grounded in educational research and draws directly from the experience of K-12 teachers successfully using the Internet themselves. It is based on educational theory, but gives plenty of practical examples for using the Internet inside and outside the classroom. As with any tool, mastery of the Internet will require practice. We'll provide ideas and advice for making that practice worthwhile. We hope that after reading and *using* this book you will find the Internet to be a valuable and versatile tool for your teaching, just as we have.

Douglas R. Steen
Mark R. Roddy, Ph.D.
Derek Sheffield
Michael Bryan Stout

E-mail: teaching.with.the.internet@pobox.com
World Wide Web: http://www.halcyon.com/ResPress/teacher.htm

Contents

Section 3 — Internet for communication

SECTION 1

Introduction

▼▼▼▼▼▼▼▼▼▼▼

When we started writing this book, a few of us were in the same position that many of you may be in now; we were teachers interested in the Internet who knew very little about it. We ventured online with the help of a few teacher friends, and with the right mix of instruction and awe, we now feel comfortable using the Internet in and out of the classroom. Like learning how to swim, learning how to negotiate the Internet requires thoughtful assistance; just jumping in the water doesn't work.

▲▲▲▲▲▲▲▲▲▲▲

CHAPTER 1

New teacher on the Net

▼ ▼ ▼ ▼ ▼ ▼ ▼ ▼ ▼ ▼ ▼

DEREK'S EXPERIENCE

We believe that with this book, a helpful friend or two, and some time and patience, you too can become comfortable with the Internet. The story below is an account of how one of us went from novice to net-user. We hope that it provides you with an example of the process you might find yourself going through, and lets you know that you are not alone. Here's how it all happened.

▲ ▲ ▲ ▲ ▲ ▲ ▲ ▲ ▲ ▲ ▲

The New World

I t was the first week of the Master in Teaching program at Seattle University. I was going to be a teacher. I had quit my marketing job, and there I was, packing lunches, heading back into the classroom. Early in the quarter, I met Michael Stout. From the beginning of our friendship, I called him Michael. He is not a Mike.

While eating lunch one day, we had a conversation that went something like this: Michael asked me, "So, what's your e-mail address so I can send you an e-mail?"

"My what? What do you mean e-mail ?" I asked, munching a carrot.

"You know, the Internet," he smiled.

"I must be missing something here. What's the Internet?" Michael explained something about computers all over the world in hyperspace (I have since learned that he actually said cyberspace), and that I had my very own access through Seattle University waiting for me.

This sounded interesting, especially after I found out there were no extra fees involved. Michael said he used the Internet a lot (for what, I wasn't sure). He was obviously excited about it and wanted to share it with me.

Even though the graduate teaching program was intense, I had a little time to explore the Internet. Following Michael's

advice, I managed to log in to S.U.'s computer and sign up for an account.

Initially, however, I didn't spend much time online because not only did I have to be on campus to use my account, but I also had to be there within the operating hours of the computer lab. Whenever I had a little spare time, I didn't feel like driving to Seattle U. just to get lost and confused online. I did, however, use my account enough to take one big step—I memorized my password.

A month later, we started the educational technology component of the curriculum with Dr. Mark Roddy. We had to explore a site on the Internet related to education. This turned out to be a baptism of fire for the fifty teachers in training. While Michael was busy playing fireman for everyone else, I joined another friend to complete the assignment using his computer at home. After witnessing the ease of logging in from home, and hearing about all the intriguing sites my classmates had explored, I knew I needed two things: a computer and a modem. Within a week, I acquired a used Apple Macintosh PowerBook 145 complete with a 2,400 baud modem.

Exploring the New World

The modem provided me access to the Internet from home. I was able to log some hours online in the evenings and on the weekends. This is where I really began to feel comfortable with the Internet. I explored any Internet resource that Michael threw my way. I did not fully know what I was doing or where I was going, but such mystery was part of the allure of the Internet for me. It was like a large, inductive lesson. I remember being amazed again and again at the amount of information I glimpsed. In my exploration I learned some useful commands, and amazingly, didn't break the Internet. If I took a wrong turn all I had to do was e-mail Michael, Dug Steen or Mark Roddy. They were an eager support group, and what better group to have than one composed of teachers?

I saw the Internet as a potential classroom tool, and I wanted all the tools possible to help me survive the infamous first year of teaching. Also, at this stage, I was in the grips of shiny object syndrome. I was fascinated by the Internet much as a raccoon can be entranced by a shiny piece of metal. In other words, the Internet was an end in itself for me. Even if I hadn't planned on using it in the classroom, I would still have spent a few Friday nights wrapped in screen light simply because it intrigued me. This has been helpful in that it has made me "Net-fluent." However, as you should see by the end of this story, I have come to understand the Internet is a powerful tool for us to use. In this respect, it is like a textbook. As teachers, we don't sit at our desks and tell students to open their books and learn; rather, we use it as one tool in our curriculum to help communicate information and develop thinking skills. The main differences are that the Internet has much more information and often talks back.

The next significant step in my education of the Internet took shape in a woman named Allison. I met Allison briefly at a play in Portland, Oregon. She was a friend of a friend, and we conversed long enough for me to find out that she was a computer training specialist at a local college. Because of the novelty of the Internet, I was not shy in asking for her e-mail address. We swapped and through e-mail I grew close to Allison, or Red, as my e-mail address book reads. She has made me laugh aloud at my computer screen many times. We have counseled each other through relationships, and shared discoveries about the Internet.

Since our first meeting in person, I have seen her on two other occasions. Beyond that, we have a novel detailing the progress of our friendship floating somewhere in cyberspace. It's difficult for me to decipher how much of our relationship is due to the Internet. Given the same two people in the same physical vicinity, would the same interaction occur? I don't know. That's one for the philosophers. What is certain is that this red-haired person, this friend, this reliable ear and voice is woven into my online experience.

Homesteading

As my knowledge about the Internet grew, I continued to find time to work with the various Internet services described in this book.

E-mail was a constant source of communication with friends, colleagues, and even family. This network of people grew as I met more people who had access to the Internet through educational institutions and commercial services. During my student teaching, I barely had time for e-mail. My top priorities were survival and finding a school that wanted to help repay my student loans.

I've ended up teaching at the same high school where I did my student teaching, and I'm paying off my loans with this book ;-).[1] My timing is good. Our school district has just acquired access to the Internet for its staff. I'm teaching district personnel how to use the Internet in special classes. What a difference a year and a good support group makes; it wasn't long ago that I was in the same place my students are now. I'd like to give them the same experiences I had, but time constraints have restricted me to the basics of Internet and e-mail. I have seen that these three-hour classes are not enough. People need more. They need what I had—Michael Stout, Dug Steen, Mark Roddy, or any friend who knows their way around the Internet.

---

1   This is a "smiley," a written wink. We'll explain more about them in *Expressing yourself on the Net* on page 87.

Staff in my building see me as the Internet person. Some ask me questions during our spare time as we pass in the hallway. One P.E. teacher bought me breakfast for individual tutoring. The teachers in our district know there are resources, friends, and avenues in cyberspace, and they want in.

In the spring of my first year of teaching, my primary use of the Internet was e-mail because for me, e-mail means people. I use e-mail to maintain long distance relationships: Allison in Portland, Lowell in Los Angeles, a friend from high school, Matt, in South Africa, and my aunt and uncle in Seldovia, Alaska.

In addition to these distant correspondents, e-mail fuels my writing. I have a friend who lives near me, teaches at the same school, and yet, e-mail adds to the communication in our friendship. Besides emergency lesson plans, we send each other poems back and forth, and have even written a poem together, line by line, through e-mail.

The Internet has aided my classroom activities by providing resources. For example, one student needed information for a debate topic. In fifteen minutes of searching the World Wide Web, I found a small library's worth of data on "censorship." Because one of the classes I teach is required for all juniors, and the six of us who teach it cover the same curriculum, there is a resource shortage for students. To help alleviate this, I provided a cursory introduction to the Internet in a fifty-five minute lesson, and then worked with students in pairs to help them locate resources.

I'm fortunate that I know the Internet well enough to use it in this way, and yet I know that it is like using a powerful computer only for word processing. There is much more that my students could do with the Internet, and I have some goals in mind. Currently, our building has one computer in the library which is hooked up to a modem. Even with this limited access, there is much that may be done. In particular, I have one project in mind. I think it is feasible to make use of what my Short Fiction/Poetry class already does. This class creates a school literary journal every year showcasing the poetry, fiction and art of students and staff. To provide another venue for this project, and thus increase the students' sense of audience, they can, in essence, publish the journal online and receive feedback from online readers. This would also be a great way for them to share their journal with students from other schools.

This is where I am now, typing on my PowerBook, my 2,400 baud modem a cord's length away, soon to be traded in. I remember my first, confused attempts at learning the Internet. I am reminded of the time it demands when I work with each new Internet class. In my experience, the difficult beginning has been well worth the friendships that the Internet has fostered and renewed, and the options it is beginning to create for my students. A year-and-a-half ago, I had lunch with Michael Stout.

Now, I know my way around the Internet.

CHAPTER 2

Inside this book

▼ ▼ ▼ ▼ ▼ ▼ ▼ ▼ ▼ ▼ ▼

SNEAK PREVIEW

*Here's a sneak preview of what we'll cover in
the chapters ahead and how we hope this
book and its special features can help you,
the educator, enhance your teaching. This
chapter also acts as a checklist, pointing out
what you'll need to use this book and how to
make it work for you. As in any project, before
you start you should make sure you have the
necessary equipment, and read the
instructions so you'll understand how to use
your tools.*

▲ ▲ ▲ ▲ ▲ ▲ ▲ ▲ ▲ ▲ ▲

What this book and the Internet can do for you

Experienced teachers know that education trends can be like fashion trends; just because it's chic doesn't mean it's worth buying into. The Internet is currently one of the hottest education trends around, but the hype has come mainly from people using the Internet, not textbook publishers or even Internet providers. All sorts of people are out there right now using the Internet in all sorts of ways. Teachers from around the world are using the Internet:

In their personal lives

- to **keep in touch** with friends and loved ones who live far away.

- to **obtain advice** on anything from travel accommodations to computer repair.

- to **find software freebies** they can use on their home computer.

In their professional lives

- to **keep up-to-date** in their subject area.

- to **find lesson plans** and teaching ideas.

- to **discuss educational issues** with teachers, parents, and researchers.

In their classrooms

- to **enable** their students to make connections across borders.

- to **provide** their students with opportunities to gather and analyze primary source information.

- to **involve** their students in national and international projects.

What you'll need to use this book

If you've ever read a computer manual, you know that right in the front you can usually find the system requirements: what you need to make the program work. This book is *not* a computer manual for the Internet (thank goodness!), but it does require a few things from you to really make it work. So here is our list of system requirements.

You'll need a connection to the Internet

You can start this book without a connection to the Internet, with the idea that you're evaluating the possibilities, deciding whether or not to invest in a connection. By the time you get to the fourth or fifth chapter, however, we expect you'll be wanting to try it out. We provide plenty of examples and suggestions for hands-on activities in this book, and if you don't have anything to put your hands on, well ... they fall a little short. So if you don't have one already, go out and get yourself a connection. It may not even cost you anything. Many Internet service providers give new customers a week or two on a free-trial basis.

Here are some recommendations for the kind of connection you should have:

Computer. It doesn't matter whether you are using a Macintosh or an IBM-compatible computer (running Windows or DOS), as long as it is able to access the Internet. If your computer is at home (which we recommend), this means it needs a modem[1] and the proper communications software. If you're using a school computer, you should probably talk to the resident computer expert about what you'll need to get connected to the Internet.

One of the nice things about the Internet is that you don't need the fanciest computer available to be connected. Older computers like the Mac Plus or the IBM XT will work just fine (although they may not be able to handle the newest Internet services).

---

1   We'll be describing what a modem is and what it does on page 52. In the meantime, please see the *Glossary* on page 315 for any technical definitions.

Connection. There are two types of connections, text-only and graphical, and either one is fine (although the graphical connection is *much* easier to use). We do recommend that you get your own Internet account, one that allows you to send and receive electronic mail. Also, if you can, get a connection from your own home. Most teachers find that using the Internet at home is easier and much more relaxing.

If you're not sure whether you're connected or how, or if you don't understand some of the recommendations above, don't worry. We'll spend more time describing the different types of connections in *How to gain access to the Net* on page 51.

You'll need someone who understands computers

Teachers are by-and-large a pretty independent bunch, and sometimes it's hard for us to ask for help, but we recommend that you do so when starting out on the Internet. The Internet is a relatively new creation, and therefore it is mostly unstandardized. This means that everyone's set-up is a little bit different, and it is impossible for this book (or any other) to be a *complete* reference, especially when things go wrong. So it's important to have a real, live person you can depend on when you need help. And it's important to find the *right* real, live person to help you as well.

How do you know if your person is the right one? Here are some handy guidelines:

You should be able to reach out and touch this person, literally. Trying to explain things over the phone can be more hassle than it's worth (especially if your computer needs the phone line, too). Sometimes the school's acting computer person is just too busy to sit down and work with you, and as a rule, salespeople and technical support people don't come and sit next to you unless you pay them *gobs* of money.

You should feel comfortable asking this person stupid questions. You may say that there's no such thing as a stupid question, but you might also change your mind once you start using the Internet.

If you ask your person to help you do something on the computer, and they elbow you out of the way in order to get to the keyboard, you've got the wrong person. The only way you're going to learn the Internet is by working on it yourself, so even if they're *directing*, make sure you're *doing*.

Beware of techno-junkies. These are the people who are so excited by the technology that they have sixteen answers (and hey, look at these interesting miscellaneous features!) for every one of your questions. It's very easy to get sidetracked, so it's important to find a person who can answer a simple question simply.

You'll need much time and patience

The Internet, like fine wine and teachers, will improve with age. By the time your students are using it in the workplace, the Internet will be, well... at least somewhat standard, if not completely intuitive. But for now, it's still pretty complex; and the only way to really learn how to use it effectively is to practice, practice, practice! That means spending time using the Internet, and spending time using the Internet often means being patient with the Internet and with yourself.

You'll need an interest in teaching

This last requirement is unique to this book; it is not an essential element of most other books about the Internet. However, we wrote this book to share what we have learned about using the Internet effectively *as teachers*, and we have structured the book towards that end. We are not interested in promoting the Internet for its own sake, our goal is to improve *teaching*, not Internet skills. So if you, too, would like to learn how you can use the Internet to improve your teaching, read on!

What this book contains

When you finish reading this Introduction, we'll take you straight into *The Internet*, the first section of this book, which provides a simple description of a complex entity: the Internet. We'll explain exactly what it is, how it works, and how you can get connected to it. If you already have a basic understanding of the Internet, or if you just don't care, you can skip it and no one will be the wiser. On the other hand, you can probably glean enough factoids and buzzwords from this first section to impress just about anybody!

Once you have some concept of what the Internet is, you'll be ready to learn how to use it. In the second and third sections we describe the most effective ways of using the Internet for its primary purposes: communication and research. The chapters in these sections do *not* contain classroom lesson ideas (they come later). Instead they concentrate on using the Internet in your personal life and your work outside of the classroom. This means sharing ideas, discussing issues, and collaborating with teachers and other professionals, as well as finding lesson plans and gathering information for personal and classroom use.

As we describe these approaches to using the Internet, we'll also describe the Internet services you'll need to make them work. By the end of the second section you'll be able to use electronic mail, mailing lists, newsgroupss, the World Wide Web, Gopher, file transfer, remote access, and a variety of Internet search tools. More importantly, however, you'll be able to use them *effectively* as a teaching professional.

One might argue that using the Internet in your work outside of the classroom is just as worthwhile as using it during classroom lessons (in fact, we argue just that), but it's hard to ignore the clamor for putting the Internet into the hands of the students. The fourth section, *Internet in the classroom*, addresses that issue, but from an educational standpoint. Designing lessons which incorporate the Internet simply because the school has access to it makes as much sense as designing lessons to incorporate the copier because there's one in the main office. Even if your objective is to teach *about* the Internet, just turning on the computer and letting the students go is unlikely to create a productive learning environment.

Internet in the classroom describes how you can use the Internet to enhance learning in your classroom. We start the section by reviewing educational philosophies, giving you a chance to reflect on your personal goals for your teaching. When you have a clear picture of the philosophy which guides your teaching, you are better prepared to incorporate the Internet into your work. We'll finish this section with some case studies: narrative accounts of teachers like yourself who are using the Internet in their classroom, and the tips and techniques they suggest for doing it well.

In the final section, *Internet resources* offers a list of places to go and things to see on the Internet. We've provided descriptions and pictures of some of the more important mailing lists, news groups, and World Wide Web pages. The Internet is changing so rapidly that we couldn't possibly enumerate all of the resources for teachers, so we chose to include only the most important (and we hope the most permanent). This list of Internet sites will give you a starting point for your travels, and also serve as a reference for when you're a veteran Internet user.

How to make this book work

In the preface we described the Internet as a huge library: plenty of people to talk to and lots of information, all essentially free-of-charge.[2] Unfortunately, this library has a poor card catalog and directory of services. These days, however, you can find any one of several dozen books that will fill this void at your local bookstore. They contain thousands of references for millions of interesting resources on the Internet. Although you will find the same sort of references to Internet resources throughout this text, being your Internet card catalog is not our primary goal.

We'd rather be your friendly Internet librarian. Like any good librarian, we are just as interested in helping you determine what you might need as we are in helping you find it. We want to help you learn what the Internet is good for, and what it isn't good for. As you learn *why* you'd use the Internet, you will also learn *how* to use it. We hope that this book will eventually become unnecessary; you will be comfortable enough with the Internet to use it effectively the best way you

---

2   Actually, that isnt quite true. For more discussion on who really pays for the Internet, see *Who pays for all of this?* on page 43.

see fit, and you'll only use this book for reference or to refresh your memory.

To start with, though, we recommend that you begin at the beginning and work your way through. We arranged the chapters in this book deliberately. After introducing some important concepts and terminology in the first section we spend most of the rest of the book taking you one-on-one with the Internet. It isn't until the penultimate section that we address how you can help your students use the Internet. There's good reason for this.

When it first became practical to bring computers into the schools, many administrators, policy-makers, parents, and even teachers believed that the first objective should be to get as many computers into as many kids' hands as possible. A computer on every desk, was the rallying cry. It wasn't long, however, before these same people (or at least some of them) realized that computers, like any technology, are not effective educational tools in and of themselves. To make them work, the *teachers* must first understand how to use them. Initially, only a few teachers knew how to use computers as educational tools; in fact, only a few teachers knew how to use computers *period*.

Today's hot new technology is the Internet, and it looks as though the same mistakes are being made. Teachers often look for ways to bring the Internet into their classroom before they bring it into their own work. If you use the Internet first as a person, then as a professional, and *then* (once you are comfortable with it yourself) introduce it to your students, you may find that they get more out of it as well. Even if you *never* introduce your students to the Internet, we think you'll find it a useful tool for your teaching.

There are as many ways of using the Internet as there are teachers to use it. We can't pretend to know what application will work best for you. What we can do is to show you how we and other teachers have used the Internet, and explain why we think these uses are especially effective. We'll start with the simplest applications of the simplest services and work our way towards more complex services as we go on. Along the way we'll provide examples of how teachers use these Internet services, quote the opinions of actual teachers, and give you some activities to try yourself.

If and when you do take it into the classroom, we can help you there, too. In Chapter 16, *Case studies*, we model some effective classroom use of the Internet and contrast it to ineffective use. We'll also give you advice straight from the teachers who use it, so that you can avoid their mistakes and benefit from their wisdom.

We and thousands of other teachers have found the Internet to be an indispensable tool for our teaching. Whether you read it from cover to cover, or browse only the sections you find most useful, we hope that this book will help you determine how *you* can make use of the Internet in *your* teaching. We think you'll find the Internet to be an incredible boon for yourself and your students, but if you don't, that's okay too. Were out to help teachers, not Internet service providers, so take what works for you and leave the rest behind.

The Internet

▼ ▼ ▼ ▼ ▼ ▼ ▼ ▼ ▼ ▼ ▼

The Internet does two things well: It allows people to communicate, and it stores information. In the first chapter of this section, *The Internet*, we'll discuss the importance of these two major functions of the Internet, and then we'll get into the nitty gritty of how the Internet works. Finally, we'll describe the different ways of accessing the Internet, and how you can get yourself "connected".

The second chapter, *Perils of the Net*, addresses some of the fears that are widely shared by those who first journey onto the Internet: Is it appropriate for children? Is it offensive to adults? What should I watch out for? We'll tackle the issue of free speech vs. Internet abuse, and let you know just what's out there and what you can do about it.

▲ ▲ ▲ ▲ ▲ ▲ ▲ ▲ ▲ ▲ ▲ ▲

CHAPTER 3

What is the Internet?

▼▼▼▼▼▼▼▼▼▼▼

MORE THAN COMPUTERS

The Internet is a vast collection of computers linked to one another. But more importantly, the Internet is a vast community of people sharing information and ideas. In this chapter, we'll take a look at the Internet as both a community of people and a warehouse of information. We'll also describe how it all works, and how you can get connected.

▲▲▲▲▲▲▲▲▲▲▲▲

The Internet as community:

Who's connected to the Net

Most descriptions of the Internet start by explaining how computers connected to computers make up the Internet. This is true, of course, technically speaking. But the Internet is more than a collection of computers. The Internet is a collection of people. With the Internet it is possible to send personal messages from Seattle to your family in North Carolina, plan conferences with people in Norway, and discuss censorship with educators all over the world. Because the Internet connects people to people it feels more like a community than a computer network.

For this reason, some folks like to describe the Internet as a virtual community. Although the word virtual may be the most overused (and misused) adjective of the 1990s, in this case its use is appropriate. The Internet is a community only in effect: there are no schools, no community meetings, and no sign posts that delineate community boundaries. In a sense, there is no true physical embodiment of the Internet. The Internet community is people sitting at their computers all over the world communicating with one another.

The Internet community, like the Internet itself, is still a fledgling entity. Originally, it was a haven for academic researchers and the computer-minded. These early pioneers developed their own social customs for the new territory, a set of unwritten rules governed primarily by a spirit of cooperation. Many of the services provided on the Internet are run entirely by volunteers. The software necessary to make the Internet work is often written by graduate students who get little or no compensation for their efforts (other than the fame that comes with having written a piece of the Internet software). Even the boards which govern certain aspects of the Internet (such as technical problems and standards) are all-volunteer.[1]

---

1   If you'd like to learn more about Internet governance, see the Internet Society's World Wide Web page at *http://www.isoc.org/*. Directions for accessing this resource can be found in Chapter 10 , *The World Wide Web*, on page 137.

NET FACTS

▼▼▼▼▼▼▼▼▼▼▼

Is the Net really a community?

Not everyone agrees that the Internet is the promised land of human community that some have made it out to be. A few well-respected Internet writers have been calling for the end of this hype, wondering if the Internet is "not a tool for conviviality but a life-denying simulacrum of real passion and true commitment to one another."

One area in which the Internet falls decidedly short, for example, is diversity. The population on the Internet does not mirror the world population, or even the population of developed nations like the United States. Women, children, the elderly, and the poor are under-represented, as are the illiterate and people from most developing nations.

On the other hand, the Internet is still young. As its population increases, so will the diversity. And this "inhuman" medium can provide for very human interaction. Even Internet critics usually have a personal tale of bonding over the Internet: friends found or adversity shared. The absence of visual clues in correspondence allows for connections which might not be as easy face-to-face. We are witnessing the beginnings of a technical revolution, and its effect on our culture, and on our communities, has yet to be determined.

The quotes on this page are taken from Howard Rheingold's The Virtual Community *(Addison-Wesley, 1993); for other discussions on the Internet as a community see* Silicon Snake-Oil, *by Clifford Stoll (Bantam/DoubleDay, 1995), and "Is There a There in Cyberspace?" by John Perry Barlo* (Utne Reader, *March-April 1995), as well as other articles from that issue.*

▲▲▲▲▲▲▲▲▲▲▲▲

The Internet community may not be altogether unfamiliar to teachers, as it has grown in large part from the efforts of the academic community. There is that spirit of cooperation: expe-

NET FACTS

▼▼▼▼▼▼▼▼▼▼▼▼

Super-inter-info-what?

With all the talk about the Internet and the information superhighway and online services, it's no wonder people get confused. Here are some definitions to help you sort it out.

Information Superhighway: (a.k.a. the "Infobahn" or the "I-way") An as-yet-unrealized vision of global networking. This is the term people use when they want to include all networking possibilities now and in the future.

Internet: The current collection of networks of computers stretching around the world. Because most of the costs of the Internet are paid for by universities, large research corporations, and the United States government, the Internet is generally considered a public entity. No single corporation, institution, or government owns or manages the whole Internet.

Commercial networks: (e.g. CompuServe, Prodigy, America Online) These networks (sometimes called online services) are owned and managed by specific companies. The companies charge you for the use of their networks, usually at an hourly rate. They generally provide access to the Internet as well as other services.

▲▲▲▲▲▲▲▲▲▲▲▲

rienced users often take time to help out the new users, and even stupid questions or social infractions are usually met with polite suggestions. Also, there is a feeling on the Internet that information deserves to be free. That means both available to all, and without cost. Blatant commercialism is frowned upon, and (issues of intellectual property rights notwithstanding) most of what you can find on the Internet is there just for that reason so that you can find it and use it. Teachers especially are encouraged to use what they find in their work.

As a newcomer to the Internet community, however, its important that you respect the rules (official and unofficial) set by the people who came before. Official rules are set by the company (or school or district) which provides your connection to the Internet, as well as by government agencies and international treaties. You can obtain a copy of what is called the **acceptable use policy** from whomever provides your Internet service; in fact, they'll probably have you sign one before you can use the Internet.[2] (For a sample policy, please see Appendix B on page 295.) It is important to read and understand the policy before signing it, of course, but it need not be a point of concern. Accidentally violating the acceptable use policy is about as likely as accidentally committing mail fraud.

On the other hand, unless you take the time to learn about etiquette on the Internet, you may inadvertently violate one of its unofficial rules. Barging into certain corners of the Internet without any sense of what is expected of you can generate as much resentment as crashing someone's wedding. Luckily, the unofficial rules of the Internet are not unwritten rules (in fact, we've included a number of them on page 131), and they're based on common sense and courtesy. Unfortunately, some of the new Internet users seem to be unwilling to take the time to learn the ropes, and this is beginning to frustrate the veterans. Throughout this book we will concentrate heavily on Internet etiquette (commonly known as netiquette), so that you can be on your best behavior as you make your way through this new environment.

The Internet as warehouse:
What's out there?

The Internet is not only a community, but also a huge warehouse for information. By some estimates, there are close to 5 million host computers holding information on the Internet (host computers are generally larger computers found at colleges and corporations). If you consider that each of these

---

2   If your school or district does *not* make you sign an acceptable use policy, you might want to talk to your school/disctrict computer person about creating one.

computers contains an average of a couple gigabytes of accessible files (a conservative estimate), then you have 10 *petabytes* (or 10 quadrillion bytes) of information at your fingertips on the Internet. If this means nothing to you, consider that the computers on the Internet could hold the complete works of Shakespeare two hundred million times over and still have room for a couple hundred million copies of the King James Bible. Thats a lot of information.[3]

Actually, the figures above are a little misleading, since much of the information on the Internet is duplicated from one computer to the next. Nevertheless, there is still a wide variety out there. This isn't surprising when you consider that almost every industrialized nation and every college and university in the United States, Canada, and western Europe has a computer on the Internet. It is also becoming more common for regular users like yourself to add whatever they choose to this collection. You *can* find the complete works of William Shakespeare and the

---

3   The number of host computers is estimated as of January 1995. If you would like to see the latest figures, see the Internet Domain Survey produced by Network Wizards at *http://www.nw.com/*. Directions for accessing this resource can be found in Chapter 10, *The World Wide Web*, on page 137.

NET FACTS

▼▼▼▼▼▼▼▼▼▼▼▼

Who pays for all of this?

One of the first questions asked about the Internet is: Who pays for it? Right now the answer is everybody, to some extent. Different people pay for different parts. If you get a connection through your school district, for instance, you will pay the phone company because you'll be using your phone line to connect to your school district's computer. The district has paid for their computer, and they may pay a private company to connect it to others on the Internet. The private company may be connected to the National Science Foundation's network, which is funded by the United States government. Universities, corporations, and other governments also connect and contribute. Right now, trying to answer "Who pays for the Internet?" is like trying to answer "Who runs the world's economy?"

The important thing to remember is, for now at least, once you are connected to the Internet, the services it provides are free. No one will charge you for each electronic mail received, or each World Wide Web page visited. Because we all pay for the Internet to some degree through our government, some people are fond of declaring, "The Internet is *not* free!" To most Internet users, however, it sure *feels* free.

▲▲▲▲▲▲▲▲▲▲▲▲

King James version of the Bible on the Internet (heck, you can even find the King James Bible in *Pig Latin*), but you can also find a variety of lesson plans, all White House press releases, lists of poker variations, collections of famous sound recordings, and pictures of our (the authors') families, as well as plenty of guides to the Internet and software for your computer.

This is not to say that the Internet will replace your public library. There is no acquisitions director for the Internet, no one to make sure that the Internet has enough information about eastern Europe, for instance. Instead, there are simply eastern Europeans, and people who are interested in the study of eastern Europe, providing what information they choose. This means that what you get from the Internet is usually unfiltered primary source material; an incredible boon to researchers and history teachers, but something of an obstacle for those who want concise and reliable information.

When the Murrah Building in Oklahoma City was destroyed by a car bomb in April 1995, for instance, information was available on the Internet almost immediately. Lists of the dead and missing, sketches of the suspects, and electronic mail addresses for sending support were distributed by government authorities; local schools provided pictures of the devastation and eyewitness accounts; and thousands of Internet users discussed the implications of the tragedy with each other online.[4]

Unfortunately, other people on the Internet used the bombing as an opportunity to propagate rumors that middle-easterners were responsible, and some spent their time online detailing the procedures for making such car bombs. There is no single authority checking the appropriateness, the accuracy, or even the reasonableness of information on the Internet, so this kind of misuse can and does occur (although it is generally the exception, not the rule).

All of this means that, as far as the information warehouse idea goes, the Internet is less like one humongous library system than it is like millions of people opening their own home libraries (and picture, and sound, and software collections) for you to browse through. We'll discuss what this means for Internet users, teachers and students in particular, in later sections of the book. Right now, let's take a look at how the Internet can be both a communications device and an information repository.

---

4   You may still be able to find information about the Oklahoma City
    bombing on the American Red Cross page at
    http://www.ionet.net/~graham/redcross.html, or on the FBI's page at
    http://naic.nasa.gov/fbi/okbomb.html. Directions for accessing this
    resource can be found in Chapter 10, *The World Wide Web*, on
    page 137.

A brief history of the Internet

Students of history know that successful projects frequently begin as a bright idea in the minds of visionary people. The Internet is such a project.

In the late 1950s, during the infancy of computer networking, data was sent between computers by first moving the data from computer memory to 80-hole punch cards (each about the size of a legal envelope). The words on this page would fill a 25- to 30-card stack. A fully punched stack of cards was carried by hand to a very specialized card reader that was attached to a telephone line using a rudimentary modem. The cards were read with a mechanical sensor and the information was sent across a telephone connection as bits (binary digits) to a distant card punch at a rate about 50 bits-per-second. The stack of cards punched at the distant site would then be transferred to computer memory by reversing the process. There was a clear need to improve this complex and time consuming technique.

In 1962, Paul Rand came up with a better way. He published a paper on a new approach which broke the text or data up into packets to be transmitted directly on telephone wires (for example, the 200 words on this page would have been broken up into four 50-word packets). The packets were sent to a packet switch which could forward the data over other telephone lines to additional switches until it reached a remote computer. A Department of Defense (DoD) program under the Advanced Research Projects Agency (ARPA) was established and the first packet switch was designed by Bolt, Beranek and Newman under contract to the DoD. This packet switch arrived at UCLA, one of the first three ARPA-Network sites, in early September 1969. ARPA had a vision that packet switching would revolutionize military communication systems. Over the next three decades, however, it became clear that its value outside the military field would be even greater. This was the birth of the Internet.

In the 1970s ARPAnet grew slowly at first and then more rapidly. During the 1980s the National Science Foundation (NSF) undertook to provide researchers with five supercomputer centers at various places around the United States. Since

▼▼▼▼▼▼▼▼▼▼▼▼

What about my privacy?

Information exchange on the Internet is not a two-way street. Just because your home computer has access to computers around the world, it does not mean that computers around the world have access to your home computer. Those other computers are set up specifically to provide access for people on the Internet. There is a slight chance that the computer you use at school is set up this way, but your home computer is not.

If you are connected to the Internet over the phone line, it is difficult, if not impossible, to allow others access to the information on your personal computer—even if you want to. Unless you send your files across the Internet (via electronic mail, for instance), or place them in special directories on large Internet computers, the only way for some unauthorized person to get access to the information on your home computer is to break into your house.

Of course, if you do place them in those special directories or send them via electronic mail, all bets are off. Although you will certainly have some privacy in such transactions, the security measures are by no means foolproof. For this reason, we suggest that you never include private information, such as credit card numbers, in electronic mail. For more about this issue, see *E-mail is not as private as it seems* on page 83.

▲▲▲▲▲▲▲▲▲▲▲▲

these supercomputer centers were to be used by all researchers, they were connected to an upgraded ARPAnet. The NSF created this new network of packet switches connected by telephone lines operating at 56,000 bits-per-second (1,000 times faster than the 1960s). Actually, this new network was constructed from regional networks connected to other regional networks. This inter-networking of networks gives the Internet its name.

In 1987, Merit Network, working with IBM and MCI, provided the NSF with a backbone network to connect regional networks over telephone lines operating at the blazing speed of 1.5 million bits-per-second. The 200 words which would have taken close to a minute to transmit in the 1960s, would now take less than one one-hundred-thousandth of a second.

Today the NSF is searching for a way to turn the Internet over to a commercial company which would continue to meet the rapidly growing needs of the community of users. The full extent of the current Internet is not known, but it is an international network made up of an estimated 5000 regional networks interconnected with telephone lines as fast as 45 million bits per second and with as many as 20 million people within its reach. The growth of the Internet is unprecedented in the history of computer networks and seems likely to continue until most people on earth are connected.

Technically the Internet:
How it all works

Internet junkies call the Internet a network of networks. Simply stated, a network connects at least two computers, and the Internet connects hundreds of thousands of networks. There's no telling how many people have access to the Internet, although some folks estimate that there are 20 to 30 million users from over 70 countries. We do know that this number is growing at a phenomenal rate: One analyst has predicted that 550 million people will be connected to the Internet by the year 2000.

The number of Internet users from developed nations is disproportionately high. In most countries, Internet connections for average people are hard, if not impossible, to come by. Outside of the United States, Canada, Australia, and most of western Europe, the Internet is restricted to people in government, universities and large corporations. This is changing rapidly, as the Internet continues to gain international attention. Right now, the United States has the best Internet access for the average person. Connections are available through national as well as local providers, as well as many schools and school districts.

As the Internet grows, so does corporate interest in the Internet. Many companies now have a presence on the Internet: Some contribute to discussions about their products, others maintain Internet showrooms which you can browse from your computer, and some even let you order products via electronic mail. Other companies, such as CompuServe, Prodigy, America Online, and Microsoft, have created their own global networks. These commercial networks are paid for entirely by subscribers (no government or industry subsidies), so they are usually more expensive, although they do provide extra services (like stock market trading and travel planning) which aren't available on the Internet.

How do you fit in?

To understand how your computer becomes connected to the Internet, it's useful to think of a highway system. This analogy works (although it is something of a cliché by now) because the Internet does consist of a system of thruways, secondary highways and private roads. Like the highway system, no one owns the entire system. Different parts of the sys-

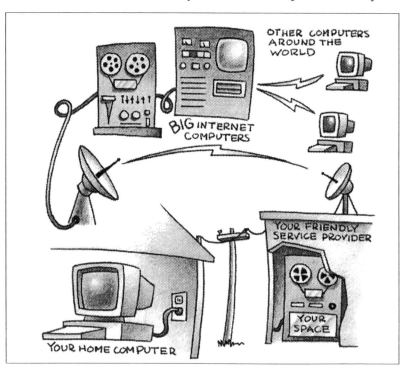

tem fall under different jurisdictions. These different parts are paid for and maintained by different companies, schools, government agencies, and regular people like yourself.

Let's take an example. Suppose your school system has announced that it will provide you with an **Internet account**. What this probably means is that a state-wide network has been connected to the Internet and some of the space on one of the computers in this network will be set aside for your use.[5] You can use this space to store personal files, but usually it acts as a mailbox it holds your electronic mail until you are ready to read it. With your Internet account you will also get the right to use software programs on the big, state computer. These programs will let you search for and retrieve information from other Internet computers, let you join in world-wide discussions about a variety of topics, and much, much more. This is what we will call **Internet access**.

Schools that offer Internet access don't always provide teachers with their own accounts. Some schools have one shared account for all of their teachers. This means that the electronic mail is communal, and only one person can access the Internet at a time. Other schools or districts will offer access to the Internet without an account. This means that you get to use the software programs which provide **Internet services**, but you won't be able to send and receive electronic mail. In either of these cases, you may

Buzzwords

Internet access: The right to use software programs on a large computer which is connected to the Internet. These software programs provide Internet services such as file transfer, remote computer access, and newsgroups.

Internet account: Personal space on a large computer which is connected to the Internet. Having your own Internet account means that you can send and receive electronic mail, as well as store personal files.

want to consider paying for your own account from an In-

---

5   The amount of space (or disk storage) available to you depends on the provider.

ternet service provider. Internet service providers act just like the state provider in the scenario above, except you pay for the Internet account yourself. It will cost you more, but it also means you aren't beholden to the school system for your use of the Internet. You can probably find an Internet service provider in the computer section of your phone book or newspaper.[6]

Whether or not you choose an Internet service provider, you should be sure to have access to your account from home. Teachers we've talked to say that its much easier to find the

---

NET FACTS

▼▼▼▼▼▼▼▼▼▼▼▼

Internet services

electronic mail: Text communication between people on the Internet.

file transfer: Moving information from a distant Internet computer to your own.

gopher: Simplified, menu-oriented system for file transfer and remote access.

mailing lists: Automated electronic mail, allowing multiple recipients of a single message.

newsgroups: Subject-oriented group discussions on the Internet.

remote access: Using the services of a distant Internet computer from your own.

search tools: Special services which allow you to search for information anywhere on the Internet.

World Wide Web: Graphical, point-and-click system for file transfer and remote access.

▲▲▲▲▲▲▲▲▲▲▲▲

---

6 Note that Internet service providers are different than commercial networks (like America Online, Prodigy, or CompuServe) in that they *only* provide access to the Internet. For this reason they are usually less expensive.

time at home than it is at school, and that this extra time allows them to get comfortable with their own use of the Internet before trying it with their students. We'll describe how to get connected from home in the next section.

Connecting to the Internet:
How to gain access to the Net

Before we start into the nitty-gritty of getting connected to the Internet, we want to reiterate that you should probably find someone who knows about computers to help you with this. Getting connected to the Internet is becoming easier all the time (what took several days last year takes just a few hours now and will probably take minutes next year), but there are so many different possibilities for mistakes that it would take an entire book just to get you started. In fact, you can probably go to a bookstore and buy just such a book. However, we recommend you find a person instead; they're more likely to respond to your questions.

What types of access are available?

As described in the example above, the way to get connected to the Internet is to get connected to a computer already on the Internet. If we continue the highway analogy, you need to put in a driveway between your garage (your home computer) and the street (a commercial provider, your school, or district) so that you can eventually get out to the highway (the Internet). This driveway is usually a phone line: Your computer sends information through its modem to the Internet providers computer. This is what is known as **dial-up access**. Most universities, research centers, large corporations, and even some schools have **direct access** to the Internet. This is less common for teachers (or any single individual) because it requires special wiring and loads of money. Since it is really the province of more technical Internet books, we will leave the issue of direct access behind, and concentrate on how you can get dial-up access to the Internet.

First, you'll need a computer at home. Fortunately, just about any Macintosh or IBM-compatible computer will do.[7] The computers speed has little to do with how fast you will be able to access the Internet, so don' feel obligated to buy a state-of-the-art system (a Lambourghini is nice, but it doesnt help much if you're on 35-mph roads). What *does* matter is the **modem**—the piece of hardware which connects your computer to the telephone line. The current standard for new computers is 14,400 bits per second (abbreviated as 14.4, and called

 Buzzwords

dial-up access: Using a phone line to communicate between your home computer and the Internet. This is slower, but far cheaper, and therefore almost universal for individual users.

direct access: A special high-speed connection between a local computer or computer network and the Internet. Businesses and schools which can afford this type of access prefer it because it is much quicker than dial-up.

graphical connection: A connection to the Internet which allows for point-and-click access, similar to the Windows or Macintosh operating systems.

text-only connection: A means of accessing other computers on the Internet using only text. Often called a "UNIX shell account."

fourteen-dot-four). If you are planning to use the Internet on a regular basis, we recommend you get a modem at least that fast. Faster modems are available as well, but you should probably ask a knowledgeable friend (or trustworthy salesperson) for advice if you are planning to buy a modem.[8]

Once you have a computer and a modem, you'll need to find someone who will provide you with an Internet account and/or access to the Internet. As a teacher, you are likely to find low-cost (possibly no-cost) Internet access through a local

---

7   If you are using an IBM-compatible PC, it is best to have one which runs the Microsoft Windows or IBMs OS/2 operating system. This will allow you to use a graphical Internet connection.

8   This goes double if you're planning to buy a new computer. Which computer system is the best system may be the most hotly contested debate among computer users today. In fact, what is the best varies so widely from person to person, we couldn't possibly take sides.

school district or university. Sometimes even newspapers or other businesses will provide free accounts for teachers. Your best bet is to find someone knowledgeable (like your school or district technology person) and ask how to get a free account. If all else fails, local commercial Internet service providers are usually available for $10-$30 per month.[9] You may also consider trying one of the **commercial networks** like Prodigy, CompuServe, or America Online. These companies will usually give you a few hours of trial time free of charge. When you sign-up, you may want to ask them how to access the Internet through their service.

What kinds of connections are available?

Technically, there are all sorts of connections to the Internet, but they fall into two major categories: **text-only** and **graphical**. If you decide to use a commercial Internet provider, you will be asked to choose between the two, but if your service provider is a school or commercial network commercial network, the choice will probably be made for you. A general description of each is given below.

Text-only connection

This is the oldest, most basic, and least expensive type of connection; it is also the connection most commonly provided by universities and school districts. It is known as a UNIX shell because it connects you to a machine running the UNIX operating system.[10] Although it may provide almost all of the services of a more expensive connection, these services can only text. Even if you use a mouse in a graphical environment (like Windows or the Macintosh), you will be limited to the keyboard when you are on the Internet. There are no buttons, pull-down menus, pretty fonts, or helpful graphics in a text-only connection, so getting around the Internet is more difficult. On the other hand, you will never need to obtain any more software than what comes with your modem. If you'd

---

9   There are national providers as well, but the cost of connection is usually substantially higher.

10 The operating system is the software which runs your computer at the lowest-level. The UNIX operating system is similar to the DOS operating system run on IBM-compatible computers.

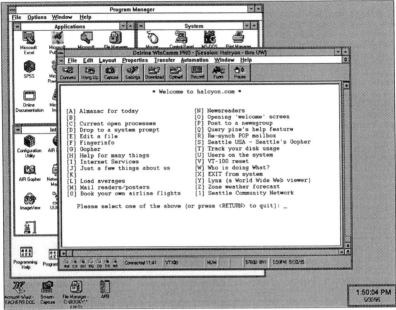

A computer with a text only interface in the foreground and a graphical interface in the background

like to be surfing the net you'll probably want more, but if you plan only to use electronic mail (which is text-based as well), you might as well stick with this inexpensive connection.

Graphical connection

This newer (and more expensive) connection allows you to point and click your way around the Internet making the experience much more pleasant. It also means that you'll need special software to run on your computer in order for it to communicate with your Internet provider. You can buy this software in a package at your local computer store, or you can find it for free by asking a connected friend to get it from the Internet.[11] Sometimes the free software can be a hassle to set up (especially on IBM-compatibles), but once it's set correctly it usually works just fine. If you're using a commercial In-

---

11   This isn't stealing. The software were referring to is called freeware because it is simply given away. There is also shareware, which is also distributed for free, but the creators ask you to send a nominal fee if you decide to use it on a regular basis. If you use shareware, please send the fee. It is important to encourage such practices.

ternet provider (and you probably will be in this case), that provider will be happy to give you advice on what software to get and how to set it up (in fact, they sometimes offer a package deal at reduced rates to help entice new customers). We'll provide directions for getting some of the free software when we describe the different Internet services in chapter 10.

If you want the graphical connection, you have three options: **ISDN, SLIP** and **PPP**.[12] The first, which stands for **I**ntegrated **S**ervices **D**igital **N**etwork, is a high-speed connection used only for direct access, not dial-up. For this reason, it is unlikely that your Internet service provider will even mention it. The second, **S**erial **L**ine **I**nternet **P**rotocol, is essentially an older version of the last, **P**oint-to-**P**oint **P**rotocol. Either SLIP or PPP will work, but PPP gives you the advantage of being able to do several things at once (for instance, you can download lesson plans while you read your electronic mail). It is

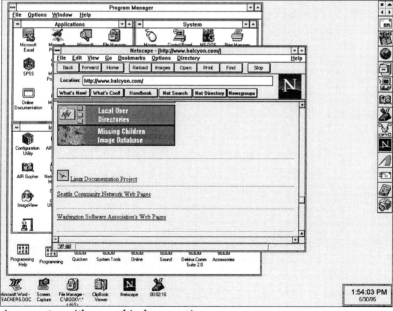

A computer with a graphical connection

---

12   Actually, there is a fourth option. You can obtain software which will turn your text-based account into a graphical account. For more information, see *Web surfing from a text-only account* on page 145.

usually more expensive, but not by much. Generally, PPP is where the market is going, and unless it is out of your price range, it makes sense to follow.

This last maxim holds true for all decisions about connecting to the Internet. The computer industry has an awful reputation for pushing the latest model as the only solution, but in this case it's justified. Remember, individual Internet connections are a relatively new phenomenon, and each advance in technology is leaps and bounds ahead of the last. The difference of ease of use between clicking with your mouse around the World Wide Web (which is possible only with a graphical connection) and typing out Telnet or FTP commands (which are text-based) is incredible. Of course, if the district is giving out free text-based accounts there's no reason to snub them, but if you're doing this on your own, you may want to think seriously about taking the plunge.

What next?

So now you've badgered your principal and buttonholed the district technology person so many times that they've finally provided you with an Internet account. You've bought a modem for your home computer, and you've got everything hooked up properly. You can even dial up your account, enter your name and password, and ... hey, you're connected to the Internet! Great! Now what?

CHAPTER 4

Perils of the Net

▼▼▼▼▼▼▼▼▼▼▼

CONTROVERSIAL ASPECTS OF THE INTERNET

The Internet is chock full of all sorts of things: words, pictures, sounds, movies. Most of what you find on the Internet is ... well, if not useful, at least fairly harmless. Some of it, however, would probably be confiscated if it were found in a classroom. These are the things which generate controversy among parents, teachers, and policy-makers. In this chapter, we'll give you a sense of what's really out there and what you can do about it.

▲▲▲▲▲▲▲▲▲▲▲▲

Who's afraid of the big, bad Internet?

Unfortunately, the people who are most concerned about the so-called "prurient aspects" of the Internet are usually the least informed about them. Before you consider how to keep your students away from the perils of the Internet, it's important that you understand what those perils are. The controversial stuff on the Internet can be generally divided into three broad categories:

Conversation

Since the Internet is primarily a tool for communication, it stands to reason that most of the problem is one of adult conversation. In this respect newsgroups are probably the prime offender (although Inter-Relay Chat comes in a close second).[1] These Internet services are provided to allow people to talk about specific subjects, and there are dozens of newsgroups devoted to R- and sometimes X-rated topics. The discussions in these groups range from immature ramblings to scientific debates, but the vast majority would probably offend the average parent. For this reason schools usually do not choose to carry any of these newsgroups. This will keep all but the most intrepid child away from these conversations.

There are other places in the Internet, however, for discourse. The World Wide Web, for instance, is quickly becoming a forum available to anyone who has the proper equipment and an opinion. Not only are there people posting their favorite dirty jokes or providing access to their nude photo collection, but there are white supremacists spouting hatred and racism and anarchists describing bomb-making procedures. Here we get into the sticky issue of free speech. Parents and teachers may agree on keeping students away from such Internet sites, but they may be split amongst themselves over sites promoting safe and legal abortion or meeting places for gay teens. This is a difficult issue for most conscientious Internet users who would like to restrict children's access

---

1   See *Newsgroups* on page 107 for a description of newsgroups, and *IRC* on page 184 for a description of Inter-Relay Chat.

NET FACTS

▼▼▼▼▼▼▼▼▼▼▼▼

In a newsmagazine near you

An excellent example of the kind of hot-button treatment this subject gets was the Time Magazine cover story entitled "On a Screen Near You: Cyberporn" (Elmer-Dewitt, 1995). The article, based on an "exhaustive study of online porn," describes objectionable material on the Internet as "ubiquitous" and "hard-core," and was cited on the floor of the United States congress during a debate over censorship on the Internet.

In the days after it was published, however, this article, and the study on which it was based (Rimm, 1995), was systematically torn apart by experienced researchers over the Internet. Not only was the study conducted by a lone undergraduate, using suspect methodology and publishing in a non-peer-review journal, but the figures quoted in the cover story are for adult bulletin board systems which aren't even part of the Internet (*Congressional Record* via Government Printing Office, *http://ssdc.ucsd.edu/gpo/index.html*). In fact, the study itself found only nine out of 11,576 sites examined on the World Wide Web contained R- or X-rated pictures (Rosenberg, 1995).

It is this sort of high-profile, unfounded scare story that makes many Internet users more cynical about the media than the Internet. No one is arguing that everything available on the Internet is suitable for young children, but neither is anyone sure what to do with the parts that aren't.

For more information about this topic, and the Time Magazine article in particular, see:

The cyberporn debate
http://www2000.ogsm.vanderbilt.edu/cyberporn.debate.cgi

Censorship and the Internet
http://dis.strath.ac.uk/people/paul/Control.html

Electronic Freedom Foundation
http://www.eff.org/

▲▲▲▲▲▲▲▲▲▲▲▲

to inappropriate material without destroying the democratic idealism of the Internet. This debate will not subside anytime soon.

Pictures

With the emergence of the World Wide Web comes the ability for people to download sounds, pictures, and movies with relative ease. This has increased the likelihood that your students will be able to find "dirty" pictures on the Internet. Usually, however, these pictures are relatively tame compared to what can be found at most large newsstands or on pay cable channels. Also, the sites which carry such pictures often become victims of their own success. Internet service providers rarely remove Web pages because of content, but if too many Internet users find and use a certain Web page, the service provider will often remove it because it slows down the entire system.

NET FACTS

▼▼▼▼▼▼▼▼▼▼▼▼

Making the Internet safe

Some companies offer software programs which will restrict access to the Internet. Among these are:

SurfWatch Software
http://www.surfwatch.com/

theLinq
http://www.qualitycomp.com/thelinq.html

There are also groups on the Internet dedicated to making the Internet safe for kids. For more information, see:

SafeSurf
http://www.safesurf.com/wave/

Children Accessing Controversial Information (CACI)
http://www.zen.org/~brendan/caci.html

▲▲▲▲▲▲▲▲▲▲▲▲

People

Possibly the scariest thing about the Internet can be the people on the other end of the connection. Teachers have described episodes in which students have been followed and harrassed over the Internet after meeting someone in an electronic forum. Granted, these instances are rare and should not outweigh the benefits of most electronic exchange, but you should be sure that you and your students are taking certain obvious precautions:

☑ **Remember that communication** over the Internet is not private or secure. Imagine that you are communicating via postcard, not letter!

☑ **Never give out your address** and phone number in an open forum such as a newsgroup or mailing list. If your students wish to correspond via the postal service, have them give the school's address.

☑ **Never accept an invitation** to a clandestine meeting, requests for personal information, or any other entreaties that may suggest unsafe situations.

☑ **If you are being harrassed** by electronic mail, get the e-mail address of the offending person and write to their Internet service provider.[2]

Who can get it?

There is a (possibly apocryphal) story about a group of high school seniors on a college tour with their parents. One of the parents asks the undergraduate tour guide, "Is there a drug problem on this campus?" "No, ma'am," the tour guide replies, "No drug problem at all. You can get just about anything you want here."

---

2   You can usually write to a person's service provider by sending a message to *postmaster@* their host computer. For instance, if you wanted to complain about someone whose e-mail address was *chris@dne.org*, you'd write to *postmaster@dne.org*.

Unfortunately, the same is currently true for the Internet, and this is exactly what stokes the fears of many non-Internet users. Most everything that is available on the Internet to adults is available to children; there is currently no way to completely regulate who is getting what. However, there are a number of new companies appearing which will help you restrict your students' access to certain inappropriate sites. These companies generally provide software which checks incoming information against a list of restricted sites. Anything on the list can not be accessed. Of course, at the rate the Internet is growing, no single list can encompass all objectionable material. However, these same companies will regularly update the list for a monthly fee. Or you can get more restrictive by allowing only a list of approved sites to be visited by your youngsters.

You should know, however, that any student with sufficient Internet skills can get just about anything that is available on the Internet, no matter how many safeguards or barriers to their access you erect. The teachers we talked to, though, generally agreed that students can find far worse stuff far more easily off the Internet than on. Children in today's society are exposed to sexually explicit material regularly, and they face risks to their person from neighbors and sometimes even family members. The chances that they'll find hard-core pornography on the Internet or be lured away from home with online conversations are small in comparison.

An important thing to keep in mind is that none of this comes unbidden to your computer. Really the only thing that you don't have to actively search for and retrieve on the Internet is your electronic mail. And, for now at least, no one is sending out unwelcomed messages to strangers on the Internet. The worst that you might get is a message with a political agenda (asking you to support a particular cause) forwarded to you from a friend who thinks you might be interested.

What can you do about it?

☑ **Talk to your provider.** If you are planning to let your students use the Internet in the classroom, you may want to talk to your school's technology person to find out what precautions have been taken and what access the students will have. If you are concerned about your own children, talk to your Internet service provider.

☑ **Talk to your students' parents.** Before you begin using the Internet in your classroom, you may want to broach the issue with your students' parents. Beware though, this is a hot issue, and many parents may not have any understanding of the Internet beyond the scare stories they see on TV.

☑ **Talk to your students.** Set up clear guidelines for what the students can do and what they can't. Many schools adopt acceptable use policies which clearly outline responsible behavior on the Internet. See page 295 for an example of such a policy.

SECTION 3

Internet for communication

▼ ▼ ▼ ▼ ▼ ▼ ▼ ▼ ▼ ▼ ▼ ▼

Although the Internet was originally designed for information storage and retrieval, early users quickly discovered its importance as a medium for long-distance communication. Today, the Internet is probably used more for communication than for any other single purpose.

In the next several chapters we'll explore the ways you can correspond with other people over the Internet, as well as the reasons you might want to do so. Chapters 5, 7 and 8 describe particular Internet services specially designed for Internet communication: electronic mail, mailing lists, and news groups. We give examples of how other teachers are using these services, provide directions and tips for using them yourself, and outline some ideas for practicing what you've learned.

Chapters 6 and 9 explore the means and methods of Internet communication. The Internet is an entirely new medium for communication, and Internet users have created an entirely new culture within the constraints of the technology. These chapters act as a guidebook might, explaining how the natives express their feelings, what you should and should not say, and how best to work and play in this new environment.

▲ ▲ ▲ ▲ ▲ ▲ ▲ ▲ ▲ ▲ ▲ ▲

CHAPTER 5

Electronic mail

▼▼▼▼▼▼▼▼▼▼▼

SENDING PERSONAL MESSAGES

Many teachers are being given electronic mail accounts at school. But what can you really do with electronic mail—and what can it do for you? How do your messages get to the right people? And how do you actually use it? In this chapter we'll describe how electronic mail works, give some strategies for using it effectively, and provide examples for you to try at home.

▲▲▲▲▲▲▲▲▲▲▲▲

Corresponding with other Internet users

Electronic mail (often called e-mail) is the most common and one of the most useful Internet services. It allows Internet users to send messages among themselves. Each person with an Internet account is given a unique e-mail address which identifies him or her to the rest of the Internet. Once you have an Internet account and an e-mail address, you can use any of a number of e-mail programs to write a message, address it to a friend on the Internet, and send it off.

The message goes from your computer to your Internet provider's computer to another computer in the network to yet another computer and so on, until it finally reaches your friend's computer where it sits and waits for your friend to read it. Messages addressed to people nearby or half-way around the world will arrive within hours or even minutes of sending them.

What can you do with e-mail?

The vast majority of Internet-proficient teachers use electronic mail, and that's not too surprising.[1] Although electronic mail is one of the simplest Internet resources, it is also one of the most powerful. Imagine being able to:

- **Send out a quick announcement** to all of your students' parents—one that you know will get home!

- **Keep in close contact** with former students who have moved on to different cities or countries.

- **Send daily impressions** back to your class during your vacation abroad.

- **Ask the author** of a journal article or textbook questions about her work directly.

---

1   According to one study, 91% of teachers using the Internet in the United States also use electronic mail. (Honey & Henríquez, *Telecommunications and K-12 Educators: Findings from a National Survey*, Bank Street College of Education, 1993)

- **Make your views** on educational policy known to your local and national representatives quickly and easily.

- **Keep in touch** with long-distance friends and family, without long-distance bills.

How does electronic mail work?

In today's fast-paced society of overnight mail and fax machines, the idea of sending someone a message from your computer to theirs does not require much stretch of the imagination. Electronic mail is much like these other modern communication mediums, with one important difference: E-mail messages are composed entirely of what is known as . This means that what you see on your computer keyboard is what you can use in your messages. You get all letters and numbers, punctuation, a few important symbols (like $ and @) and that's it. No fancy pictures or sound files, no fun fonts or styles. [2] If you have been using computers for a while, you'll find that working with your e-mail software is reminiscent of the early days of word processing in DOS or on the Apple II computer.

NET FACTS

▼▼▼▼▼▼▼▼▼▼▼▼

What is ASCII text?

American Standard Code for Information Interchange defines a standard set of characters numbered from 0 to 255. Computers around the world communicate by sending ASCII text to each other, so that they need not worry about conflicting file formats. Unfortunately, it also excludes any possibility for different fonts or font styles, such as **bold**, *italic*, or underline.

▲▲▲▲▲▲▲▲▲▲▲▲

---

2   Actually, that's a bit misleading. You *can* include other files with your e-mail, but it's not yet an easy process, and most teachers we know avoid it if possible.

Luckily, most Internet providers these days offer fairly sophisticated software programs for writing and reading e-mail. Even the software programs provided with text-only accounts offer an impressive array of features, and still remain easy to use.[3] With a single keystroke you can submit a new message, delete an old

Buzzwords

electronic mail (or **e-mail**): An Internet service which allows users to send messages to each other.

e-mail address: The unique identifier computers on the Internet use to identify a specific Internet account.

e-mail program: The software program which allows you to send, receive, and process e-mail messages.

domain name: The part of an e-mail address which names the *computer* which will get the message. It is found to the right of the @ sign.

message, or reply to the person who sent you a message. It seems likely that it is this simplicity as much as anything which has made e-mail so popular.

The e-mail programs for text-only connections have another advantage: They are kept on your Internet service provider's computer. This means that you won't have to buy any software beyond that which came with your modem. Graphical mail programs aren't expensive (see below), but you will have to find one and install it on your own computer if you'd like to be able to point-and-click your way around your electronic mail.

Using electronic mail:

Reading messages

Because not all e-mail programs are alike, the best way to learn about your e-mail program is to have an experienced

3   These programs have been in existence for many years, and are therefore better refined than most of the programs available for graphical connections.

NET FACTS

▼▼▼▼▼▼▼▼▼▼▼▼▼▼▼▼▼

Creating your own e-mail signature

In most e-mail programs, the signature is simply a text file which is added to the end of every e-mail message you write. You can put anything you want in your signature file, but remember: It will go out to everyone you ever send an e-mail message to.

Most people include their name and e-mail address, and possibly their occupation and hometown, in their signatures. Full postal service addresses and phone numbers are usually left out (unless you happen to be a business). A lot of people like to include a favorite quote, or sometimes a picture drawn with ASCII text, but keep in mind that somebody is paying for you to send this. Anything more than a few lines is considered bad manners. Here's an example of a signature file:

```
*********************************************************
Anne Educator            / A teacher affects eternity; he
Nullity High             / can never tell where his
aeducator@horace.dne.edu / influence stops. - Henry Adams
*********************************************************
```

▲▲▲▲▲▲▲▲▲▲▲▲▲▲▲▲▲▲▲

friend lead you through it.[4] Reading and writing e-mail is not a difficult process, but it may take a while for you to learn the intricacies of your own program. To give you some idea of how to work your e-mail program, we'll take you on a quick tour of a generic e-mail program. Our descriptions may not match your own set-up exactly, but chances are they will be similar enough to be helpful.

---

4   Or you can take a class on the subject. You may want to check with your district technology person to see what is available. Often a school or district will offer free classes on the Internet for interested teachers, and e-mail is usually the first subject covered.

NET FACTS

▼▼▼▼▼▼▼▼▼▼▼

Deciphering an e-mail address

mroddy@seattleu.edu

The e-mail address above, which belongs to one of the authors, is a good example. To the left of the @ sign is his user name: mroddy, which is short for Mark Roddy. To the right, you'll see the domain name: seattleu.edu. The first word, seattleu, indicates that his account is on the main computer at Seattle University (i.e. the "domain" of Mark's account), and the second, edu, indicates that it is a school or university site.

The fact that we used all lower-case letters for Mark's e-mail address is arbitrary. E-mail addressing on the Internet is "case-insensitive," meaning that you can use upper-case or lower-case at will and not have to worry about getting the address wrong.

When someone speaks her e-mail address out loud, the @ becomes "at" and the period become "dot". Therefore, the e-mail address above would be pronounced:

"m roddy **at** seattle-u **dot** edu"

The last word in a domain name is usually a tip-off for the kind of host computer, also known as the "domain type:" *edu* refers to any school, college, or university; gov is a government site, and com means a commercial Internet provider. You may also see country-specific endings, such as us (United States), au (Australia), and jp (Japan). For a regularly updated list of country codes, see the *news.answers newsgroup.*

▲▲▲▲▲▲▲▲▲▲▲▲

When you first start your e-mail program, it will present you with a list of the messages in your "IN" box, i.e. messages that have been sent to your account. The message list tells you which messages are new and which you've already read, as well as specific information about each message such as who sent the message, when you received the message, and what the message is about. This last bit of information is called the **subject** of the message, and it is an important part of most Internet communication.

If you open one of the messages in your "IN" box, you'll see it comes in two parts: the **header** and the **body**. The message header is mostly for the computer. It contains information about where the message came from, the message format, and so on—stuff that would go on the outside of a regular mail envelope. The body of the message is the text for you. E-mail programs usually let you hide the message headers when you read your messages, but most people just get used to ignoring it.

Some messages have a third part: the **signature**. This is a few lines of text which are added to the end of every message a person sends. Usually it has the person's full name, their e-mail address, and perhaps their occupation or a pithy quote. Internet users create their own signatures, so they can vary quite dramatically from person to person.

Using electronic mail:
Writing messages

There are two ways of writing an e-mail message: writing a **new message** or writing a **reply**. We'll talk about what goes into a new message first.

Writing new messages

The most important part of a new e-mail message (for the computer at least) is the **e-mail address**. This tells your computer, and other computers on the Internet, where to send your message. An e-mail address comes in two parts: the **user name** and the **domain name**, which are separated by an "@" (pronounced "at"). The domain name is the name of the *com-*

NET FACTS

▼▼▼▼▼▼▼▼▼▼▼

Talking to people through computers

If you are like most teachers who use the Internet, you will find it to be an invaluable communications tool. With it you can talk to one person or a group of people thousands of miles apart at any time of the day or night. It provides what experts call "computer-mediated communication" (understandably abbreviated to CMC). As the name implies, CMC encompasses any communication in which computers are the medium. It is much more than an ultra-quick postal service: It is a new form of communication.

CMC, for the time being, is text-only; thus, it lacks all of the sensory clues we use when talking face-to-face or over the phone. Conversation is based on what you say, not who you are or what you look like. Because of this aspect of CMC, it is important to say what you mean. Miscommunication can happen easily because the person on the other end of the keyboard can't see you wink, hear your tone of voice, or see that you haven't slept in two days. It is especially difficult to convey humor and sarcasm in a

puter which should receive the e-mail, and the user name is the Internet account of the *person* who gets the e-mail.

To the uninitiated, e-mail addresses look like some kind of computerized newspeak. User names are usually just what they say — the user's name, sometimes cropped to eight letters or a first initial and a surname. Domain names are also decipherable if you understand the code, but it doesn't really matter. The important thing is that the Internet computers are able to decipher the domain name as well as the user name and get your e-mail where it needs to go. The only time you'll have to deal with addresses is when you're addressing your e-mail.

Actually, with most e-mail programs, you won't have to deal with them at all. Most e-mail programs allow you to keep text-only environment. This deficiency is partially alleviated by humor marks like :-) for a smile, and ;-) for a wink (see page 87 for more of these marks). However, the danger of misinterpretation still exists. Think before you type.

Through CMC, you will communicate with friends, associates, family, and even people you've never met before from all over the world. In this way it humanizes our relationships by increasing communication and shedding light on different lines of thought, perspective, and opinion. If, however, you lock yourself away in a dim room and limit your communication to CMC, then you've gone too far. CMC is only a supplement to our physical interactions, not a replacement.

When you were young, there was a first time you picked up a ringing phone and didn't know what to expect; there was a first time you dialed a phone number to talk to a friend. Now we take this technology for granted, and, along with it, the subtle way it brings us closer to each other. There was a time, however, when it filled us with wonder.

Be prepared to experience this feeling again with CMC.

an address book: a list of nicknames which are much easier to remember than full e-mail addresses. For instance, instead of writing out my dad's e-mail address (which is completely unintelligible), I just type "Dad" in the address space. The e-mail program substitutes Dad's e-mail address, and I never even think about it. Nicknames can also be used for groups of people, so that you can send one message to all of your school colleagues or students' parents at once. As you begin explore your e-mail program, be sure to learn how to make and use nicknames—you'll find them indispensable.

Now that you've got an e-mail address, you'll need a **subject**. The subject can be very important—especially if you're writing to someone who gets a lot of e-mail. The subject

NET FACTS

▼▼▼▼▼▼▼▼▼▼▼▼

Eudora: An electronic mail example

If you have a graphical connection to your Internet account, you may be using Eudora to read and write your electronic mail. (Eudora is an e-mail program distributed for free to students and teachers by Qualcomm. You can find out more about Eudora at http://www.qualcomm.com/quest/QuestMain.html. Directions for accessing this resource can be found in chapter 10, *The World Wide Web*, on page 137. In the example below, my friend Derek is responding to a message I wrote him about having dinner. The subject of my message was "Saturday going to meeting." Since his message is a response, the subject of his message reads "Re: Saturday going to meeting".

The first seven lines of the message from Derek are part of the header. The header is mostly for Eudora to sort out, but it can also tell me when he wrote the message, to whom he sent it, and so on (on the Cc: line, for instance, you can see that "Mark R. Roddy" got a copy as well). Below that is the actual message, which in this case reads only "Dinner sounds fine with me." Underneath his message, Derek's electronic mail program has included his signature. Derek's signature shows some mountains, rain, and snow (all done with only ASCII text)—an appropriate signature for someone living in the Great Northwest!

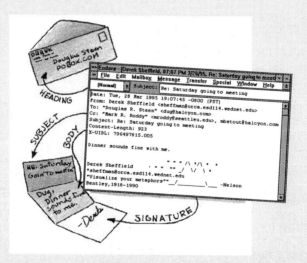

NET FACTS

▼▼▼▼▼▼▼▼▼▼▼▼

Finding people on the Internet

Unfortunately, there's no good way to find a friend's e-mail address on the Internet. There are a few Internet services (such as `finger` and `netfind`) which might help, but the directories they reference are usually so incomplete as to be worthless. If you want to know someone's e-mail address, we recommend that you call them up on the phone and ask them for it. If that doesn't work, you can try the services at:

http://www.nova.edu/Inter-Links/phone.html

or ask your Internet service provider for help.

▲▲▲▲▲▲▲▲▲▲▲▲

should be a clear and concise summary of your message, like "Important: Can't make Tuesday's meeting." Since people see the subject lines before reading the messages, they may skip over ones which don't look important, especially if they're in a hurry. Of course, if you're just writing to friends who know you, you can write anything you want in the subject line. Good friends will read your e-mail no matter what you say.

There are other spaces for you to fill in if you wish: **Cc:** to send someone a "carbon copy" (an antiquated term for computer users!), **Bcc:** to send a "blind carbon copy", i.e. one which is not seen by the other recipients, or **Attachments:** to send files with your e-mail. For the most part, though, once you've added the appropriate e-mail address or nickname to the **To:** line, and an appropriate subject to the **Subject:** line, you're ready to write the message. Type away!

▼▼▼▼▼▼▼▼▼▼▼

Teacher on the Net:

Broadening your perspective

David R. Lineweaver
High school computer science
and math teacher
Harrisonburg High School
Harrisonburg, Virginia
Teaching experience: 23 years
Internet experience: 2 years
E-mail address: dlinewea@pen.k12.va.us

Teacher David Lineweaver says he prefers e-mail over regular mail for several reasons, including cost, ease of use, and immediate response time. Most of his correspondence goes to his daughter who just started college. In David's opinion, this is an excellent way to make use of the Internet:

❝I feel that anything that aids in communication aids in teaching. Even when the correspondence I have has little direct educational value, I am still learning more about what is going on in another location. This gives me a wider perspective, a broader view of the world. I gain more insight into college life and requirements so that I can pass them on to my students and if necessary modify my teaching. While it is not direct one-to-one correspondence I feel that Internet information gathering is a great value to me, my teaching, my students and the learning in my school.❞

For teachers starting on the Internet, David has this advice:

❝For the beginner it is important to practice. Find someone you are familiar with who has an e-mail address and start to correspond with them. Maybe this is a friend or relative and you can exchange family news and updates. Maybe this is a fellow educator in your subject area and you can swap teaching activities, ideas, as well as the frustrations. In short you must invest the time and it will pay dividends.❞

▲▲▲▲▲▲▲▲▲▲▲▲

Writing replies

If someone sends you a message and you'd like to respond to it, you can write a **reply**. Automatic replies are a very useful and common feature of e-mail programs. Just click the appropriate button or enter the appropriate command, and your e-mail program will create a new message already addressed and with the subject line filled out. All you have to do is type your response and send it. Most e-mail programs will even allow you to imbed the previous message in your reply, so that you can make direct references if necessary. Watch out, though! If someone replies to your reply and then you reply to their reply of your reply, and every single reply contains the entire text of the last message sent, you can get some pretty long messages. It's usually a good idea to edit out all of the unnecessary text before sending a reply.

Other things your e-mail program can do

Electronic mail programs have gone from being mere message processing stations to full-fledged filing systems, allowing you to keep folders of e-mail you have received or sent and to search through them for important old messages. You can also print out your messages or save them to a file that you can read on your word processor, although sometimes that's more of a hassle than it's worth. And of course, e-mail programs let you delete e-mail. As your list of e-mail correspondents grows, and your "IN" box fills to overflowing, you might find this last feature to be the most useful of them all!

How to get started with e-mail

When you first get an e-mail account, find a few colleagues or friends who have one too and start sending messages. You can start off with general greetings, catching up, etc. and then gradually move into something approaching letter-writing. If you know someone who works or studies at a college or university in the United States, chances are that person has an e-mail account (although it doesn't mean they use it). Start reading and writing e-mail on a daily (or so) basis; get used to writing quick replies, or filing away messages for later use. This sort of technological efficiency will serve you well as your experience on the Internet grows. If you can sort through your electronic mail quickly, you'll be more likely to read it frequently; and if you read it frequently, you'll have less mail and will be able to sort through it more quickly!

You may argue that this exhortation to use e-mail for personal messages contradicts a major theme of this book: that the Internet is an educational tool. As we've mentioned before, however, we've found that most teachers feel more comfortable with the Internet if they start by using it for their personal needs, then use it for their work outside the classroom, and only bring it into the classroom when they are completely comfortable with it. The Internet, like any tool, is used most effectively (and efficiently) when the user is familiar with its workings.

E-mail is the best way we know of to start getting familiar with the Internet. Almost all of the Internet-using teachers we've spoken to are experienced e-mail users. This doesn't mean that becoming an e-mail expert will make you an effective Internet user, but it may mean that as you become a more effective Internet user, you will find your e-mail practice was worth the time and effort.

What can e-mail do for you?

Being able to send personal messages via electronic mail was one of the first available Internet services, and it is still probably the simplest. This simplicity, however, masks a power which makes it one of the most effective tools on the Internet. Here are some of the ways in which sending personal messages can help improve your teaching.

Posting electronic Post-It® notes

Teachers are some of the few professionals who do not have regular access to a phone as they work. The classic problem of teacher isolation is only compounded by the fact that it is so difficult to reach anyone, even other teachers, during the school day. If you simply want to ask a colleague (especially one from another school) for a recommendation about a specific lesson, you're stuck. Letters seem too slow and phone calls to the main office seem too urgent for mundane correspondence.

Sending personal messages with electronic mail offers a simple solution. You can read your messages or type out a quick note before school, on the weekend, during a break in your day, or whenever it best fits your schedule. E-mail becomes something of an electronic Post-It note: a handy messenger for simple correspondence. In corporate America, it has all but replaced the interoffice memo. Some schools and school systems have also begun to realize its usefulness and efficiency and are beginning to make it available to teachers and administrators. It would not be at all surprising if e-mail were as prevalent in ten years as P.A. systems are now.

Putting it in writing

Electronic mail can handle longer personal messages as well. Many teachers are finding that e-mail discussions with colleagues and friends give them that time they need to reflect upon their work. This reflection is an important part of growth, both personal and professional. Writing down what you want to say before you say it also helps to codify your thoughts and feelings. It means that you can look over what you have said, reflect upon and edit your words before they go out to the world.

Of course, the same good things can be said about regular old-fashioned letter-writing. But sitting down to write a letter, addressing an envelope, and finding a stamp are tasks that few of us can find the time for anymore. E-mail is fast and easy; it combines the speed of the telephone with the clarity of written correspondence.

You've got the whole world ...

Many teachers, upon realizing the wide reach of the Internet, imagine their students connecting with other students across the country or abroad. They imagine what a wonderful adventure this inter-cultural dialog will be for their students: how their minds will broaden, their hearts will open with the experience of meeting new people, of sharing ideas and feelings. What is forgotten, or possibly even dismissed, is what a mind-opening adventure it could be for the teachers themselves.

One of the central tenets of school reform is that we must break the isolation of the classroom. Teachers need more opportunity to share what they know with each other, to discuss broad questions which affect their profession, and to give each other the support they need to teach to their potential. This is happening, now, on the Internet. Teachers are finding a culture which goes beyond the walls of their school, and are learning that the problems they face are also being faced in New York, New Mexico, and New Zealand.

Strategies for using electronic mail

Be polite. Even the most well-intentioned personal messages can take on new meanings when stripped down to a text-only medium. Those of us who like our humor dry find it difficult to add cutesy smileys and "just kidding!" remarks, but they can help keep nice messages from going awry. Also, it is good "netiquette" to sign all your messages and, if you are replying to an earlier message, to include short references to that message. Remember, the person reading your message won't start with the same train of thought you had as you wrote it.

E-mail is (semi-)forever. Learn how to use your electronic mail software to file away your messages for later reference. This can be a life-saver for those times when you "know you had it here somewhere." E-mail addresses aren't that easy to remember, but if you file away e-mail messages with their corresponding header information, you'll always have that to return to. Also, if you're corresponding with old friends or relatives, saving both the messages you receive and the ones you send can make a journal of sorts. So far I haven't heard of anyone publishing the "The Collected Electronic Mail of Anne Author," but who knows?

E-mail is not as private as it seems. Although some people feel that the fear of "hackers" and other techno-miscreants is overblown, it is important to remember that electronic mail is not completely secure. E-mail programs make it simple for someone who has received your message to broadcast it to the world; and you have no guarantee that they won't. Especially in our heavily litigious society, it is important that you be careful about what you say over the Internet.

Be gentle with the unconnected. This warning may seem exaggerated, but you should be aware of the dividing line that falls between the e-mail haves and the e-mail have-nots. One newly connected friend told me that she is happy to have rekindled relationships with old friends on e-mail, but that she now finds herself neglecting her unconnected friends. Most teachers find that their in-school colleagues are usually interested in ideas brought from others on the Internet. However, these same colleagues can become somewhat jealous if the out-of-school culture is viewed as replacing the existing in-school culture.

Beware the time drain. Many teachers who use electronic mail to send personal messages suggest that it is very easy to spend far too much time each day with your electronic mail. It is important that you learn early on how to read and write electronic mail efficiently. You will need to balance this efficiency with writing worth-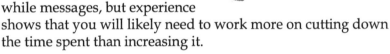 while messages, but experience shows that you will likely need to work more on cutting down the time spent than increasing it.

Things to try at home

Write, write, write. The only activity we can recommend for practicing e-mail is to get out there and write. If you start looking for electronic mail addresses, you're sure to find them everywhere. Here are some examples:

 Write to your friends. Maybe someone you know has e-mail, perhaps even someone you haven't talked to in a while. Call and ask for their e-mail address, and then try sending them a message. If you send out a yearly letter to friends and relatives, include your e-mail address. You may be surprised to learn who is connected.

 Write to your government. The legislative branch of the U.S. government has slowly, but surely, been moving online. Many U.S. Representatives now have e-mail addresses (see *http://www.house.gov* to find yours), and some Senators do as well. The executive branch has an impressive presence online. You can write to the President or Vice President at the following addresses:

| The President | president@whitehouse.gov |
| The Vice President | vice.president@whitehouse.gov |

You won't actually get through to the president, of course, but you will get a nice letter in response describing what the White House will do with your e-mail, and what other Internet services the White House provides.

 Write to reporters, columnists, or cartoonists. Newspapers, magazines, and radio stations are getting e-mail addresses, and they're doing it so that you can write with your comments. If you look through an issue of *Newsweek, Time,* or *People,* or listen to National Public Radio, you'll find that they've set up e-mail addresses for you to use. Even if all you read is the comics, you'll see that cartoonists like Scott Adams (*Dilbert*) are including their e-mail addresses in every strip.

Newsweek	letters@newsweek.com
Time	timeletter@aol.com
People	74774.1513@compuserve.com
NPR's All Things Considered	atc@npr.org
Scott Adams (*Dilbert*)	ScottAdams@aol.com

 Write to us. Our e-mail addresses are listed below. Write to us and let us know how you think the book is so far. We look forward to hearing from you!

| Authors | internet.for.teachers@pobox.com |
| Publisher | rbpress@halcyon.com |

E-MAIL BALANCE SHEET

Reasons to use electronic mail	Reasons not to use electronic mail
✔ **To be more efficient.** It enables you to keep in touch with colleagues, friends, and relatives on a regular basis.	✘ **If you don't want it in writing.** The person who receives your message to can save it, print it, or send it to others. So if you'd rather not have a record of what you said, then don't send an e-mail.
✔ **To think things over.** You can use it to reflect on your life and work, as you might in a hand-written letter.	✘ **If you wish to send confidential information,** such as credit card numbers, student records, or classified documents. Remember, e-mail is generally safe, but not completely secure.
✔ **To save time and money.** It's a simple and inexpensive way to communicate with people all around the world.	✘ **If you want an immediate answer.** Most people read their e-mail *at most* once a day, and often more rarely. You may find yourself waiting for a response, especially if the person you're writing is particularly busy.
✔ **To keep information in order.** Once you understand how your e-mail program's filing system works, you can save and retrieve messages with important information.	✘ **If the contents of your message warrant face-to-face contact.** If it would be rude to fax or leave such a message on someone's answering machine, it would be rude to e-mail it to them.

CHAPTER 6

Expressing yourself on the Internet

LOL   **ROTFL**

▼▼▼▼▼▼▼▼▼▼▼

SMILEYS AND OTHER TECHNIQUES

It's hard to cram the full range of human emotions over a network based mainly on text, but folks on the Internet have been doing their best. Over the years, Internet users have developed a number of conventions for expressing themselves efficiently using only letters, numbers, and punctuation marks. These shorthand techniques go a long way toward eliminating the need for proper word choice and eloquent phrasing; you wouldn't really want us to have to use a thesaurus, would you? ; -)

▲▲▲▲▲▲▲▲▲▲▲

Internet punctuation

Most Internet writers don't have a range of fonts to choose from, or even special character formats like *italics*, <u>underline</u>, or **bold**. Instead, they must rely on new punctuation techniques to provide emphasis. For instance, by typing an underscore before and after a certain word or phrase, Internet writers imply an underline.

```
Whew! That took a _long_ time!
```

Internet writers have also made use of angle brackets <> to provide commentary upon their own writing. You can think of these asides as stage directions; if you want the full effect, you can even perform the action for yourself (although you might want to do so in the privacy of your own home!). Some common examples are:

`<grin>` or `<g>`	when you make a joke.
`<groan>`	when you make a *bad* joke!
`<hug>`	when you're feeling warm and fuzzy.

Internet acronyms

There's no telling why Internet communications are such fertile grounds for acronyms, but more than a few have sprung up, and if you're going to be reading and writing in cyberspace, you may end up using them yourself. Some are obvious (once you've deciphered them), but others have evolved an Internet meaning which transcends their simple translation.

Acronym	Meaning
BTW	**B**y **T**he **W**ay
IMO (also IMHO or IMCO)	**I**n **M**y **H**umble or **C**onsidered **O**pinion *(a disclaimer)*
LOL	(I'm) **L**aughing **O**ut **L**oud
OIC	**O**h, **I** **S**ee! *(okay, it's not really an acronym, but we like it)*

Acronym	Meaning
OTOH	**On The Other Hand** *(useful for debates)*
OTTH	**On The Third Hand** *(even more useful for debates)*
PMFJI	**Pardon Me For Jumping In** *(when you want to contribute to a conversation in progress)*
ROTFL	*(I'm)* **Rolling On The Floor Laughing**
RSN	**Real Soon Now** *(said of bug fixes, new software products, or educational reform—in other words, it's usually meant sarcastically)*
RTFM	**Read The #@%! Manual** *(a reply to someone who is asking an obvious question; it can be meant politely, despite the pejorative, but usually isn't)*
TTFN	**Ta Ta For Now** *(an Internet sign-off)*
YAA	**Yet Another Acronym**

Smileys

The most common form of Internet shorthand is the "smiley" (or as it's sometimes called, the "emoticon"). These little wonders have been catching on outside the Internet lately, and you can even see people wearing them on buttons & tee shirts (no tattoo sightings, as of yet). In case you've never seen one, here's a handy guide for viewing smileys:

1. Tilt your head to the left.

2. Use your imagination.

There are literally hundreds of smileys, but most people use only the basic versions. We've listed a few below, and if you'd like to see more we recommend the book *Smileys*.[1]

---

1   Sanderson, David W. (ed.) *Smileys*. O'Reilly & Associates. Sebastopol, CA. 1993. Or see *http://www.eff.org/papers/eegtti/eeg_286.html*, for the

Smiley	Meaning
:-)	The Basic Smiley. It can mean anything from you're happy to you're joking, but generally indicates lightheartedness. For example: I'm signing off now, because it's Friday and I've got a hot bath waiting for me at home! :-)
=)	Variation on the Basic Smiley
;-) or ;)	The Wink. A smiley with a sly connotation. For example: I'll write when I come back from vacation. _If_ I come back! ;-)
:-D	The Open-Mouthed Smiley. For when you're really happy, or outright laughing. For example: The lesson ran right on time, and the kids ate it up! :-D
:-(	The Inverted Smiley. Things didn't go quite the way they should have. For example: They forecasted snow, but all we got was rain. :-(

The smiley quiz

See if you can match these smileys to their descriptions below.

A.	:-o	1.	Apathetic Smiley
B.	:-		2.	Bartholomew Cubbins
C.	7:-)	3.	Left-handed Smiley
D.	8-)	4.	Ronald Reagan
E.	<<<<<<<<<:-)	5.	Smiley with glasses
F.	(-:	6.	Surprised smiley

Answers

1. B; 2. E; 3. F; 4. C; 5. D; 6. A

Electronic Frontier Foundation's Guide to Smileys. Directions for accessing this resource can be found in Chapter 10, *The World Wide Web*, on page 137.

CHAPTER 7

Mailing lists

▼▼▼▼▼▼▼▼▼▼▼▼

SENDING MESSAGES TO GROUPS

Mailing lists have long been one of the most popular resources on the Internet, especially among educators. In this chapter we'll explain what a mailing list is and how you can use it personally and professionally. We'll also describe the different kinds of mailing lists, give you some mailing list examples you can use immediately, and show you where to go to find other mailing lists that might suit your needs.

▲▲▲▲▲▲▲▲▲▲▲▲

▼ ▼ ▼ ▼ ▼ ▼ ▼ ▼ ▼ ▼ ▼

Teacher on the Net

Teacher finds it on the Net

Connie Mark
Fourth-grade teacher
Waiau Elementary School
Pearl City, Hawaii
Teaching experience: 25 years
Internet experience: 4 years
E-mail: *conniem@kalama.doe.hawaii.edu*

Teacher Connie Mark is new to the fourth grade, but she's not new to the Internet. She's done projects with her first and second grade students, and she knows how to get what she wants out of the Internet. "When I want to learn about something," she writes, "I go and search for it on the Internet." Here's how she has been using mailing lists to improve her teaching:

❝I join by subscribing and lurking [reading messages] to see what the discussion is about. I get ideas or question educators as to what they do in the classroom. I also find other educators who are willing to exchange information about certain lessons that my class is studying, thereby enriching one's teaching and learning. This is the most important place where one can meet people. I did a Day in the Life... project and exchanged writings with educators in Minnesota, Nevada, and New York. I met an educator in Pittsburgh and we did a multimedia project using the concept of autobiographies. ... I conducted a states multimedia project where we exchanged the same questions about our state and then added it to a slideshow to be exchanged through snail mail. ... An educator in New York sent us rocks that his class had studied, thereby enriching our curriculum on the earth. I, in return, sent him informational pictures about volcanoes and rocks in Hawaii.❞

▲ ▲ ▲ ▲ ▲ ▲ ▲ ▲ ▲ ▲ ▲

Keeping in touch

I t doesn't take a long time using electronic mail to realize that being able to send an e-mail message to several people at once is a very useful feature. One way of doing this we've already described: You can set up your own nicknames for groups of people on the Internet. For instance, one of the authors made a group named "Katie News" which includes his parents, his wife's parents, his brothers and sisters, and a few other relatives who don't live nearby. Whenever he has news to share about his daughter Katie, he simply writes an e-mail message to "Katie News" and then all of his relatives can share in the joy of that first molar.

Any or all of them could reply to such a message, and even include all the other recipients in the reply, so that everyone who got the first message would get the reply as well. If they want to write a new message to this group of people, however, they'd have to do what he did: gather everyone's e-mail address and make a nickname for the entire group. Later, when a cousin gets her own e-mail address, everyone involved would have to add her name to their own lists, and then she'd have to make a list. This would happen any time anyone wanted to join.

Buzzwords

listserv: The most popular mailing list software program. This program is run on your service provider's computer—you do not have to buy one for yourself.

mailing list: Automated electronic mail which allows messages to be sent to a group of subscribers rather than specific e-mail addresses.

subscribe: To join a particular mailing list so that you will get all the messages sent to that mailing list.

Automating such mundane tasks is the *raison d'être* of our friend the computer. Software programs called **listserv**s (spelled without the "e" and sometimes in all capitals) residing on big Internet computers keep track of lists of e-mail addresses and act as a distribution centers for any e-mail messages sent to the main list address. This type of Internet service is called a **mailing list**.

What can you do with mailing lists?

E-mail automation was the impetus behind creating mailing lists, but they have grown to be far more important and useful than this simple description would imply. Imagine opening your electronic mail each morning to find:

- **Funding opportunities** for yourself, your classroom, and your school.

- **A daily report** on the progress towards the educational Goals 2000.

- **Information about new Internet resources** as they become available.

- **A word-a-day** vocabulary builder.

- **Ways of conferencing** with groups of people over great distances during your spare time.

What kind of mailing lists are available?

Mailing lists are set up to address a group of people who have a similar interest, like the relatives interested in Katie's development, or a group of science teachers. Some mailing lists are simply free-form discussions, anyone who wants can send any message they wish to the entire list of people. We call these **unmoderated discussion lists**. Others, **moderated discussion lists**, have a human administrator who filters the messages so that only appropriate ones are sent out to the group.

Buzzwords

unmoderated: A mailing list which has no human intervention. Messages sent to such a list will be automatically distributed to all subscribers.

moderated: A mailing list run by a human (the moderator). Messages sent to such a list will be read by the moderator and distributed only if they are appropriate.

As membership for any mailing list grows, so does the volume of messages on that list. As you may imagine, mailing lists with a few thousand subscribers can generate a lot of e-mail, even if they're moderated. For this reason, some moderated mailing lists have ceased to be discussions at all. Instead, they distribute announcements about a particular topic or periodic e-mail (like a word-a-day or educational news of the week). These mailing lists do not allow subscribers to submit e-mail messages for distribution at all, so we call them **announcement lists**.

How do mailing lists work?

You can think of mailing lists as mechanical office secretaries, with one secretary for each group of people you wish to address. For instance, suppose there's a mechanical secretary for science teachers named "Bill Ology" *<groan>*. Bill keeps a list of everyone who teaches science. If you wish to write a message to all of the science teachers, simply place the message in Bill's mailbox, and he'll make as many copies as necessary, putting one into every list member's box. Mailing list programs act just like Bill, distributing a copy of every e-mail message they receive to every member of the mailing list. In order to send an e-mail message to a mailing list, simply write to the main list address and the software program on the other end will take care of everything.

Now assume that a student teacher, who is particularly interested in science, starts working at the school. She'd like to be on the list, so she places a message in Bill's mailbox which says "Please put me on the science teacher's list." She was hoping that Bill would read this message and do what she asked. Unfortunately, Bill is an entirely mechanical secretary. He copies her message and puts one copy into every science teacher's box. Now when the list members check their mailboxes, they'll find a message from the new student teacher which doesn't make any sense. Whoops!

Most mailing lists, like Bill, are entirely automatic. *Anything* you send to the mailing list will be automatically distributed to hundreds or thousands of people (depending on the size of the list). For this reason, mailing lists have a separate, administrative e-mail address for requests regarding the mailing list itself. Usually e-mail messages sent to the administrative address are read by a computer as well, so they must be written in a specific format in order to be interpreted correctly. Unfortunately, this format varies depending upon the mailing list software used.

How do you find the right mailing list?

One of the nicest things about mailing lists is that if you know how to use e-mail, then you already know how to use mailing lists. Once you've subscribed to a particular list, messages from that list will come directly to your mailbox, and writing a message to the list is as easy as writing a message to a friend. Sometimes it takes a little doing to get on or off a mailing list (the computers reading the administrative mail are very picky about details like spelling and format), but once you're subscribed it's a piece of cake. *Finding* the right mailing list is another thing altogether.

Anyone with the necessary software and space on a big Internet computer can set up a mailing list, and sometimes it seems as though they all have! There are thousands of mailing lists available, providing everything for discussion forums for teachers of English as a second language to the daily distribution of David Letterman's Top Ten List from his show the night before.

So how do you find a mailing list (or two) which meets your needs? The best answer is, once again, ask a friend to recommend one. Or you may want to get the directory of mailing lists available for download[1] at:

```
ftp://rtfm.mit.edu/pub/usenet/news.answers/mail/mailing-lists/
```

Be ready: it's a fourteen part list (files *part01* through *part14*) and contains brief descriptions of almost twelve hundred mailing lists. If you have World Wide Web browsing capability you can find similar lists of mailing lists, this time divided nicely into subject areas, at:

```
http://www.neosoft.com/internet/paml/
```
```
http://www.tile.net/tile/listserv/index.html
```
```
gopher://dewey.lib.ncsu.edu/11/library/stacks/acadlist
```

Despite their length, these lists are not comprehensive. Also, the descriptions are sparse and relate only to the intended purpose of the list, leaving out important information like how many messages are distributed each day or the level of discussion taking place. If you'd like more in-depth analysis of mailing lists especially appropriate for teachers, try downloading:

File name:	IRD-listservs.txt
From URL:	ftp://tcet.unt.edu/pub/telecomputing-info/IRD/IRD-listservs.txt

It contains comments about each of a couple dozen mailing lists, as well as specific descriptions of how to subscribe and other services provided by each mailing list. Unfortunately, the information is already a year old, and by Internet standards that's an eternity. We've listed a few of our favorite

---

1   Directions for accessing this resource can be found in Chapter 10, *The World Wide Web*, on page 137.

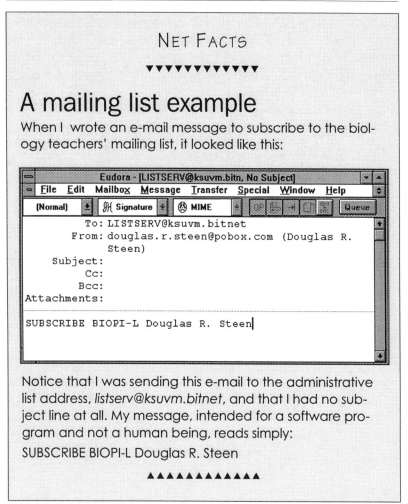

NET FACTS

▼▼▼▼▼▼▼▼▼▼▼

A mailing list example

When I wrote an e-mail message to subscribe to the biology teachers' mailing list, it looked like this:

```
         Eudora - [LISTSERV@ksuvm.bitn, No Subject]
 File   Edit   Mailbox   Message   Transfer   Special   Window   Help
 (Normal)        ℋ Signature        MIME                              Queue

        To: LISTSERV@ksuvm.bitnet
      From: douglas.r.steen@pobox.com (Douglas R.
            Steen)
   Subject:
        Cc:
       Bcc:
Attachments:

SUBSCRIBE BIOPI-L Douglas R. Steen|
```

Notice that I was sending this e-mail to the administrative list address, *listserv@ksuvm.bitnet*, and that I had no subject line at all. My message, intended for a software program and not a human being, reads simply:

SUBSCRIBE BIOPI-L Douglas R. Steen

▲▲▲▲▲▲▲▲▲▲▲▲

mailing lists in Appendix A, *Internet resources*, starting on page 267, and you're welcome to try those out as well.

How to subscribe to a mailing list

Let's say you want to join a mailing list for high school biology teachers. You can send an e-mail message to *listserv@ksuvm.bitnet* which reads only *SUBSCRIBE BIOPI-L your name*. In this case, *BIOPI-L* is the name of the mailing list, and *SUBSCRIBE* indicates your intentions. Soon after sending your subscription message you will receive an automatic reply from the mailing list program indicating that you are subscribed to the list. You will then start getting any messages that anyone writes to *BIOPI-L@ksuvm.bitnet* These messages could include announcements of grant possibilities, questions about the best methods for teaching environmental science, or discussions about the issues involved in teaching AIDS education in the biology curriculum.[2]

Notice that there are two different e-mail addresses given above:

listserv@ksuvm.bitnet

is for administrative messages, and:

BIOPI-L@ksuvm.bitnet

is for writing to the group of subscribers. Sending a message to *BIOPI-L@ksuvm.bitnet* asking to be removed from the list is a sure way to mark yourself as a neophyte, and possibly to generate some grouchy replies as well.

In order to subscribe to a mailing list, you need to know two things: the administrative e-mail address and the directions for writing the subscription message. In the example above, the administrative e-mail address is:

listserv@ksuvm.bitnet

and to subscribe you send an e-mail message with:

SUBSCRIBE BIOPI-L your name

in the message, leaving the subject line blank.

This format is common to all mailing lists run by listserv software. If you are ever given the administrative e-mail address for a mailing list, but not given directions for subscrib-

---

2   All of these subjects came up on this mailing list within the first week of
    1995.

ing, try writing:

SUBSCRIBE mailing list name your name

It may not work, but the worst that can happen (assuming that you are mailing it to the *administrative* address and not the main list address) is that you'll get a message from the software program complaining that it can't understand. In that case, an e-mail message which simply reads *HELP* will sometimes work.

What can mailing lists do for you?

We've already described some of the ways that mailing lists can go beyond simply automating e-mail. Below we've divided the types of mailing lists into three categories: unmoderated discussion lists, moderated discussion lists, and announcement lists. We'll describe each in more detail and give you a sense of what each can do for your work.

Unmoderated discussion lists

The most common form of mailing list is the unmoderated discussion list. You can think of unmoderated discussion lists as telephone poles with posted notices. Anyone can put anything up, and usually they

do! These mailing lists have human administrators, but their job is purely technical—they do not restrict the flow of the messages coming through the mailing list. You can send any message you choose to everyone on the mailing list (this could be hundreds of people, remember) and any message any subscriber sends to the list will end up in your mailbox. Each unmoderated discussion list will have a particular topic, but the dialog which ensues is open and sometimes strays far wide of its intended focus.

Unmoderated discussion lists, especially those with a large and garrulous membership, can overwhelm your mailbox. However, a forum for hearing others and expressing yourself can be rewarding and enriching. Taking part in discussions about teaching may help you improve your own teaching by opening your mind to new ideas and allowing you time to reflect on your own work.

We will explore the growth possibilities inherent in group discussions in Chapter 8, *Newsgroups*, on page 107.

Moderated discussion lists

Moderated discussion lists have all of the advantages of unmoderated discussion lists, and one more: Someone is in charge. This someone, the moderator, reads the incoming messages and only forwards those which are appropriate to the entire list. This kind of list is more like a display box in a school hallway than a telephone pole, since someone decides what will go in it and what won't. Usually, though, any reasonable request is honored. If you join a moderated discussion list you should have a far more  manageable number of messages coming to your mailbox, and you may find the discussion is more likely to stay on-topic.

Of course, the quality of a moderated discussion list depends largely on the moderator. Also, moderating a large discussion list is a difficult and time-consuming task. Very few discussion list moderators are paid to moderate, which accounts for the relatively few moderated discussion lists, compared to the huge number of unmoderated discussion lists.[3]

---

3   Commercial networks, like CompuServ and America Online, can afford to pay for moderators. For this reason they often have more

Announcement lists

Some mailing lists send out periodic reports to their subscribers. You can imagine these lists to be like the public service announcements on television. They come out at a certain time each day (usually), and they contain specific messages written for the viewing public. Like public service announcements, the communication goes in one direction only: from the ones in charge to you. Many are just for fun (such as the *TOPTEN* and the *WORD.A.DAY* lists described in *Internet resouces* on page 267), but a few are set up to send educational announcements to teachers and other education professionals.

Educational announcement lists are much like miniature electronic newsletters. Each "issue", or e-mail message, contains a handful of reports (usually about a particular educational topic), and each report is only a few paragraphs long. Anything more would make the e-mail message too cumbersome to receive and store efficiently. Therefore, you won't find the kind of depth or detail you would expect from a true newsletter in a announcement list.

On the other hand, getting a newsletter (even a small one) via electronic mail means that you can easily scan, save, or delete it. If something catches your eye, you can save it away for later, print it out, or pass it on to another friend who has e-mail. If nothing interests you, then you can get rid of it with a keystroke. This kind of efficient handling capability makes you wish all of your newsletters arrived via e-mail.

---

moderated discussion lists than the Internet.

Strategies for using mailing lists

Because they are an extension of electronic mail, mailing lists are fairly simple to use. However, there are a few important points that you should keep in mind:

 There are two addresses for each list. Anything administrative, such as subscribing and unsubscribing, is handled by sending e-mail to the administrative e-mail address. This address usually starts with *listserv@* or *majordomo@*. The other mailing list address (which usually starts with the name of the mailing list itself, like *BIOPI-L@* is for sending messages intended for other mailing list members.

 Don't use your signature file. When you subscribe to a mailing list, a computer program reads your e-mail message and adds you to the list. Some of these programs become confused if they see your signature at the bottom of your message. If you are unable to subscribe to a mailing list, try disabling the "include signature" option in your e-mail program.

 Save the welcome message. The first message you get after subscribing to a new mailing list will be a welcome message which describes the mailing list and the methods for subscribing and unsubscribing. *Be sure to save this message.* You may even want to save it in a special folder for mailing list welcome messages, so you'll know where it is when you want it.[4] The welcome message will come in handy when you wish to unsubscribe, or if you want to let a friend know how to sign up.

There are also strategies for joining in discussions over mailing lists, but these strategies are similar enough to the ones for joining a newsgroups discussion, that we will save them until Chapter 8, *Newsgroups*, on page 107.

---

4   If you don't know how to save an e-mail message, read through the instructions which came with your e-mail software, or talk to a friend who uses the same e-mail package.

Finally, there are a few caveats we should mention before you start subscribing to mailing lists:

 Subscribe from your own account. The software programs which run the mailing lists take your e-mail address from the message you send, so if you send a message from a friend's account, that friend will be subscribed. Therefore, make sure you are using your own account when you subscribe to mailing lists for yourself.

 They may not be there. Mailing lists, like almost all other Internet services, come and go. The larger mailing lists are likely to be more stable, but you can never tell. If you read about a mailing list, try to subscribe, and can't, it may mean that the mailing list has been disconnected, or possibly that it has moved. Unfortunately, there's no easy way to discover what happened to a missing mailing list.

Things to try at home

Subscribing to a mailing list is simple: just write an e-mail message and you're in. Finding one which suits you can be more problematic. Appendix A, *Internet resources*, has descriptions of several mailing lists which we've found useful, interesting, or fun. Find one among them which looks good and give it a whirl. If you decide it's not for you, you can always unsubscribe (if you kept the message which tells you how!)

MAILING LIST BALANCE SHEET

Reasons to use mailing lists	Reasons not to use mailing lists
✔ **To discuss common interests.** You have a personal hobby, political agenda, medical condition, etc. and you'd like to talk with other people about it. On a mailing list you can find people worldwide who share your interest.	✘ **Too much e-mail.** If you subscribe to too many mailing lists, or even a few voluble ones, you may find yourself completely inundated with e-mail. After a while it gets hard to find the important, personal messages with all of the discussion going on.
✔ **To collaborate.** You are working on a collaborative project over the Internet. Mailing lists are often the best way to hold "meetings" without getting everybody together. We'll talk more about this subject in *Working with people on the Internet* on page 209.	✘ **No mailing lists you like.** Although there are many mailing lists out there, and many more being added all of the time, there's no guarantee that there's one for your particular interest.
✔ **To keep up.** You would like to keep informed about a particular topic, such as national education goals or your favorite TV program. Announcement lists run by non-profit groups and for-profit companies are becoming more and more common.	
✔ **To find people to e-mail.** You'd like to start getting mail, and no one is writing you! You may laugh, but we have a sneaking suspicion that many people start subscribing to mailing lists just for this reason. Announcement lists which send out messages daily will ensure that your mailbox isn't empty.	

CHAPTER 8

Newsgroups

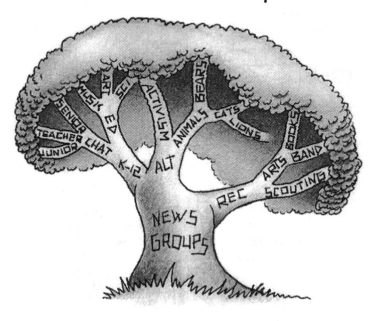

▼▼▼▼▼▼▼▼▼▼▼

READING ARTICLES IN A FORUM

The Internet is alive with discussion and debate. People the world over argue controversial issues, post interesting information, and ask one another questions on Internet newsgroups. Newsgroups are one of the oldest Internet services, and they have in large part contributed to what the Internet is today. In this chapter, we will show you what's available to you and how newsgroups work, as well as how to use them effectively and what they can do for you in and out of the classroom.

▲▲▲▲▲▲▲▲▲▲▲

Mailing lists on demand

Mailing lists are handy because they allow you to communicate with a group of people with a specific interest, without knowing each person's individual e-mail address. However, they can also be intrusive. If, every time you read your mail, you have to read through 10 or 15 messages that don't interest you to find the few that do, it can become tiring. Also, mailing lists are more appropriate for a continued interest in a subject (like physical education) than a transient one (like people who might have an old modem for sale).

There is a solution to these problems: **newsgroups**. Newsgroups are mailing lists on demand. Instead of getting messages each day from a mailing list, you must run a special software program called a **newsreader**, choose a newsgroup from the list of those available, and sort through the messages (or **articles**) which have been posted to that newsgroup. If this seems like more of a hassle than mailing lists, it is. However, newsgroup articles are available when you want to read them, not simply when they are sent. Also, the newsgroups available to you are listed by your Internet service provider, which makes finding a newsgroup on a particular topic much simpler than finding a mailing list.

 Buzzwords

article: A message in a newsgroup.

newsgroup: A place to post articles about a particular topic.

newsreader: A software program which will let you subscribe to a particular newsgroup, read newsgroup articles, post articles to a newsgroup, and so on. If you wish to use a graphical newsreader, you will need to find the software for your own computer. If you are using a text-only connection, the software will be available for use on your Internet service provider's computer.

post: To place an article in a newsgroup so that all subscribers can read it. (Sometimes "post" is used as a noun, in that case it is a synonym for "article.")

subscribe: To mark a newsgroup as one you will read frequently. Some newsreaders force you to subscribe to a newsgroups before reading the articles within, others do not.

What can you do with newsgroups?

Although there are some newsgroups which simply disseminate information, the vast majority are discussion groups: people sharing information, ideas, and opinions with each other. These discussions are joined by people from all walks of life living all over the world. Imagine sharing in discussions which include:

- **First-hand reports** of important news stories as they happen: During the spring 1995 outbreak of the Ebola virus in Zaire, newsgroups provided information needed to find newswire stories and interviews, daily developments in the crisis, and even electron micrographs of the virus itself.

- **Philosophical debate** about the future of teaching with educators from around the globe: Censorship, AIDS education, race and I.Q. ... if its been a hot issue, its been discussed in newsgroups.

- **Specific suggestions** for real classroom use: One new teacher substitute wrote to ask for ideas to keep her students in line; she got several tried and true techniques from experienced teachers.

- **Educators reaching out** find resources for their students: One school librarian in Colorado used a newsgroup to find a pen pal for an 11-year-old Korean-born student who wanted to learn more about her country of origin.

- **Announcements** about exciting projects for yourself and your classroom: A German producer posted an article asking for students who had foreign penpals to be part of a new television series.

- **Answers to questions** on a particular topic: In the K-12 teacher chat group, people have asked for everything from international cooking lesson plans to gift ideas for favorite teachers.

How do newsgroups work?

Newsgroups can be likened to big bulletin boards, much like the kind that are found in school faculty rooms or main offices. Each bulletin board has its own purpose. One newsgroup might be for messages about health and physical education (*k12.ed.health-pe*), and another for messages about selling or trading modems (*misc.forsale.computers.modems*). Internet users can read the articles in any newsgroup, or post their own message to that group (i.e. display it for all to read). This allows for continuing discussions about issues regarding

---

NET FACTS

▼▼▼▼▼▼▼▼▼▼▼▼▼▼▼▼▼

A (very) brief history of newsgroups

Newsgroups started as their own network, User's Network, or Usenet (which is why they are sometimes referred to as "Usenet groups" or "Usenet news"). The software behind the newsgroup service was written by graduate students and high school students in the early 1980's. Since that time, Usenet has grown far beyond the first connection (between Duke University and the University of North Carolina). There are currently more than 10,000 newsgroups, and Usenet has become an important part of the Internet itself.

Now that Usenet is available over the Internet, any computer directly connected to the Internet (like the one your Internet provider uses) can access any given newsgroup. Each Internet provider decides which newsgroups to access, and then you can subscribe to any of the newsgroups in its list.

If you'd like to learn more about the history of Usenet, see:

Amdahl Corporation's USENET History Page

http://www.amdahl.com/internet/events/usenet-history.txt

▲▲▲▲▲▲▲▲▲▲▲▲▲▲▲▲▲▲

the newsgroup topic, as well as announcements, offers, questions, and so on.

Buzzwords

moderated: A newsgroup run by a human (the moderator). Articles sent to such a list will be read by the moderator and posted only if they are appropriate.

unmoderated: A newsgroup which has no human intervention. Aritcles posted to such a newsgroup can be read by anyone subscribing.

In order to read the articles in a newsgroup, you must have a special software program called a **newsreader**. Like e-mail software programs, newsreaders are usually provided by your Internet service provider, or they can be found for free on the Internet.[1] Newsreaders allow you to subscribe to a newsgroup, read the articles in that group, post new articles, post responses to others articles, or respond to others articles via e-mail.

Depending on your connection to the Internet, newsreaders can be simple to use or a real pain in the neck. The most common newsreaders for text-only connections, *tin*, *rn*, and *trn*, have an impressive array of functions for managing your newsgroup articles, but they force you to use esoteric commands and arcane keystroke combinations. Graphical newsreaders, on the other hand, provide most of the same functionality, but in a user-friendly way. One of our favorite graphical newsreaders, Netscape, is also a World Wide Web browser. It is free for educators; we'll describe how you can get it in *Using Netscape as a newsreader* on page 115.

What kind of newsgroups are available?

Newsgroups, like mailing lists, focus on a particular topic, and like mailing lists, they can be **moderated** or **unmoderated**. For the most part, however, newsgroups are for discussions,

---

1   Also like e-mail software programs, you'll need to get one for your own computer only if you wish to use a graphical newsreader. If you're on a text-only connection, your Internet service providers computer will have the necessary software.

not announcements or periodic reports. For this reason, they are often called discussion groups.

How to get started with newsgroups

Each time you start your newsreader, you will be presented with a list of subscribed newsgroups. These are the newsgroups in which you have indicated an interest. The first time you start your newsreader, this list will probably include newsgroups such as *news.announce.newusers* and *news.answers*: newsgroups specifically designed for new users.

From this point it is usually a simple step to find a list of available newsgroups.[2] This list will *not* be a complete list of all possible newsgroups, but instead a list of all the newsgroups to which you have access. Your Internet service provider determines which groups are on this list; in this way it is something like your local cable television provider. Which newsgroups are carried is a decision based on any number of criteria. If you are connecting through a commercial Internet service provider, they may carry as many as they can. Just as with cable providers, the more they carry, the more attractive they are to potential customers.[3] If you are connecting through a school or district, however, you may have only appropriate newsgroups. School providers are unlikely to carry the newsgroup equivalent of the Playboy Channel.

Deciding which newsgroup(s) to read can be quite a chore. Our Internet service provider, for example, carries over 6,000 groups! Fortunately, newsgroups are divided hierarchically by name, and these names give you an idea of what kind of discussions take place in each newsgroup. At the top of the hierarchy are general subjects: *comp*, for computer discussions; *rec*, for recreational discussions; *alt*, for alternative discussions;

---

2   If you are using Netscape as your newsreader, you should press the
     View all newsgroups button.

3   If you find that a newsgroup which interests you is not carried by your
     Internet service provider, you should ask the provider to carry it. They
     are much more likely than your local cable provider to take these type
     of requests to heart.

sci, for scientific discussions; *k12*, for education discussions; and so on.

The next step down the hierarchy further delineates the discussion. Anything in *k12.chat* (such as *k12.chat.teacher*) is for miscellaneous chatting, whereas newsgroups in *k12.ed* are for specific educational discussions (*k12.ed.math* is a good example). By the time you've gotten to the bottom of the hierarchy, you have quite a number of disparate newsgroups whose topics range from the general (like *alt.adoption*) to the specific (like *sci.bio.entomology.lepidoptera*) to the silly (like *alt.barney. dinosaur.die.die.die*). There's even a newsgroup which is supposedly devoted to the destruction of the Internet itself (*alt.destory.the.internet*) although no one in the group has discussed this topic for quite some time!

So how do you go about finding the right newsgroup for you? If you are interested in gardening (perhaps because you've been enlisted to run the school's Pea Patch program), you can start by searching for the word garden among all of the available newsgroups.[4] This will give you *rec.gardens, rec.gardens.orchids*, and *rec.gardens.roses*. The first of these is a newsgroup for all gardeners, and the next two are set aside for orchid and rose aficionados respectively. Once you've found a group that looks interesting, you can subscribe to it, or just begin to read the available articles.

Subscribing to a newsgroup is different than subscribing to a mailing list (see page 98). Subscribing to a mailing list gives you access to the messages in the mailing list; you cannot read the messages unless you are subscribed. Some newsreaders force you to subscribe to a newsgroup before reading the articles there, but on many you can read the articles whether or not you subscribe. Subscribing to a newsgroup simply indicates that you'd like it on your hot list of newsgroup favorites. When you tell your newsreader that you want to subscribe to a newsgroup (a simple process for most newsreaders—no special messages to write or formats to follow), your newsreader will add it to the list of favorites. Whenever you start your newsreader, you will be presented with that

---

4   For information on how to search through the list of newsgroups, see
     your newsreader documentation, or an experienced friend.

list; thus you can quickly and easily jump to your favorites without having to wade through thousands of others.

When you go to read the articles in a newsgroup (either a subscribed newsgroup, or a newsgroup from the list of all available newsgroups), your newsreader will retrieve a list of article **headers**. These headers, like e-mail headers, contain information about the article: such as when it was posted, who posted it, and its subject. From this list of headers you can then choose the specific articles which interest you the most and open them to read. When you finally open an article, you'll find that it looks much like an e-mail message. In fact, e-mail messages and newsgroup articles are essentially the same thing; they are just written for different audiences.

When you open a newsgroup article to read, your newsreader will mark it as having been read. Articles that have been read will not appear the next time you open your newsreader.[5] When you finish reading the articles which interest you from a newsgroup it is a good idea to **catch up**. Catching up is a newsreader term for marking all of the articles in the newsgroup as if they had been already read. This will mean that you won't have to sort through the articles you have already seen (and dismissed) the next time you open that newsgroup. Catching up can be accomplished with a single click or keystroke (see your newsreader instructions for details).

You can do many of the same things with a newsgroup article that you can with an e-mail message. For instance, if it's something you're interested in, you can save it as a text file, or you can print it out. If you're not interested in the article, you can simply ignore it (unlike e-mail, it is not taking up any of your personal space, so there is no need to delete it). If you'd like to respond to what was said, you can **reply** to the person who posted the article via e-mail, or you can post a **follow-up** article to the newsgroup. By posting a follow-up article you are continuing the **thread** of the discussion, and others may choose to read and reply to your follow-up. Because your article will be posted for anyone on the Internet to read, you should be extra careful about what you write. Guidelines for

---

5   This is the case for most newsreaders. Some, however, like Netscape,
     will simply mark them in a different color.

when to reply via e-mail and when to post a follow-up article are described below.

Using Netscape as a newsreader

Netscape is a popular World Wide Web browser (more about that in Chapter 10, page 137), but it also doubles as a graphical newsreader. Below you see the screen which appears after clicking the Newsgroups button. This screen shows you your list of subscribed newsgroups. Notice that *news.announce.newusers*, a moderated newsgroup, currently has 50 articles, while *news.newusers.questions*, an unmoderated newsgroup, has almost 6,000!

From this screen you can click the View all newsgroups button, which would give you a list of all the available newsgroups. You could then choose a few and subscribe. From then on, those newsgroups would also appear on this first page.

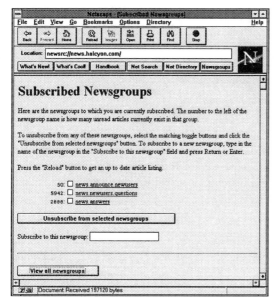

The default newsgroup home page in Netscape.

Viewing existing articles

After finding the *k12.ed.science* newsgroup and clicking on it to get a list of the available articles, a screen like the one below appears.

Here you see the subject lines of the first dozen articles. Articles with solid round bullets are original; articles with empty squares are replies. If you are curious what Elizabeth A. Keator has said about vinegar and baking soda, you can simply open her article (by clicking on it) and read it.

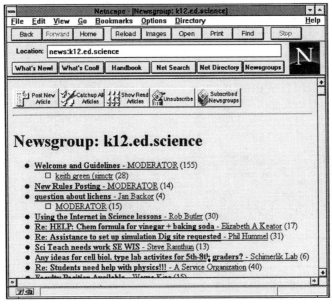

Indented lines in the list of articles in the k12.ed.science newsgroup show that someone has responded to a question or issue.

Responding to a message

If you did open Elizabeth Keator's article, you would see the screen below. The first part has header information: the subject of the article, when it was posted, who posted it, etc. Below that the article itself. In this case, Elizabeth is replying to Mark Boehlen, who asked for the chemical formula for vinegar and baking soda. Not only does this article provide you with information about chemical reactions, it also gives you the names and e-mail addresses of two teachers interested in chemistry (Elizabeth Keator and Mark Boehlen). If you had something to add to this information, you could post a follow-up to the entire newsgroup by clicking the Post Reply button. If you'd rather just e-mail a private note to Elizabeth, you can click Mail & Post Reply.

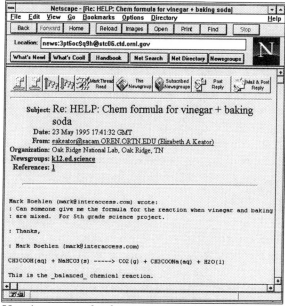

Here is an example of a newsgroup reply in Netscape.

What can newsgroups do for you?

You can stay on top of your field. Subscribing to a newsgroup is like subscribing to an educational journal: You can browse it for information and inspiration, but you rarely read it straight through. Teachers can find all sorts of information simply by subscribing to a newsgroup and reading the articles on a regular basis. Conference schedules, lesson ideas, new Internet sites, and more are often distributed through these channels. Newsgroup discussions often focus on current issues as well as philosophical debates, and you may find that the Internet helps you keep abreast of the teaching profession or your favorite subject area. It's important to remember, however, that nobody is authenticating what is written on the In-

▼▼▼▼▼▼▼▼▼▼▼

Teacher on the Net

Keeping up-to-date on the Internet

Eric Hendrickson
High school chemistry teacher
Presque Isle High School
Presque Isle, Maine
Teaching experience: 21 years
Internet experience: 8-10 years
E-mail: *hendrie@pirtc.pihs.sad1.k12.me.us*

Eric Hendrickson keeps himself up-to-date in the fields of education and chemistry by joining newsgroup discussions. This is especially important to Eric because "as an educator in a rural area, with my nearest peer with common interest more than three hours away, it gives me access to people with common interests at any time of the day." He had this to say about his favorite newsgroup:

❝While I commonly use a number of different newsgroups in various areas, my favorite group is called *sci.chem.* ... The main reason that I use this group is that it allows me to stay current in chemistry while at the same time expanding my knowledge in the area of common chemistry, making it more interesting and relevant for my students. It is through the use of this group that I was able to explain to my students in class about the discovery of element 110, including how it was discovered and how long it lasted, long before it was made public on the evening news. The information that I was able to give the students came directly from the place where the element was discovered written by the people involved in the discovery. If I had to wait to read about the discovery before I could bring it to the attention of my students it would have been some time, and then only in bits and pieces. ... I have in the recent past asked a question about topics in a certain textbook and had the author of the book respond to the question including an explanation of why it was presented in that fashion in the book.❞

▲▲▲▲▲▲▲▲▲▲▲▲

ternet. The old adage about not believing everything you read holds doubly true for newsgroups.

You can find a community of enthusiasts. Using Internet newsgroup discussions as a means of collecting information can be interesting, but it's not that efficient. Often the information that comes through is something of a grab bag, and useful ideas are serendipitous. If you are joining a newsgroup solely as a source of information, you may be disappointed; these discussions often satisfy emotional more than technical needs. What makes them worthwhile is becoming involved. The Internet provides a collegial atmosphere which allows you to share experiences and thoughts with a variety of others. The number and depth of in-school philosophical discussions and hot-topic debates are limited by time constraints. The Internet is an out-of-school forum for these professional and recreational dialogs.

You can ask specific questions. Many people, teachers included, like to use Internet group discussions as a means of getting answers to specific questions. As an example, suppose that you'd like to find a specific board game to teach your kids history; one you remember enjoying when you were their age. It simulated pre-World War I Europe and it involved a lot of bargaining and deal-making, but you just can't remember its name! There's no reference book that would help and the school librarian just shrugged his shoulders. You've already tried everyone in the teachers lounge; now try the Internet.

In your list of newsgroups you'll probably find *rec.games.board*, a newsgroup for people interested in board games. If you read the articles in this group you'll find a host of messages about war games and fantasy games, but every once in a while someone jumps in with a does-anybody-remember-the-game-where...? question. The regular participants of this newsgroup are quite friendly and helpful; they'd probably let you know that the board game you're thinking of is called Diplomacy, it's still available in stores, and it even has its own newsgroup: *rec.games.board.diplomacy*.

On the surface, it may look as though the ability to have this sort of instantaneous access to experts on thousands of diverse topics is the single most useful aspect of the Internet. Indeed, this kind of helpful interaction has encouraged a lot of people to start using newsgroups in this fashion. If they've got a question, they find an appropriate group, jump in and ask. Unfortunately, the subject you are interested in doesn't always have a newsgroup. If you want to talk about a specific computer platform, or anything having to do with *Star Trek*, you'll have no problem, but if youd like to ask questions about the

---

NET FACTS

▼▼▼▼▼▼▼▼▼▼▼▼▼▼▼

What to learn in your newsreader

Most newsreaders have a host of features ranging from the mundane to the complex. Although we can't tell you how to do everything on your specific newsreader, we can point you to some common, important features. We suggest that when you first start learning to use your newsreader, you concentrate on the following:

subscribing: Setting up which newsgroups you want to see regularly is a first step to reading the articles within them.

reading, posting, and replying: Obviously, being able to read articles and send out new ones is the most important use of any newsreader. It is especially important that you learn the difference between posting to the entire newsgroup and writing to an individual.

catching up: Marking all of the articles in a newsgroup as "read" can save you time and effort when you next log on.

searching newsgroups: When the articles in your newsgroup number in the hundreds, it makes sense to search for just the subject lines which interest you.

following a thread: Learning to read the articles in the order they were written takes a little work, but makes the discussion much more sensical.

editing your "kill" file: Newsreaders can be set to ignore articles written by specific people. This is a useful way to avoid getting caught up in a "flame war."

▲▲▲▲▲▲▲▲▲▲▲

cavalier poets (as opposed to the romantics), you're out of luck. Even if you find an appropriate newsgroup, you are not guaranteed an answer. Regular readers of some newsgroups get tired of questions which are asked by each new user. Almost every newsgroup has its own frequently asked question (FAQ) list, and you would do well to read it first (see more about FAQs below).

You can meet people in newsgroups. Newsgroup discussions on the Internet can also be an excellent way of meeting people. If someone distributes a message about a certain topic which interests you, you are able to reply to that person through the discussion group, or personally, via electronic mail. This can lead to professional relationships and friendships with people across the country and around the world. Some teachers who use newsgroups recommend keeping track of the people who seem to be knowledgeable about particular subjects. Then you can send a specific question in an e-mail message to someone who seems to be on top of things. Of course, you dont want to abuse their generosity, but if they've been kind enough to answer questions in the newsgroup, they're likely to be kind enough to answer specific questions directly as well.

Strategies for using newsgroups

Get the FAQs

Almost every newsgroup has a **FAQ**: a list of frequently-asked questions and their answers. Not only does this list contain a large number of answers to simple questions, it will tell you who's in charge of the newsgroup, why it was set up in the first place, etc. The FAQ is usually posted as an article in the newsgroup once every few weeks. Also, it is often available for download from an Internet computer. Most newsgroups keep a copy of their FAQ for anonymous download at

ftp://rtfm.mit.edu/pub/usenet-by-hierarchy/

NET FACTS

▼▼▼▼▼▼▼▼▼▼▼

A FAQ example

The following are taken from the "FAQ about FAQs" written by Russell Hersch, and can be downloaded from:

ftp://rtfm.mit.edu/pub/usenet-by-hierarchy/news/newusers/ questions/FAQs_about_FAQs

1 WHAT ARE FAQs?

1.1 What does FAQ stand for?

FAQ is an acronym for Frequently Asked Questions. It is also sometimes used as the singular Frequently Asked Question (although when was the last time you only heard one question?).

1.2 How is FAQ pronounced?

FAQ is pronounced three ways:

1. By pronouncing the letters individually: F - A - Q
2. As a word: fack
3. Obscenely: *figure it out on your own*

1.3 What do FAQs contain?

FAQs are compilations of information which are [usually] the result of certain questions constantly being asked (posted) in a newsgroup - hence the name FAQ (Frequently Asked Questions).

It seems that those who frequent USENET are a polite bunch. In my house, the "frequently asked questions" that my three rug rats come up with are usually referred to as stupid questions or pestering. There is a lesson to be learned from this... before asking a question in a newsgroup or mailing list, make sure that you've checked out the appropriate FAQs. A frequently asked question can be a stupid question if the answer is posted right in front of your face in one or more FAQs.

Sometimes a FAQ or periodic posting is compiled as a result of extensive research on a specific subject. A convenient way to share the information with others is by posting the article. In this case, the article might not really be a FAQ - that is, it isn't necessarily based on frequently asked questions. However, the term FAQ is sometimes used as a catch-all term for articles, periodic postings, compilations, etc.

© Copyright 1995, Russell Hersch. Reprinted by permission of the author.

From there you can look in the appropriate directory for the newsgroup you are interested in.[6] For instance, the FAQs for the *news.announce.newusers* newsgroup (which cover the basics of newsgroups and the Internet) can be found at one of the following:

```
ftp://rtfm.mit.edu/pub/usenet-by-hierarchy/news/announce/newusers/
```

```
http://www.cis.ohio-state.edu/hypertext/faq/usenet/FAQ-List.html
```

If you want to ask a question in a newsgroup, please read the FAQ first. You may be surprised by what questions they have already answered. Even if you aren't interested in asking a question, the FAQ can give you important insight into the workings of this particular newsgroup. If you want to join a newsgroup, first get the FAQs!

Wipe the slate clean

If you choose to read a newsgroup or two on a regular basis, we recommend that you start by immediately marking all of the articles as already read (i.e. catch up). This way you won't have to wade through all of the articles waiting on the system for you (which can easily be several hundred). Of course, you may want to take a look at a few of the articles to see if the newsgroup is really what you wanted; but if you try to read them all, it could take hours. Then, if you check the group regularly, you will find a manageable number of unread articles to sort through each time.

Lurk

When you first subscribe to a newsgroup, you should lurk for a while. Lurking does not have the same sinister connotations on the Internet as it does in monster movies. It simply means reading articles without posting your own. This gives you a sense of the newsgroup. Lurking helps you understand who is contributing to this particular newsgroup and why, what is appropriate to discuss and what is not. Because of the

---

6   Directions for accessing this resource can be found in Chapter 10, *The World Wide Web* on page 137.

vast numbers of people who can access a newsgroup, this is considered a courtesy for experienced users and is a must for those just starting out. One newsgroup user we know of is still apologizing months after joining for misusing the newsgroup in ways he might have avoided had he simply waited and watched before posting his own articles.

Take ... and give

Once you have spent some time lurking, and are comfortable with what is going on, it is important that you *share your knowledge*. By sharing what you know (or what you think) with others in a newsgroup, you become a part of that discussion; you make the group your own. Those who contribute to discussions build an online reputation and find it easier to work in the environment. Also, by joining in discussions you are much more likely to reflect upon your own work and internalize the ideas of others for your own use, two key aspects of professional development. It is unfortunate (but certainly not uncommon) when new Internet users spend all of their time in the background allowing some of the more experienced users to dominate discussions.

Don't be discouraged

Once you have joined a group discussion, you should be aware that things will not always be as easy as you would like. You can find the different threads of conversations difficult to follow. Sometimes, for instance, you may read the response to an article before you read the article itself. Other times, you may find that an article you have sent receives few or no responses. Do not be discouraged. Often this is more a factor of unfortunate timing than anything else. Think about your message again; if you decide that it was important to you, you can try sending it again after a few days. Or you can pick up on another conversation and send a new message. As we mentioned above, though, people are more likely to heed your requests or respond to your messages if you have been heeding and responding to theirs.

When you decide to send a message in a group discussion, be sure you are doing so in an appropriate manner. Some key things to remember are:

Do not send test messages

Sometimes it is hard to believe that contributing to a newsgroup will actually work. New users will occasionally send out test messages which say, in effect, "I'm just trying this out!" Please don't do this. It may seem harmless, but it is wasteful of computer resources, and quite annoying to more experienced Internet users. You can either wait until you actually have something to say before you test, or you can find the newsgroups which are specifically designed to let people test their posting capabilities (such as *misc.test*).

Include a brief synopsis

People reading your article may not know what has transpired before, and most newsreaders makes it easy for you to include portions of the previous messages. Make sure, though, that you include *only important selections*. If you include everything said so far (or even most things), you will wind up with more of the previous discussion than what you have added. This is not only rude, it will often be rejected by the computers which run the newsgroups.

To whom should you reply?

Newsgroups are not appropriate places to send personal messages; that can be done via electronic mail. Writing to a friend using a newsgroup is like carrying on a private conversation during a class debate: It is done, but nobody appreciates it. Similarly, when you see an article you wish to reply to, think about whether it is appropriate to reply to the person directly (via electronic mail) or to everyone (through the newsgroup).

For instance, suppose someone posts an article asking people to e-mail him information they have about working with learning disabled students in group projects. You would like to get the same information, but are afraid it won't be posted to the newsgroup. It is much better to send a personal message (via electronic mail) to the person who posted the original request, asking him to forward the information to you as well, than to post an article to the entire group saying, "Send all your info to me, too, please!"

Be aware of what you write

If it's important to be polite in your regular e-mail correspondence, its doubly important for newsgroups. You can assume that any article you post will be read by hundreds or thousands of people from all different cultures and backgrounds. For this reason, it is also essential that you not include private information in your articles. A good rule of thumb: *Don't* write anything you wouldn't want printed in the newspaper.

Make your requests specific

New users of newsgroup discussions sometimes start by asking things like, "Please send any information you have about gifted children" or "Please, everyone, send me electronic mail." These messages sometimes get responses, but experienced users are likely to ignore them. As you become familiar with newsgroup discussions, you will find that you are often faced with hundreds of messages daily (even if you only read a few groups), and responding to such general messages is simply not efficient. On the other hand, if you were to ask for "a good magazine for gifted children," experienced users could quickly respond with their favorite.

Use the subject appropriately

Newsgroup articles, like e-mail, have a one-line subject heading for you to describe the content of what you've written. Since most other readers will decide to read your article depending on the subject, you should be sure that it is concise, specific, and appropriate. The subject "Please Help!" will more than likely be ignored (despite its urgency), but "Need gifted students journal" may not.

Make personal contacts

Newsgroups can be like after-school clubs: places for people with similar interests to meet and get to know each other. In this sense, you have an array of clubs to choose from, and you don't have to worry about scheduling conflicts, meeting agendas, or other limitations. Although the club members might be friendly even if you barge in and start asking questions, everyone will appreciate it if you take the time to watch how the club operates, start contributing where you can, and then ask appropriate questions succinctly and politely. Even if you don't make any close e-mail pals, you'll have a professional networking arena that wasn't available before.

Things to try at home

Subscribe and lurk

Try finding one newsgroup for your teaching, and one newsgroup for you personally. Skim through the group on a regular basis, reading a few articles that catch your eye, then marking them *all* as already read so you dont have to wade through the same ones twice. If you read the groups every few days, you should be able to keep the number of new articles to a manageable size, and therefore keep the time you spend online to a bare minimum while still reaping the benefits which newsgroups afford.

Here are some newsgroups that might interest you:

- *k12.teacher.chat* In this newsgroup teachers discuss whatever is on their minds. Discussion threads seen recently include school reform plans, what to do about students misbehaving for substitutes, and even an instructor who wanted to carry teachers' concerns to his custodial service students who will soon be out cleaning classrooms.

- *k12.ed.** All of the newsgroups which start with *k12.ed.* are for K-12 teachers. Some are busier than others, but

they all have an air of professionalism. For a list of
k12.ed.* newsgroups, see Appendix A, *Internet resources,*
on page 267.

● *news.announce.newusers* Not the most exciting newsgroup on the Internet, but a useful one for new users. It
has articles with frequently asked questions about
newsgroups, newsgroup etiquette, and how to start
your own newsgroup.

● Search for *forsale* or *marketplace.* If you're the kind of
person who enjoys browsing the want ads, you'll love
the newsgroups devoted to buying, selling, and trading. For instance, if you need more memory for your
IBM computer, try the *misc.forsale.computers.
pc-specific.memory* newsgroup. If you're going to be buying and selling over the Internet, it's a good idea to
check out the How to post / buy / sell on *misc.forsale.**
FAQ available at[7]:

> http://www.cis.ohio-state.edu/hypertext/faq/usenet/
> misc-forsale-faq/top.html

● *rec.** There are hundreds of newsgroups which start
with rec. and they cover all sorts of recreational per-
suits. When you browse through them you'll find general groups like rec.animals, as well as specific groups
like rec.arts.marching.band.high-school, rec.food.his-
toric and rec.music.indian.classical.

● *alt.fan.** The newsgroups which start with *alt.fan.* put
the word fanatic back into fan, but if you're a devotee
of anyone or anything from the founder of Microsoft
(*alt.fan.bill-gates*) to the trial-of-the-decade judge
(*alt.fan.judge-ito*) you may find some like-minded people on the Internet.

---

7   Directions for accessing this resource can be found in Chapter 10, *The
World Wide Web,* on page 137.

Write a follow-up article, or post your own

After you've been lurking for a while, you may find something you'd like to comment upon, or an issue you'd like to raise. If so, go ahead and try posting an article. If you don't have anything worthwhile to add to your favorite newsgroup, use *misc.test*. This group is set up specifically for you to test your newsreader. You can post test messages there and no one will mind. Try a test anywhere else, and they might get a little peevish.

NEWSGROUPS BALANCE SHEET

Reasons to read newsgroups	Reasons *not* to read newsgroups
✔ **To find a sense of community.** If you find the right group, you can spend time talking about subjects that interest you with other enthusiasts.	✖ **Time and effort.** Reading a newsgroup regularly can take a lot of your precious time. Until you become adept at skimming subject lines for information important to you, you'll find yourself reading a lot of material which really doesn't help that much. Also, newsgroups dont come to your mailbox like mailing lists do; you have to go out and get them.
✔ **To find serendipitous info.** Announcements about new Internet resources, conferences, breaking news; all of these things are regularly posted in newsgroups.	✖ **Too confusing.** Imagine several thousand people reading and posting messages on a mile high bulletin board and you'll understand why newsgroups can be confusing. Discussions can go veering off into incidental topics or fade away into nothing. Following your favorites requires a good memory and a fair amount of concentration.

Reasons to read newsgroups	Reasons not to read newsgroups
✔ **To ask specific questions.** Regulars of a newsgroup are often happy to answer questions from people who are just passing through. Be polite, though, and read the FAQ first to see if your question has already been answered.	✖ **None you like.** The list of available newsgroups is still slanted heavily towards techies and trekkies. If you know that a newsgroup you'd like exists, but isn't carried by your Internet provider, you can try talking them into carrying it. However, it may just be that your favorite discussion topic is simply not a newsgroup.
✔ **Meeting people.** After reading a newsgroup for awhile, you can usually find the people whose interests and attitudes match your own. Since people post their e-mail addresses with their newsgroup articles, this is a good way to start an e-mail dialog.	

CHAPTER 9

How to behave on the Internet

▼▼▼▼▼▼▼▼▼▼▼

A QUICK GUIDE TO NETIQUETTE

"Netiquette" is short for etiquette on the Internet. Over the years, the folks who use the Internet most often have developed some accepted rules of courtesy, some do's and don'ts of cyberspace. As a newcomer to the Internet, it's important that you understand what is expected, so that you don't end up with an electronic foot in your mouth. We've collected some of the most important rules of netiquette for you in this chapter.

▲▲▲▲▲▲▲▲▲▲▲

Electronic mail

☑ **Be brief.** Keep your message concise, and if you are replying make sure that you include only what is necessary of the original message. Also, keep your signature short (a few lines at most).

☑ **Be polite.** Sending insults online is known as "flaming," and is unacceptable. If someone sends you something inflammatory, take a few minutes before responding, or better yet—don't respond!

☑ **Be correct.** As a teacher, you may already understand the importance of proper English, but it is especially important in a purely written forum. A sloppy message on the Internet sends the same signals as wearing shabby clothing in a crowd, so use a spell checker if you've got one.

☑ **Be direct.** Most humor (especially sarcasm) doesn't work very well online. Be sure to include a smiley or some other disclaimer when you're just kidding—you'd be surprised at what people take seriously.

☑ **Be quiet.** Typing in all capitals makes it look like you're SHOUTING! This can be useful for emphasis, but it should be used sparingly. Typing subject lines in all capitals, for instance, is frowned upon.

Mailing lists and newsgroups

☑ **Read the FAQ.** There is usually a Frequently Asked Questions document for each newsgroup, and some of the larger mailing lists have one as well. Reading it before contributing will save you the embarrassment of asking something obvious. For more information on obtaining the FAQ for your favorite newsgroup, see page 121.

☑ **Use the subject line.** People will decide whether or not to read your message based on your subject line, so make it specific and concise.

☑ **Restrict your audience.** Newsreaders allow you to restrict the distribution of your article to your city or country. If you're asking for local field trip ideas, you don't need to be talking to Kenya, so don't post your message to the whole world.

☑ **Respond via e-mail.** You can use newsgroups and mailing lists very effectively by just reading other peoples' messages and responding to them privately. If the entire group doesn't need to see your response, don't send it to the entire group.

For more netiquette do's and don'ts, see the following newsgroups:

news.announce.newusers

news.answers

There you'll find useful articles such as "Rules for posting to Usenet," "Hints on writing style for Usenet," and "Emily Postnews answers your questions on netiquette."

Section 4

Internet for research

▼ ▼ ▼ ▼ ▼ ▼ ▼ ▼ ▼ ▼ ▼

The Internet can be a wonderfully effective research tool—sometimes. The information on the Internet is generally up-to-date primary source material. Furthermore, it comes in many formats (text, pictures, sound) from many different people. Unfortunately, the Internet is not an electronic encyclopedia. It makes no claim of completeness or reliability. The Internet can be as much of a grab-bag as a treasure trove. In the next few chapters we'll explain how to reach into that grab-bag with your computer, and why you might want to.

Chapter 10, *The World Wide Web*, describes the most well-known Internet service: the World Wide Web. When people talk about "surfing the Internet," they usually mean browsing through the Web. We'll explain how it works and why you might use it in your personal life and in your teaching. In Chapter 11, we'll show you how to create your own Web pages. Chapter 12, *Other research services*, details other, older Internet services, such as Gopher, Telnet, and FTP. Although the World Wide Web is quickly making these services obsolete, there is still a lot that can be done with them, especially if you have a text-only connection.

▲ ▲ ▲ ▲ ▲ ▲ ▲ ▲ ▲ ▲ ▲

CHAPTER 10

The World Wide Web

▼ ▼ ▼ ▼ ▼ ▼ ▼ ▼ ▼ ▼ ▼

INTERCONNECTED INFORMATION

The World Wide Web is the newest and fastest growing service on the Internet. It's an information retrieval system that offers an eclectic mix of up-to-the-minute reports, primary sources, and useless trivia. In this chapter we'll see how it works and discover ways of using it for educational research. We'll show you how to move beyond mere "surfing" and use the Web as an effective research tool.

▲ ▲ ▲ ▲ ▲ ▲ ▲ ▲ ▲ ▲ ▲

▼▼▼▼▼▼▼▼▼▼▼

Teacher on the Net

Don't leave home without Net surfing

Bonni L. Katona
11th grade, Legal Office Training
Northeast Career Center
Columbus, Ohio
Teaching experience: 16 years
Internet experience: 1½ years
E-mail: bkatona@magnus.acs.ohio-state.edu

Although Bonni Katona uses the Internet for her classes, she also uses it for herself. She's found the Internet to be a wealth of information and services. As she puts it,

❝Much of the information I gather is for my own use. This includes recipes, travel information, graphics, and computer utilities. As a teacher, I make examples out of the types of information I've gathered to illustrate how we are continuing to become an information-processing society.

❝For instance, last summer I was planning a trip to the Pacific Northwest and needed to find a reasonably priced hotel in Vancouver. Most of the places listed in the AAA book were pretty expensive. By reading through the rec.travel newsgroup, I learned about the Sylvia Hotel, which was reasonably priced and located in a safe residential area of Vancouver. A number of people had posted messages about this hotel stating that they had a pleasant experience staying at that hotel. These people were not travel agents and had nothing to gain monetarily by endorsing this hotel, so I felt I was getting an objective opinion. We made a reservation at the Sylvia Hotel and had a wonderful time. Without the Internet, I probably would have paid a lot more money for hotel accommodations.

❝When I tell this story to students or adults who attend some of my Internet discussion groups, they begin to understand why I'm so excited about the potential benefits of using the Internet.❞

Pulling it all together

The Internet consists of millions of computers around the world each containing all sorts of information: text files, pictures, sounds, and movies. Much of this information is available to any Internet user, at no extra cost. To take advantage of this bonanza, you must find the information you need, get it to your own computer, and display it. The World Wide Web is one of the most popular Internet services for doing all three.

What can you do on the Web?

The World Wide Web provides a display case for any government agency, corporation, school, or individual to show what they want to the rest of the world. The possibilities of the World Wide Web have not yet been fully realized, but already you can:

- **Submit English words** and phrases to a Japanese/English dictionary and have it return Japanese characters as pictures: *http://www.wg.omron.co.jp/cgi-bin/j-e/*

- **See the largest known prime number** (which is 285,716 digits long!):
  http://www.utm.edu/departments/math/largest.html

- **Read reports and enjoy pictures** created by students at schools around the world (e.g. Hillside Elementary School): *http://hillside.coled.umn.edu*

- **Operate a robotic telescope** at the University of Bradford in West Yorkshire, England, from your own computer: *http://www.telescope.org/*

- **Browse electronic "brochures"** of community colleges, four-year colleges, and universities (e.g. Seattle University): *http://www.seattleu.edu/Home.html*

- **View maps** of everything from Tajikistan (*http://www.lib.utexas.edu/Libs/PCL/Map_collection/ commonwealth/Tajikistan.GIF*) to the current traffic slowdowns in your area (e.g. the Los Angeles Traffic Report. *http://www.scubed.com/caltrans/la/la_transnet.html*

- Get reviews of popular books and movies, e.g. "Book Recommendations of Real Folks", *http://www.best.com/~yylee/homespun/booktop.html* or HollyWeb, *http://www.ingress.com/users/spease/hw/hollyweb.html*

What is the World Wide Web?

The World Wide Web (also known as WWW or just the Web), like many other Internet services, started out as a great idea for something else. Developers at CERN (the European Particle Physics Laboratory in Geneva, Switzerland) wanted to create an environment for scientists working with high energy particle physics to share ideas. They introduced the Web to the Internet in 1992, and in a few short years this service has all but taken over the Internet.

Why is the Web so popular? One reason is that it is the first Internet service to smoothly incorporate pictures and sound, as well as text. This is where a graphical connection to the Internet really shines. Folks who have both a graphical connection and access to the World Wide Web (they are usually a package deal), can point and click their way around the Internet finding files, viewing pictures, and listening to sounds using their mouse instead of your keyboard.

Buzzwords

hypermedia: A means of storing information in files such that any word or picture can refer to any other file in the system.

link: A connection between two files in a hypermedia system.

World Wide Web: The entire set of accessible Internet documents (containing text, pictures, sound, and more) all connected to each other with hypermedia links.

stead of your keyboard. Rarely do you have to enter an arcane command or look up how to do something. If you can use a Macintosh, Microsoft Windows, or IBM's OS/2, you'll find that the Web is a breeze.

The World Wide Web is based on the concept of **hypermedia** (originally hypertext) which organizes information by connecting documents and pictures to form a non-linear web of ideas. If you've ever seen HyperCard for the Macintosh (which was once distributed free of charge, and was therefore a common sight in schools), then you've seen an early version of hypermedia. Most online help systems (for instance, Microsoft Word's help files) and CD-ROM reference works are also written using hypermedia.

If you haven't seen any hypermedia applications already, imagine a book with footnotes. The footnotes in this book contain more than references to another book, they are a direct gateway to the whole new book! Of course, this book will have references, too, and those references may have references and so on. Some of these books have pictures as well as text, and sound and even movies; and all of the items in this multimedia extravaganza can be connected to other items in other computers anywhere around the world. If you imagine all of these connections as thin strands running between computers all over the world, you'll have a World Wide Web.

The hypermedia "books" on the Web are usually more page-length than book-length, which is why they're known as

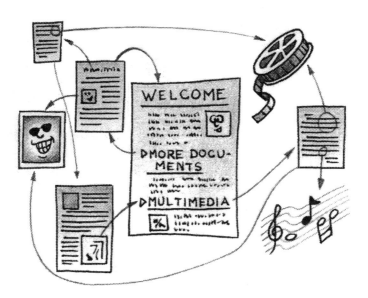

Web pages. The connection between pages is called a **link**. A link on a Web page looks like a bold word or picture. When you click on a link, your computer loads a new page of information which contains text, pictures, sound, and probably more links to different pages. The idea behind all of this clicking and loading is that it brings you closer and closer to your final goal: the information you wanted from the Internet. If you're just hopping around the World Wide Web without a

NET FACTS

▼▼▼▼▼▼▼▼▼▼▼▼

Yahoo: An example Web page

The screen below shows one of the better search tools for the World Wide Web: Yahoo. This particular Web page contains links (the underlined words near the top) as well as form entry spaces (the white boxes and buttons). More information about the Yahoo directory of the Web can be found on page 154.

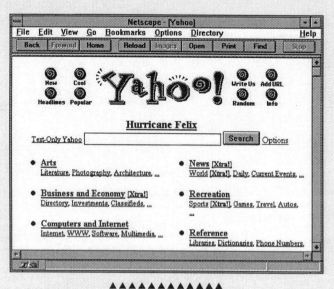

▲▲▲▲▲▲▲▲▲▲▲▲

goal or destination in mind, you are practicing a favorite sport of Internet users: you're surfing the Web.

Is it just connections?

Mostly, but not all. World Wide Web pages can also act as an interface between you and software running on other computers. Special Web pages called **forms** allow you to type in information and make choices using the same controls you might find in a word processor or gradebook application. Depending on what you type, the software can point you towards new

Buzzwords

Web browser: A software program which will find and display Web pages.

Web page: A hypermedia document on the World Wide Web.

Web pages or create Web pages on the fly. Web search pages work like that: You type in what you want to search for, and it creates a Web page containing links to what it found.

Mechanical devices can also be connected to the World Wide Web. As the popularity of the Web increases, so does the number of unusual devices connected to it. Drink machines, cameras, televisions, telescopes, and robotic arms have been connected to the Web so that Web users can operate them (or view their operation) remotely. For instance, people at the University of Southern California's Mercury Project created an "excavation site" in a terrarium at their laboratory. They then hooked up a robotic arm and video camera over the site and connected it to the Web, so that visitors to their Web page could participate in a tele-excavation. Some 250,000 of the over 2 million visitors from every continent but Antarctica moved the arm and snapped pictures while sitting at their own computers around the world. Project Mercury ended in March 1995, but they promise to have another project online again soon.

How does the Web work?

Going from your school district's Web page to an excavation site in Los Angeles to a virtual guidebook of St. Petersburg, Russia with only a few clicks of the mouse may seem like magic, but it is really quite simple. Each Web page is just a computer file on a computer somewhere on the Internet. These computer files are ASCII text documents written using a special code, called **HTML** (HyperText Markup Language).

In order to access these files, you'll need a special piece of software called a **Web browser**. Your Web browser will translate your clicks into Internet commands, make connections to remote computers, retrieve the appropriate files, read the HTML codes, and display the Web pages appropriately. Header information in the file, like the title of the Web page, will be displayed in a large font, while links to other Web pages will be shown in a different color (such as bright blue) and are usually underlined. If the Web page contains an HTML code which indicates a picture file is available, your Web browser will load and display the picture for you, too. Your Web browser will do all of this work for just a few clicks on your part.

> ## Copy it exactly!
> Unlike e-mail addresses, URLs are case-sensitive, which just means that upper- and lower-case matters. So when you are typing a URL, be sure that you type it exactly as it is written.

Your Web browser can find these files (Web pages, pictures, and more) using their **URL** (Uniform Resource Locator). The URL of a file is a pointer to its place on the Internet, sort of an e-mail address for files. A typical URL looks something like this:

```
http://www.halcyon.com/ResPress/welcome.html
```

The first word (*http*) stands for HyperText Transfer Protocol and indicates that this is a Web page. This is important because you can reach other Internet services (such as newsgroups or gopher, which we'll talk about later) on the

Web, too. Each of these services has its own keyword to start the URL. The remainder of the URL for Resolution Business Press (*www.halcyon.com/ResPress/welcome.html*) indicates which computer on the Internet holds the file, where it is located on that computer, and what the file's name is. This URL, for instance, points to the location of the home page of our publishers, Resolution Business Press. Other examples include the aforementioned excavation site:

```
http://www.usc.edu/dept/raiders/
```

and the guidebook to St. Petersburg, Russia:

```
http://www.spb.su/index.html
```

NET FACTS

▼▼▼▼▼▼▼▼▼▼▼▼

Web surfing from a text-only account

Although the World Wide Web is most easily accessed from a graphical account, it is possible to browse the Web even if your account is text-only. All it takes is some special software.

If you'd like to see a text-only version of the Web (i.e. one without pictures, sounds, and movies), ask your Internet service provider if they support "lynx." Using lynx will get you most of the information from the Web, but it's something like watching the TV news with the sound turned off. It's just not the same.

Other software is available that allows you to turn your text-only account into a graphical account (albeit a slow one). If you are interested in such a product, see:

The Internet Adapter (TIA)

http://marketplace.com/tia/tiahome.html

SlipKnot

http://www.interport.net/slipknot/slipknot.html

▲▲▲▲▲▲▲▲▲▲▲▲

Because the URL uniquely identifies any page on the World Wide Web, it is also useful for describing Web pages in print.

A recent issue of Newsweek magazine, for instance, describes the "World's First Collaborative Sentence" a Web page where artist Douglas Davis invites anyone on the Web to contribute to a sentence which is already over 25,000 words long

NET FACTS

▼▼▼▼▼▼▼▼▼▼▼

Netscape home page

When you first run your Web browser, you will begin at your home page. You can choose any Web page to be your home page, and even make your own. Netscape offers the page below as a home page for the first time you run Netscape.

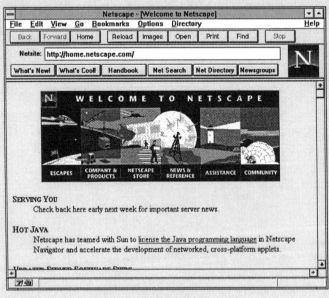

▲▲▲▲▲▲▲▲▲▲▲▲

and growing.[1] They provide a reference to the page using its URL:

```
http://math240.lehman.cuny.edu/art
```

Other mainstream publications have also begun to provide URLs for interested Internet users. Usually these references are found in the computer section of a publication (*Newsweek*'s reference, for instance, was in its Cyberscope department), but sometimes they crop up in the most unlikely places, such as at the bottom of movie ads, or even at the beginning of rental movies.

By far the most common place to find URLs, however, is on the Internet itself. Mailing lists and newsgroups are a good source for URLs, as is e-mail. People with their own Web pages often give the URL in their e-mail signature. Although there is no all-encompassing directory of URLs, there are Web pages which help you search for specific URLs. We'll describe such search tools later in this chapter.

Suppose you have a URL, how do you use it? First, you'll need a Web browser. Luckily, two of the most popular Web browsers are available on the Internet: Mosaic and Netscape. We'll describe Netscape, since it is the hands-down favorite and also because it is free of charge to all students and educators. [2] If you use Mosaic anyway, don't worry. They are simi-

---

1   See *Newsweek*, April 17, 1995, page 13

2   To learn how to get Netscape from the Internet, see page 174.

lar enough that descriptions of one translate well to the other, and they are common enough that most other Web browsers (including those available for commercial networks like CompuServe, America Online, and Prodigy) are modeled on their design.

Using the Web with Netscape

When you first open Netscape, it will take you to your **home page**. This is the starting page for your journeys on the Web. Netscape provides a home page for its users, the "Welcome to Netscape" page.

Usually your Internet service provider (be it a school, district, or commercial provider) also provides a home page, and you can choose either of these or any other page to be your "home." A good home page contains links to other pages you might find useful, such as lists of Web resources, pages which let you search the Web, and just fun pages to visit.

Buzzwords

bookmark: A means of keeping track of favorite Web pages in your Web browser.

home page: The first Web page you see when you open your Web browser.

Different Web browsers have different ways of highlighting links, but after using your Web browser for a bit it will become obvious what you can click on and what you can't. When you click on a link, your Web browser will go out and get the resource you asked it for and bring it to your computer. Depending on the size of the file, and the speed of your connection to the Internet, this can take some time. If you have a connection from your house, you will probably get used to waiting. Even good, fast modems like the 14.4 we recommended on page 52 will take some time to load pictures and sounds. If you are using a modem more than two or three years old, it may make the Web not worth using.

As you get accustomed to the Web you will start to do more than just cruise around, clicking from one page to another. Soon you will hear about specific resources available on the Web. You may get a URL from your favorite mailing list or newsgroup, or it may be sent to you by a friend. You may even find the reference in a newspaper, in a magazine, or on television. Once you have the URL, simply type that information into the box at the top of your Web browser and press Enter.[3] Your Web browser will begin to load the resource you asked for, and display it as it loads.

One of the things that makes Netscape popular is that you hardly notice it. You point and click in the Web pages it gives you, and generally forget that Netscape is involved at all. There are times, however, when you are glad it's there, such as when you get lost. Don't laugh, it can happen! One link looks interesting, so you choose it and up comes a new page which has an interesting link and another and another, and pretty soon you realize you're getting farther from your destination, rather than closer.

In times like these, you may not be able to remember where you've been, but luckily Netscape can. Press the "Back" button on the toolbar and you'll be back at the last page you visited. Press it again, and you'll be back to the page before that. If you look under the "Go" menu and choose "View History..." you will find a list of places you've been, in order. Choosing any one of them will take you right there. And using a Web browser means you can *always* go home again — back to your home page with one click of the "Home" button.

Another way Netscape, and most other Web browsers, can be of assistance is by keeping a list of your favorite pages. These references to specific pages are called **bookmarks** because they save your place between sessions. When you come across a Web page you would like to remember, simply choose "Add Bookmark" from the "Bookmarks" menu and your place will be saved. When you click on the "Bookmarks" menu again, you will see the page you saved as one of your choices. As you find more worthwhile pages, you will add more bookmarks, and your bookmark list will grow. Later you may need to organize your bookmarks into categories, remove

---

3   With Netscape you can also click the "Go" button and type in the box that it gives you.

some that you rarely visit, and so on. Netscape will let you do this as well.

What can the Web do for you?

It's easy for people to get caught up in the excitement of the Web, and lose sight of what purpose it serves, if any. Sure, you can spend several hours a day browsing the Web, finding wild and wacky Web sites, but if you end up with nothing more than several hours wasted and some eyestrain, you might as well have been watching television (okay, maybe it's better than television, but you get the point). For those who enjoy computers, cruising the Web is a pleasant diversion. For those who don't, it can still be a useful exercise.

The World Wide Web is first and foremost an information retrieval system. People using the Internet around the world have made information available in the form of files on their computers, and your Web browser can find these files and bring them back to you. This means that everything (with the exception of electronic mail) available on the Internet is available through the World Wide Web.[4] As we've described before, almost all of this information—text, pictures, sounds, movies—is out there because people believe it belongs to everyone. Considering the enormity of this conception, there are very few restrictions on your access. You'll need a connection to the Internet and the software to match, and the Web is your oyster.

With so much out there, the real question becomes how much is *useful*. A public library with all of the fiction books, oil paintings, and movie soundtracks ever made would contain a huge amount of multimedia information (just like the Web), but none of it would be useful if you were looking for ideas for using math manipulatives. Luckily, education has long been a primary interest of many Internet users (probably because of the high profile of colleges and universities on the

---

4   This does not mean that everything on every Internet computer is accessible through the World Wide Web. Some of the information on Internet computers, such as private correspondence or documents, is off-limits for the average Internet user.

Web). Much of the information for educators is aimed at K-12 teachers specifically. In fact, if you point your Web browser to the following URL:

```
gopher://ericir.syr.edu:70/00/Lesson/Math/cecmath.08
```

you'll find a document entitled "Use of manipulatives to Pre-Algebra (3-8)" from the AskEric service. This is a full-blown lesson plan, one of hundreds available through the Internet.

Getting information about subjects you teach is important, but we find the Web to be just as useful (if not more) for getting information about subjects you *don't* teach. One never knows when a student's question or interest will take you outside of your teaching strengths into areas you've never explored. Suppose you are a math teacher who has newly arrived Lithuanian students, and you'd like to learn a little more about their country. Using an online version of the CIA's *World Factbook*, you can learn all about its size and demographics, get the addresses of United States ambassadors living there, and view maps of the country as well (*http://neris.mii.lt/*).

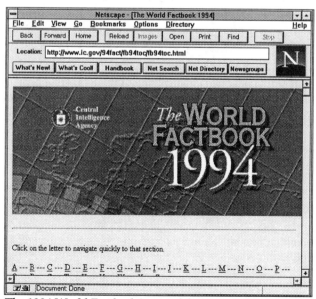

The 1994 World Factbook is one of the many reference tools available on the Web.

Big deal, you say. You can do just about the same thing with an atlas, almanac, or encyclopedia. You're right, of course, and it's a good point. Although it has some of the same information, the World Wide Web will not replace a good set of reference books. For one thing, it would probably take you twice as long (at least!) to load a full-color picture of the Lithuania on the Internet as it would to pull down an atlas and flip to the right map. Even if you're only interested in text, there's no mistaking the fact that reading something in a book is just plain more comfortable than reading it on the computer.

On the other hand, the World Wide Web has some things to offer which reference books simply can't. Documents on the Web, for instance, are being updated constantly. Your library books may be out of date: It wasn't that long ago that Lithuania wasn't even listed as a separate country! Web documents aren't always the best source for breaking news stories, but they are rarely more than a year old.

Even more important than the age of the information is its source. Not only can you find summaries of facts about Lithuania from the United States government, you can find out about Lithuania from the Lithuanians. You can get weekly reports from their parliament (*http://rc.lrs.lt/English.html*) or read about upcoming festivals, such as the celebration that takes place on St. John's Day, the shortest night of the year, when no one goes to sleep and the fête lasts until the crack of dawn (http://nemunas.sc-uni.ktu.lt/daiva/etno.html). Not only can you find primary sources on the Internet, but you can find information produced by people with an interest in the subject which goes beyond mere reporting.

That's another thing the World Wide Web can do for you: It can be your publisher. The Web is a truly democratic Internet services, because almost anyone with an Internet account can create their own World Wide Web page. Hundreds of schools and school districts have created their own home page on the Web, as have individual teachers and students.[5] These pages contain information about the pages' creators: pic-

---

5   For lists of schools and districts on the Internet see Web 66 at
     http://web66.coled.umn.edu/schools.html, which bills itself as the "oldest
     and most comprehensive registry of K12 WWW servers."

tures, artwork, poetry, links to favorite Web pages, ... anything they choose. We'll describe how you can make your own Web page in Chapter 11, *Creating you own Web page*, on page 161.

Just because people have access to this sort of resource, doesn't mean they'll come up with any interesting uses for it, of course. As Scott Adams (creator of the comic strip *Dilbert*) says on his home page,

"I think you'll agree we're using the Information Superhighway to its fullest potential: simulating the excitement of being invited to somebody's house to look at their photo album (except this takes much longer and you have to supply your own beverage)."

http://www.unitedmedia.com/comics/dilbert/

However, most people who create their own Web page try hard to make it worth seeing. There is a certain empowerment that comes from knowing that several million people could come looking at your electronic photo album. A sense of ownership that makes you want to present your best. This is exactly the kind of pride that motivates students as well as adults.

Strategies for using the Web

Get good at searching

If you want to do more than surf, if you want to really use the Web to its full potential, you'll need to get good at searching. With everyone from government agencies and libraries to elementary and graduate students to movie studios and bakeries making their own place on the Internet, its unfortunate but understandable that there is no single comprehensive directory for the World Wide Web. Luckily, there are a number of Web pages which come close.

There are two types of Web directories available, one maintained mostly by people, the other maintained mostly by computer. Each has its strengths and weaknesses. Web directories maintained by people are more organized, and can be searched by subject; directories maintained by computers (often called **robot-generated indices**) are more complete, and are usually searched by word.

For example, if you are looking for Web pages about dogs, you might try a robot-generated index called Lycos (*http://lycos.cs.cmu.edu/*). This Web page gives you access to two directories: one directory containing more than half a million Web pages, and another, more comprehensive directory containing 3.6 million Web pages. If you choose the "small" directory, and ask it to search for Web page titles containing the word "dog," it will find over a thousand. Of these it chooses fifteen and generates a Web page of links to these dog pages. Remember that this search is performed by a computer, so a Web page titled "Dog-eared Pages: A Used Bookstore" would show up on your list, even though it may have nothing to do with dogs.

On a broad category search (like one for dogs), it is usually best to use the human-maintained directories. One such directory, Yahoo (*http://www.yahoo.com/*), starts with a list of subjects such as "Art," "Business," and "Entertainment." Choosing "Entertainment" will lead you to a list of subjects generally related to leisure activities, including one called "Animals, Insects, and Pets." Clicking this choice will lead you to yet another list of subjects, one of which is "Dogs." Finally, on the "Dogs" page, you will find links to other pages such as the "Canine Web":

http://snapple.cs.washington.edu:600/canine/canine.html

which contains loads of information about caring for dogs, training dogs, specific breeds of dogs, and so on.

Notice that the title "Canine Web" would not have been found in a robot-generated search, because it doesn't contain the word "dog," even though it might be one of the better general dog pages on the Web. On the other hand, the Yahoo directory has only 39,000 entries, compared to Lycos' 3.6 million. For this reason, we recommend you start with a human-generated directory, and move to a robot-generated directory only if you can't find what you need. Another nice thing about human-maintained directories is that they often include a "Top 25" list of the most popular pages or a "What's New" list of new and interesting pages. Yahoo will even choose a page for you at random, if you like to live adventurously![6]

It's a good idea to become comfortable with a few different directories, in case your favorite can't give you what you need on a particular search. We have a number of directories listed in the appendix, some of which have been created specifically for educators. You can start with those and see what you find.

Use those bookmarks

If you find a good directory Web page, or an interesting home page, or two or three, you should keep a bookmark for each. It's simple to place a bookmark, and you'll be glad you did when you want to find it again. It's also a good idea to learn how to organize your bookmarks into categories. If you leave them all in the same general category, you'll soon have so many that it will be a chore just looking through them all to find the one you want.

Share what you find

When you do find interesting pages, don't forget to let your Internet-using friends know about them. Word-of-e-mail is one of the best ways to learn about new resources on the Internet, and a quick message with a URL and a short description of the page is often appreciated and reciprocated.

It takes time

Currently one of the most frustrating things about the World Wide Web is how long it takes to move around. You may not have this problem if you are lucky enough to have a direct connection, but for those of us working over the phone

---

6   For more information about Lycos, see page 291, and for Yahoo, see page 283.

lines, the speed is an important factor. Here are a couple of suggestions for making your work on the Web more efficient:

- **Turn off the pictures**. Loading pictures, sounds, and movies takes more time than loading text. Although pictures can come in pretty quickly if they're small enough, sounds usually take a few moments even with the fastest modems, and movies are the worst offenders—they can take up to an hour or more. For this reason, sounds and movies are rarely if ever found directly on Web pages. Instead, you must specifically click on something to download the sound or movie. Pictures, on the other hand, are often right there on the Web page, and if you want to see the page, you have to load the picture.

  Or do you? Most Web browsers (Netscape included) allow you to turn off the automatic loading of pictures. When you first see a page, it will be pictureless. You can choose to load the pictures later if you wish. This way the Web page appears more quickly because your Web browser need only load the text. Although this degrades the quality of the pages you visit somewhat (they were designed with pictures), you don't usually lose much of the content. For the most part, pictures on Web pages are logos and designs, there for decoration, not information. So turning off the pictures can speed your travels without losing sight of your destination.

- **Don't wait for it to finish**. Depending on the Web browser you use, you can often get the same effect without turning off the pictures. Some browsers will load the text first and then load the pictures, so you can read the text while you wait. If the pictures on the page don't interest you, or if you find a better link somewhere in the text, you can move on before the pictures come in completely. And if you ever feel like you're waiting too long for pictures, you can always press "Stop" to have your Web browser stop what it's doing and await your command.

You can't always get through

Sometimes you feel like you're waiting too long, and you haven't even gotten to the text! Other times, your Web browser itself will give up, telling you that the "connection timed out." This can happen because your Web browser needs to contact the host computer (i.e. the computer which holds the files you're looking for) before it loads the Web page from that computer. If the host computer already has too many other computers talking to it, or if it's not working for some reason, you may not be able to connect with it. Due to the ever-increasing load on this limited (albeit large) network called the Internet, times when you can't get through are not infrequent.

The best suggestion for alleviating this problem is to make your contacts during off-peak hours; that is, when the computers are least busy. Unfortunately, we can't really tell you when those off-peak hours are. If you are working into the late hours of the night on the west coast of the United States, it may seem off-peak to you, but if you try to access computers in western Europe, you'll be cutting into their work day. Using the Web on the weekends is probably your best shot, although now that more and more people are using the Internet recreationally, weekend use can get crowded too. Sometimes your Internet provider will recommend off-peak hours, or you might see a notice about using a particular service at a particular time, but the upshot is that if you're going to use the Web on a regular basis, you'll need to get used to waiting.

Things to try at home

 Surf's up! The easiest way to get started on the Web is to open your Web browser and start clicking. Get used to moving around on the Web, click on highlighted words or phrases, go back and forward, stop and reload. Try everything you can find; you can't hurt the Internet with your Web browser.[7]

---

7   Although this may work well for you, we've found that just getting out and surfing is not the best way to introduce students to the Web. See page 192 for details.

If you're just out for a surf, you should try out the lists of "cool" Web pages available at almost any major Web directory page. The makers of Netscape have even added a "What's cool" button to their toolbar which takes you directly to their page of "cool" Web things. Recent links included a Gilbert and Sullivan archive (*http://diamond.idbsu.edu/gas/GaS.html*), and a Web page called "Bluedog can count!!" (*http://fedida.ini.cmu.edu:5550/bdf.html*) which has a picture of a blue dog that will bark out the result of a simple math equation.

☑ **Try some URLs.** We've included a number of URLs in this section and throughout the book. Enter them into your Web browser and give them a try. If you're using Netscape, all you have to do is click the "Open" button, type in the URL and click "Ok." As long as you typed it correctly, Netscape will take you right there.

☑ **Think of a topic.** Do you have a hobby? A place you'd like to visit? A subject you'd like to know more about? Pick a topic and search for it. For instance, you could try any one of the directory search pages we list in Appendix A, *Internet resources*, and search for topics like Saturn, children's literature, *Le Louvre*, or the U.S. Congress. Ay of these topics will take you to interesting places on the Web.

WEB BALANCE SHEET

Reasons to browse the Web	Reasons *not* to browse the Web
✔ **Huge variety of information.** We can't guarantee that what you're looking for will be on the World Wide Web, but if you can't find it in any reference book, you might as well try the Web. With everything from complete editions of Time Magazine (*http://www.timeinc.com/*) to celebrity birthdays (*http://www.eb.com/ calendar/calendar.html*) the Web is an excellent reference source.	✘ **Too slow.** If you haven't got a quick modem, browsing the Web can be painstaking at best. As the number of people with fast modems or direct connections grows, large Web pages that take a long time to retrieve become more common. The number of people using the Web will slow things as well, and these problems are likely to get worse for slow modem users as time goes by.
✔ **Primary sources.** If you or your students are looking for first-hand reports, the Web is an excellent place to search. Average folks are flocking to the Web in large numbers and bringing with them unfiltered opinions, ideas, essays, and pictures. For instance, if you wanted information about the war in the former Yugoslavia, you could read reports from Bosnians in Sarajevo (*http://web.cnam.fr/Sarajevo/*) or opinions of Orthodox Christian Serbians (*http://www.maximus.com/ News/*).	✘ **No graphics.** People can and do use the World Wide Web with a text-only connection, but most prefer the graphical. You may end up turning off your pictures to speed things up, but it's always nice to know that the graphics are just a click away.

Reasons to browse the Web	Reasons not to browse the Web
✔ **Publishing opportunity.** Display just about anything you want for tens of millions of people all around the world? At no extra cost? It's a dream come true for many. We'll describe how to get your own World Wide Web page in Chapter 11, *Creating your own Web page*, on page 161.	✘ **Easier elsewhere.** The World Wide Web will not replace most of the reference materials you use regularly. For instance, although there are dictionaries on the Web (see *http://www.yahoo.com /Reference/Dictionaries/* for examples), it is much faster and easier to look up a word in your own dictionary than it is on the Web.

Creating your own Web page

▼ ▼ ▼ ▼ ▼ ▼ ▼ ▼ ▼ ▼ ▼

PUBLISHING YOUR WORK ON THE WORLD WIDE WEB

For most of this book, we have tried to avoid overwhelming you with technical details. However, in this chapter we describe the somewhat complicated task of publishing your own work on the Internet. We recommend pausing here, taking a few deep breaths and getting ready to have your friends call you a geek.

▲ ▲ ▲ ▲ ▲ ▲ ▲ ▲ ▲ ▲ ▲

What you'll need

Authoring a Web page for yourself, your class, or your school is not as difficult as it may at first sound, but before you can begin, there are a few questions that you'll need to answer.

The first thing you need to find out is: Does your Internet service provider have the necessary software? This is the software that allows other computers to connect with your account and view Web pages that you have written. If your account doesn't have this software, request it now and get a few of your colleagues to request it as well.

The second most important question that needs to be answered is: Where do you place your files so that your Internet service provider's computer can find them and make them accessible to others? Something to keep in mind is that all Web pages are just files stored somewhere out there on the Internet, waiting for someone to come take a look at them Your Internet service provider can tell you where that "somewhere" is for your account.

Why would anyone view my page?

With so much information already available on the Internet, it may seem unlikely that anyone would want to see what you or your students would put on a Web page. But sharing information is what the Web is all about. As teachers, we've all seen the excitement in the classroom when it comes time to share students' creations. Kids love to show others the work they've done. Whether it is a picture they have drawn or a story they have written, the Web enables students to show-and-tell with the world.[1] If you haven't seen a school Website yet, why not take a break right now and point your Web browser to the Web66: WWW School Registry (*http://hillside.coled.umn.edu/others.html*). This is a directory of K-12 schools on the Web compiled by Hillside Elementary

---

1   For instance, the Global Show-n-Tell Home Page is located at
     http://www.manymedia.com/show-n-tell/

School in St. Paul, Minnesota. It is a wonderful site to have students explore for inspiration before creating their own pages.

What is HTML and how can you learn it?

HTML stands for HyperText Markup Language and it is the programming language that Web pages are written in. Some of you may remember the early days of word processing when, in order to get the right printer output, we had to write the formatting codes ourselves. Documents written in HTML are very similar. In order for a Web browser to interpret the text or graphics we would like to include on our Web page, there is an underlying **source code** that formats the context.

 Buzzwords

HTML (HyperText Markup Language): The special code for writing Web pages.

source code: In this case, the HTML text file that defines how a Web page is formatted; this file is read by your web browser and interpreted to display what eventually shows up on your computer screen

tag: HTML format code

You write the source code in a text file using the HyperText Markup Language. At the top of page 164 is an example of a middle-schoolers home page; that's what you would see on your computer, if you have a connection that supports graphics. Below it is the source code (HyperText Markup Language) used to create the page.

There are special characters in HTML called **tags** that designate text style or insert objects such as pictures. For example,

NET FACTS

▼▼▼▼▼▼▼▼▼▼▼

Inside a Web page

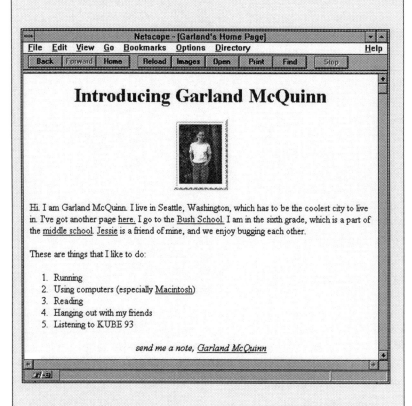

Here is a good example of a high school student's Web page, which is followed on the next page with the HTML code used to create it. While HTML offers fewer formatting capabilities than most word processors, it does offer an effective way to communicate. Recent versions of the popular word processing programs Microsoft Word and Novell WordPerfect can create simple Web pages. But these programs do require some basic knowledge of HTML, which is characterized by its tagging system. These tags instruct abrowser how to present the material.

The code behind Garland's page

Here is the code used to create Garland's homepage.
While it looks complicated, the HTML system is fairly
straight forward and can usually be learned in a matter of
hours.

```
<title>Garland's Home Page</title>
<center><h1>Introducing Garland McQuinn</h1>
<body background="garland.gif" TEXT="FFFFFF"
LINK="FFFF00" VLINK="00FFFF"><table border=4
cellpadding=3 width=0><tr><td>
<img src="garland.gif" width=72
height=97></td></tr></table></center><p>
Hi. I am Garland McQuinn. I live in Seattle,
Washington, which has to be the coolest city
to live in. I've got another page
<a href="http://www.h.com/Hi.html"> here.</a>
I go to the <a href="http://www.bush.edu">
Bush School.</a> I am in the sixth grade,
which is a part of the
<a href="http://www.bush.edu/mid.html">
middle school</a>.
<a href="http://www.bush.edu/Jess.html">
Jessie</a> is a friend of mine, and we enjoy
bugging each other.<p>
These are things that I like to do:
<ol><li>Running
<li>Using computers (especially <a
href="mac.html">Macintosh</a>)
<li>Reading
<li>Hanging out with my friends
<li>Listening to KUBE 93
</ol><center>
<address>send me a note, <a href="mailto:gar-
land@bush.edu">Garland McQuinn</address>
</center>
```

▲▲▲▲▲▲▲▲▲▲▲▲

the HTML tag for making the word "Hello" appear bold looks like this: Hello. A graphical Web browser would read the tag and follow the directions that you have requested by displaying the word in bold. Many of the graphical Web browsers now available have the ability to display a Web page's source code to you as a menu option. That is, when you are looking at a Web page and wondering how it was done, you can select a menu option that will show you the underlying HTML source code. This is what the creator of the page wrote to produce this particular Web page. We highly recommend looking at the source code of pages you like. We have found this to be one of the fastest ways to learn how to write your own Web pages.

Ready to try writing HTML?

There are a number of ways you can learn to use HTML depending on your time and interest. As the Web becomes more and more popular, we are going to see a dramatic increase in workshops centered around creating Web pages. Of course, the increase in people wanting to learn HTML is also a driving force for software developers to produce editors that have HTML formatting tools built right into them. There are both freeware and shareware development tools available as well as big business software developers such as Microsoft which are quickly attempting to meet the demand for HTML software tools.

If you are connected to the Web, you're connected to an incredible wealth of online resources that can guide you through many of the questions you'll have as you begin creating Web pages. Our first suggestion is "A Beginners Guide to HTML" (*http://www.ncsa.uiuc.edu/General/Internet/WWW/HTMLPrimer.html*). This is a wonderful collection of information on HTML tags and how to use them. It is set up with a table of contents that is easy to understand and browse. The individual sections are clearly written and very helpful when you have an idea of what you would like to do, but just don't know how yet.

From the start of your Web page education, we'd also recommend you browse through the "Yale C/AIM WWW Style Manual" (*http://info.med.yale.edu/caim/StyleManual_Top.HTML*).

Popular Web page styles are changing all the time. As you begin to spend time on the Web, you will notice that what seemed like well organized information on some Web pages is reformatted regularly, and not always for the better. We have wondered whether these Web pages change styles to excite returning visitors, or if they're just keeping up with the electronic Joneses?

Where can you find Web tools?

As you get more involved in the Web you will find that a few of the really nifty possibilities that the Web can support need additional software tools. Most Web browsers, whether purchased or downloaded as freeware, have been set to connect with a default home page usually supported by the creators of the browser. This is a great place to begin your Web explorations. The distributors of the browser software realize that a great deal of the impression you form about the product depends on what you see on the screen. Consequently, these default pages are usually highly stylized and include a variety of resources from search engines, to mega-Internet directories, to rotating personal favorite sites and critiques. Below are home page addresses from respected Web browser companies.

NET FACTS

▼▼▼▼▼▼▼▼▼▼▼

Browser home pages

Welcome to Netscape
http://home.mcom.com/home/welcome.html

NCSA Mosaic Home Page
http://www.ncsa.uiuc.edu/SDG/Software/Mosaic/NCSAMosaicHome.html

El MacWeb
http://www.einet.net/ElNet/MacWeb/MacWebHome.html

Spry Home Page
http://www.spry.com:80/index.html

▲▲▲▲▲▲▲▲▲▲▲

Style tips for authoring Web pages

☑ **Don't overload your pages** with graphics. No one enjoys waiting forever for pictures to appear. If you really feel that multiple images are necessary, learn how to use "thumbnails." These are mini-versions of your graphic; they load fast, get the basic concept of the image across without the size. They can also link to a full size version of the graphic on another page.

☑ **Check out how your page looks** using several different browsers. Each browser may alter the way the page is formatted and hence, displayed. Without checking your own pages, you'll never know how someone else may be seeing your creations.

☑ **Find examples of pages** you like and look at the HTML source code they used to create them. There is no need to reinvent the wheel.

☑ **On some pages that work well** you'll see there is no need to scroll down—everything that the page has is visible when the page opens. But you'll also see some very nice pages that are quite long. Listen to your own creative voice.

☑ **Avoid adding unnecessary links.** If it's relevant, go ahead, but you'll find that pages where every noun is linked to something get tiresome very quickly.

CHAPTER 12

Other research services

▼▼▼▼▼▼▼▼▼▼▼

GOPHER, FTP, TELNET, AND MORE

There are a number of other Internet services which provide access to information on the Internet, from Archie and Veronica to gopher and MUDs. All of them are older than the World Wide Web, and as we described before, eventually they will all be subsumed by it. In the meantime, however, you should know what these menu systems, search tools, file retrieval systems and other services can do for you.

▲▲▲▲▲▲▲▲▲▲▲

Gopher:

A menu system

I n 1991 the University of Minnesota unveiled a hierarchical menu system which greatly enhanced access to files on the Internet. The **gopher** system (named for the University of Minnesota mascot) was an almost instant hit among educators who were happy to replace the old method of file retrieval (FTP, which we'll describe below) with an easy-to-use text menu. This is still one of the easiest methods of accessing the Internet for people with text-only connections, although it has been quickly outpaced in size and scope by the World Wide Web.

To reach a gopher system with a text-only connection, simply type the word *gopher* at the command prompt. If your Internet service provider supports gopher (and most all do), you will be presented with a numbered menu. Typing the number of the item you want will take you to a new gopher page or to the item itself. Typing "u" at any point will take you back "up" the menu tree to the last place you visited.

In one sense, gopher is very much like the World Wide Web. The gopher menus are "linked" to each other just like Web pages. However, the gopher system has no ability to present pictures, sound, and movies directly; you must download the files to your computer and display them yourself. Also, gophers are usually set up by major universities, and maintained by system administrators. Private folk do not have the same access to publication on gopher as they do on the Web. For this reason, there is generally less stuff available on gopher. On the other hand, it's also better organized, and there are fewer useless items than on the Web.

Let's take an example. The first, and probably best known, gopher server is the one where it all began at the University of Minnesota. Many Internet providers start with this gopher menu, but if yours doesn't, typing *gopher gopher.tc.umn.edu* at the command prompt should get you there. The menu you see will look something like this:

```
┌─────────────────────────────────────────────────────────────────────┐
│              Internet Gopher Information Client v2.0.18                │
│             University of Minnesota (the first gopher)                 │
│                                                                       │
│   --> 1.  Information About Gopher/                                    │
│       2.  Computer Information/                                        │
│       3.  Discussion Groups/                                          │
│       4.  Fun & Games/                                                │
│       5.  Internet file server (ftp) sites/                          │
│       6.  Libraries/                                                  │
│       7.  News/                                                      │
│       8.  Other Gopher and Information Servers/                       │
│       9.  Phone Books/                                                │
│      10.  Search Gopher Titles at the University of Minnesota <?>     │
│      11.  Search lots of places at the University of Minnesota  <?>   │
│      12.  University of Minnesota Campus Information/                  │
│                                                                       │
│                                                                       │
│                                                                       │
│                                                                       │
│  Press ▓ for Help, ▓ to Quit, ▓ to go up a menu         Page: 1/1     │
└─────────────────────────────────────────────────────────────────────┘
```

This is the opening menu of the University of Minnesota's gopher on the Internet.

If you chose number seven (*News/*), by typing "7" and pressing Enter, you'll get a new menu which includes an item called *National Weather Service Forecasts/.* Choosing that item will get you a menu with each of the states in the United States as item numbers. Choosing a specific state will get you a menu of regions and choosing the region will give you the forecast from the National Weather Service (see below). Once you've found your state and region, you can place a bookmark; just like on the Web. Press "a" to add the item to your bookmark list, and "v" when you want to see the bookmark list you've made. If you find it hard to remember which key to press when, or how to go from menu to menu, you can always press "?" to get help.

```
┌─────────────────────────────────────────────────────────────────────┐
│ weather conditions at 10 pm pdt on 28 may 95 for seattle-tacoma, wa.  │
│ temp(f)    humidity(%)    wind(mph)    pressure(in)    weather         │
│ ==================================================================== │
│    71         39%        nne at 11       30.01         clear          │
│                                                                       │
│ seattle tacoma everett and vicinity                                   │
│ 930 pm pdt sun may 28 1995                                            │
│                                                                       │
│  tonight...fair. lows in the lower to mid 50s. light and variable     │
│ wind.                                                                 │
│  memorial day...sunny and continued warm. highs in the lower 80s.     │
│ wind becoming north 5 to 15 mph afternoon.                            │
│  monday night...fair. lows in the lower to mid 50s.                   │
│  tuesday...areas of morning low clouds and fog with afternoon         │
│ clearing. cooler. highs in the lower to mid 70s.                      │
│                                                                       │
│  <                      temperature   /  precipitation                │
│ seattle                52  83  54  73 /  00  00  00  10               │
│                                                                       │
│                  ************************                             │
│ --More--(55%)[Hit space to continue, Q to abort]                     │
└─────────────────────────────────────────────────────────────────────┘
```

The University of Minnesota's gopher can provide in text format a simple and concise weather forecast for an area that you select.

emember, the gopher can only handle text, so if you're looking
to get sound or picture information, the gopher can bring it to
your computer, but it can't show it to you. However, if the file
you're looking for is only text, like the weather reports above,
the gopher will not only show it to you, but let you save it to
your Internet account, download it to your home computer, or
send it to yourself via e-mail.

One of the nice things about using the gopher is that
there's no extra software; it's all run on the Internet. Also, if
you have a text-only connection, it's a very simple way of getting what you need. If you have a graphical connection and a
Web browser, you might still find the gopher handy. The gopher can be reached through the Web using a special URL. For
instance, if you set your Web browser to:

```
gopher://gopher.tc.umn.edu/
```

you'll get the University of Minnesota gopher described
above. In general, the two forms below are interchangeable:

On a text-only system:	Type at the command line: gopher some.address
On the World Wide Web:	Type in the URL or Go To box: gopher://some.address/

So, if someone suggests you check out the WELL gopher
(WELL stands for the Whole Earth 'Lectronic Link, and is one
of the first and most famous conferencing systems on the Internet), they may tell you to point your gopher towards *go-
pher.well.sf.ca.us*. Here's what you'd do:

On a text-only system:	Type at the command line: gopher gopher.well.sf.ca.us
On the World Wide Web:	Type in the URL or Go To box: gopher://gopher.well.sf.ca.us/

Either way, you'd end up in the same place.

By the way, you may be interested in checking out the WELL gopher. They have a large section for K-12 educators, right off of the main menu.

FTP:
File retrieval

The World Wide Web and gopher are just easy ways of getting files on big Internet computers back to your own personal computer. Before these services came on the scene, it was necessary to do this type of transfer "by hand." In other words, you had to connect with a big Internet computer using special commands typed at the command prompt, find the file you wanted using more commands, and then transfer it to your computer with still more special commands. This type of file retrieval came to be known as **FTP** (File Transfer Protocol).

Buzzwords

anonymous FTP: A service which allows any Internet user access to files on a given Internet computer.

login name (also **logon name** or **user name**): The name by which an Internet computer recognizes you. In the case of anonymous FTP, your login name should be "anonymous."

password: The secret word which allows you access to files on a computer. In the case of anonymous FTP, you may use any password. Most anonymous FTP sites request that you use your e-mail address as a password.

Computers on the Internet still use FTP, but now the World Wide Web or gopher interfaces can do most of the work for you. However, sometimes it's still necessary to go back to the basics and do the FTP yourself, especially if you have a text-only connection. This is true

because gopher can not retrieve *any* file on the Internet, only those which are entered into its menu system. Thus, if you normally use gopher to find and retrieve files, you will occasionally need to use FTP when the files you're looking for aren't available via gopher. The World Wide Web does not have this restriction. Any file which is available via FTP is available via the Web.

We should reiterate here that when we talk about available files, we are talking about files that were specifically made available for anyone on the Internet to use. There are a large number of these files, but they by no means comprise all of the files on all of the computers on the Internet. It's especially important to remember that they do not include your files on your personal computer. Just because you can access files on the Internet does *not* mean that people can access the files on your home computer.

If you need to use FTP, it will be because someone has given you the location of a file on the Internet, and you want to bring it to your computer. That is to say, when you start this process you should know the name of the file, the name of the Internet computer which holds the file, and the location of the file on that computer. In describing the FTP process, we will assume that you already possess those three key pieces of information.

How to download Netscape

Suppose, for instance, that you'd like to get a copy of Netscape, the Web browser described in Chapter 10. In order to bring Netscape to your computer you'll need to know the name of the Internet computer where it resides, the location of the file on that computer, and the name of the file.

Name of Internet computer:	ftp.netscape.com
Location of file:	/netscape/windows *or* /netscape/mac
Name of file:	n16e11n.exe *or* n16e11n.hqx

There are three steps involved in FTP. You must connect your computer to the Internet computer which holds the files you want, you must locate the files you want on the Internet computer, and you must bring those files from the Internet computer to your computer. When you are using a text-only connection, all three of these steps must be done by entering commands at the command line.

```
carson% ftp ftp.netscape.com
Connected to ftp1.netscape.com.
220 ftp1.netscape.com FTP server (Version wu-2.4(3) Tue Dec 27 17:53:56 PST 1994
Name (ftp.netscape.com:ssteen): anonymous
331 Guest login ok, send your complete e-mail address as password.
Password:
230-Welcome to the Netscape Communications Corporation FTP server.
230-
230-If you have any odd problems, try logging in with a minus sign (-)
230-as the first character of your password.  This will turn off a feature
230-that may be confusing your ftp client program.
230-
230-Please send any questions, comments, or problem reports about
230-this server to ftp@netscape.com.
230-
230 Guest login ok, access restrictions apply.
ftp>
```

The opening screen of the Netscape FTP server

1. Connect. To start your FTP session, enter *ftp* and then the name of the computer at your command line. For instance, to connect to the Netscape computer, you would enter:

```
ftp ftp.netscape.com
```

If your computer complains that this Internet computer is not available, you should check that you typed everything correctly, and then try again.[1] Once you have connected, the computer will ask you for your **login name**. Enter *anonymous* for the login name, and your e-mail address for the **password**. This is what is known as "**anonymous FTP.**" Entering your e-mail address as a password is not required for access, but it is

---

1   At this point, your computer may have a prompt which reads *FTP>* or something similar. In this case, you'll have to leave the FTP program by entering *quit* at the command line before trying again.

courteous. If the remote computer's administrators have any problems with the way you are using FTP, they can then e-mail you with their concerns. It also gives the administrators an idea of who is using their service. Since they're not charging you for it, it's the least you can do to let them know who you are.

2. Find the file. You are now connected to a remote computer and can browse through its directories, just like you can browse through the directories or folders on your own home computer. Unfortunately, you cannot simply point and click like you can on your own computer. Instead you have to use specific commands, such as the following:

cd (change directory)	This will move you to a new directory
ls (list files)	This will show you all of the files in the current directory

Usually it is only necessary to change to the directory which holds the file you want. In the example above the directory is /netscape/windows if you'd like the Windows version of Netscape and /netscape/mac if you'd like the Macintosh version. So the proper command would be:

For the Windows version of Netscape:	cd /netscape/windows
For the Macintosh version of Netscape:	cd /netscape/mac

3. Get the file. Finally, you need to bring the file from the remote computer to your computer. You can start this process using the **ls** command described above. Enter *ls* at the command line, and the remote computer will list all of the files in that directory. Then you can check to make sure the file you want is there. This is not absolutely necessary, but since directory holdings and file names change, it is usually a good idea.

To move the file from the remote Internet computer to your Internet account, you must use the **get** command, which gets the specified file for you. In the example above, you would enter:

On a Windows system:	get n16e11n.exe
On a Macintosh system:	get n16e11n.hqx

and the file would then be transferred from the remote computer to the Internet account on your service provider's computer. This will *not* bring the file all the way to your home computer. To do that you must use the download features of your telecommunications software. Since these features vary widely from computer to computer, it is best to read your manual or ask an experienced friend to help you with this last portion of the journey.

4. Exit FTP. Okay, we mentioned only three steps before, because step four is not really part of the process, but you'll need to exit the FTP session before you can do anything else on your Internet account. You do this by entering *quit* at the command line.

NET FACTS

▼▼▼▼▼▼▼▼▼▼▼

A few FTP commands

ftp *computer* Start the file transfer process. Replace the word "computer" with the name of the computer you'd like to access.

cd *directory* Changes directories. Replace the word "directory" with the directory which holds the file you want.

ls List all of the files in the directory. You can do this just to make sure you have the right directory and the right file name.

get *file* Bring the file from the remote computer to your account in your Internet service provider's computer. Replace the word "file" with the name of the file you want. You will still have to bring the file from your Internet service provider's computer to your home computer.

▲▲▲▲▲▲▲▲▲▲▲▲

Steps two through four of your FTP session may look something like this (the portions you would type are written after each *ftp>* prompt):

```
ftp>
ftp>
ftp>
ftp> cd /netscape/windows
250 CWD command successful.
ftp> ls
200 PORT command successful.
150 Opening ASCII mode data connection for file list.
.message
license
n16e11n.exe
n32e11n.exe
readme.txt
226 Transfer complete.
57 bytes received in 0.00 seconds (0.06 Kbyte/s)
ftp> get n16e11n.exe
200 PORT command successful.
150 Opening ASCII mode data connection for n16e11n.exe (1599738 bytes).
226 Transfer complete.
local: n16e11n.exe remote: n16e11n.exe
1606042 bytes received in 6.39 seconds (245.45 Kbyte/s)
ftp> quit
221 Goodbye.
carson% _
```

When you've finally managed to get the file from the remote Internet computer back to your own home, you'll need to know what to do with it. Some files must be decompressed, whereas other files (such as sounds and pictures) may need special software to make them accessible. All of this can be plenty confusing, which is why people find gopher and the World Wide Web so darn handy.

By the way, it is possible to access FTP through your Web browser, just like it's possible to access gopher. For FTP, the first word of your URL should be "FTP". For example, you can access the example above by giving your Web browser one of the following URLs:

ftp://ftp.netscape.com/netscape/windows/n16e11n.exe

ftp://ftp.netscape.com/netscape/mac/n16e11n.hqx

Your Web browser will then get the file and bring it to your computer. It will handle all of the necessary details without your input. See why we recommend getting a graphical connection?

Archie, Veronica, and Jughead:
Finding things on the Internet

We've already talked about Internet search tools on the World Wide Web, but there were search tools around long before the Web came into existence. Some of the most important are:

 Archie. A search tool for files available via FTP; you can access it by connecting to certain computers on the Internet. Archie works by asking each computer on the In-

Archie servers

If you live in (or near)	Use
Australia	archie.au
Austria	archie.edvz.uni-linz.ac.at
Austria	archie.univie.ac.at
Canada	archie.uqam.ca
Canada	archie.cs.mcgill.ca
Finland	archie.funet.fi
France	archie.univ-rennes1.fr
Germany	archie.th-darmstadt.de
Israel	archie.ac.il
Italy	archie.unipi.it
Japan	archie.wide.ad.jp
Korea	archie.hana.nm.kr
Korea	archie.sogang.ac.kr
Norway	archie.uninett.no
Spain	archie.rediris.es
Sweden	archie.luth.se
Switzerland	archie.switch.ch
Taiwan	archie.ncu.edu.tw
United Kingdom	archie.doc.ic.ac.uk
United Kingdom	archie.hensa.ac.uk
USA (NE)	archie.unl.edu
USA (NJ)	archie.internic.net
USA (NJ)	archie.rutgers.edu
USA (NY)	archie.ans.net
USA (MD)	archie.sura.net

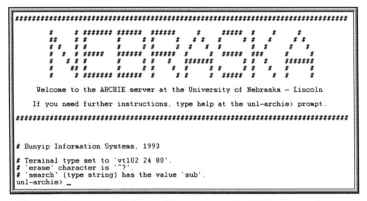

The opening menu of the Archie server at the University of
Nebraska-Lincoln

ternet what files it has available and keeping a list of all
those files and where they can be found. See below for
an example of using Archie.

 Veronica. A search tool for the gopher system; it is usually accessible through gopher itself. Much like Archie,
Veronica compiles an index to all of the menus on all of
the gopher systems available. Using Veronica is easy:
choose the menu item which says "Search the Gopher using Veronica" (or something similar). The gopher program will then ask you for a search term, and build a
menu of items which match that term. It's that simple.

 Jughead (sensing a trend here?). Also searches gopher,
but it only searches particular gopher computers. If you
use Jughead, it will probably be without knowing
it—Jughead works behind the scenes.

Telnet:
Remote access

Another Internet service which is fast becoming obsolete
due to the popularity of the World Wide Web is **telnet** (which
is short for **tel**etype **net**working). Telnet is what's known as a
"terminal emulation" program; that is to say, it makes it possible for your computer to emulate the responses of a remote
computer terminal.

You can think of this as computer "possession," like something out of *The Exorcist*. The remote computer "takes over" your computer so that anything you type goes directly into the remote computer and its responses come right back to you via your computer. The upshot of this "possession" is that you can use the Internet computer's services remotely from another computer many miles away. These Internet computers are set up specifically to let anyone access them; you do not have to worry about other people telnetting into your account and accessing your files—they can't.[2] Neither do you have to worry about having your monitor spin around and your computer speak backwards <grin>.

Certain computers on the Internet provide special services which are accessible through telnet. For instance, you can telnet to the University of Michigan's Weather Underground computer (type *telnet madlab.sprl.umich.edu 3000*) to receive weather updates and forecasts for the entire United States. This information is also available on the World Wide Web, though, and through the Web you can not only get temperatures, wind speeds, and forecasts, but also full motion sequences from weather satellites showing the clouds cluster and blow across your area of the country, exactly like the pictures on the evening news (for example, see the weather pages at the U. of Washington: *http://www.atmos.washington.edu/*). This gives you an idea of why the World Wide Web is overshadowing these other, older Internet services.

Many of the Internet services now becoming available through the Web started as telnet services. The FTP search tool Archie is a good example. Several large Internet computers around the country act as Archie "servers," meaning that they carry the Archie software and allow people to log in to their system to use it. If you telnet to any of the following computers, and enter "archie" as your username (and password, if necessary), you will be able to access the Archie software.

---

2   Like other Internet services, "telnet" has become both a noun (meaning the program itself) and a verb (using the program). Our apologies to English teachers who find this grating.

Once you've gotten into one of the Archie servers, you'll see a screenful (or two) of information about using Archie. Learning the ins and outs of Archie software can be difficult, but there are really only a couple of things you have to know. First, to find a specific file or directory on the Internet, type "find" and then all or part the file name. For instance, if you wanted to find all of the files (or directories) that contain the letters "mac" in their title, you would enter:

```
find mac
```

at the command prompt. It would then spit out a list of files with the letters "mac" in them, and the Internet computers and directories for those files. If you did this because you wanted to find files for the Macintosh, you will be overwhelmed. Remember, there are millions of computers out there, and most of them probably have a directory for Macintosh software. Archie is used best when you know the name of a specific file, but you don't know where to find it.

The other thing you should know is that if you ever get stuck, you can enter ^], i.e. press and hold the control key on your keyboard and then type a right bracket (]). This will break the connection with the remote computer.

As we mentioned above, the Archie service is now available through the World Wide Web. This graphical Archie interface is called "ArchiePlex," and is available on a number of World Wide Web pages. For a list of these pages, see:

http://web.nexor.co.uk/archie.html

Even more Internet Services:
WAIS, Talk, IRC, and MUDs

WAIS

Since finding and retrieving information from the Internet is such an important task, it is not surprising that some heavyweight thinkers have put a lot of effort into making it work. One product of such effort is the Wide Area Information Server (WAIS), a means for finding information within databases distributed among many computers on the Internet.

Although the idea is a good one, there are currently a few problems with WAIS. Because WAIS indices must be specifically constructed, there aren't many out there yet. Also, WAIS was conceived of and developed well before the World Wide Web, and does not have the same user-friendly interface. However, you can still find a lot of information on WAIS, and it's accessible via telnet (for text-only connections) and the Web (for graphical connections). You might want to give it a try if you can't find what you need elsewhere.

To access WAIS via telnet:	Type: telnet quake.think.com
To access WAIS via the Web:	Type: http://www.wais.com/

Talk

Some Internet service providers give you access to a program called "talk" which allows two people to communicate simultaneously by writing back and forth. This removes the time-delay factor of e-mail and gives you what is essentially a text-based phone. Although this seems to be a fine idea, it has certain problems.

First, it doesn't work very well unless it is well-coordinated. Both people have to be online, of course, and usually they have to coordinate the time of the call, who's going to start the process, and who's going to answer. The Internet just isn't set up to allow incoming calls and the interruptions they bring. Also, it works best if both people are using

Buzzwords

IRC (InterRelay Chat): A service which allows many people on the Internet to hold a conversation in real-time.

MUD (Multi-User Domain): An text-based imaginary world in which Internet users can act and effect their environment.

real-time: Synchronously. For example, the phone line allows real-time communication; the postal service does not.

talk: A service which allows two people on the Internet to hold a written conversation in real-time.

telnet: A service which allows your computer to emulate a remote computer. Also used as a verb.

WAIS (Wide Area Information Server): A database search engine for the Internet.

text-based connections. Finally, most system administrators frown upon the idea of "talk"ing over long distances: It takes a lot of Internet resources.

Thus, anyone who wants to "talk" should do so with someone who is using the same Internet service provider. Usually these people will be in the same area code, and therefore dialing each other on the phone is just as inexpensive as using the "talk" program. This is an excellent example of where an existing service (the phone system) is much more useful than the Internet. However, if you are still interested in trying it out, ask your Internet service provider if "talk" is supported. They should be able to tell you how to use it, and what restrictions are placed on its use.

IRC

Inter-Relay Chat is a "talk"-like Internet service which allows many people to communicate at the same time. Instead of employing a phone-like system of call-and-answer, the IRC sets up "channels": places on the Internet where people can congregrate and chat. The difference between these IRC channels and the newsgroups we've already described is that anything written by one person is immediately broadcast to every other channel member. This allows for real-time meetings and conferences on the Internet.

Although the potential for world-wide teacher conferences and the like seems exciting, in actual fact the IRC is rather vapid. Most IRC channels resemble something like a science fiction convention crossed with a single's bar, except that the anonymity of the Internet prompts some users to explore new worlds of rudeness and immaturity. For this reason, many Internet service providers (especially schools and school districts) refuse to provide access to this service.

If you're interested in exploring the possibilities for IRC, try reading the IRC Frequently Asked Questions list, which can be found at:

```
http://cbl.leeds.ac.uk/nikos/tex2html/examples/
IRCprimer1.1/IRCprimer1.1.html
```

MUDs

The closest that the Internet comes to "virtual reality" is the Multi-User Domains, or Multi-User Dimension, sometimes called MOOs or MUSHs or a whole slew of other acronyms. They come in all different shapes and sizes and names, but they're essentially the same thing: a fantasy world of text where users can interact with the environment and each other simply by typing into their computer what they wish to do.

If you know anything about fantasy role-playing games, this sort of description probably conjures images of dragons and knights (or, more likely, adolescent boys pretending to be dragons and knights). The vast majority of MUDs are "hack and slash" environments for people who want to dismember monsters and each other over the Internet. However, there are a few experiments in turning these domains into conferencing tools for research and education. If you are interested in learning more about MUDs, try:

http://www.cis.upenn.edu/~lwl/mudinfo.html

Internet in the classroom

▼▼▼▼▼▼▼▼▼▼▼

Now it's time to set aside most of the technical aspects of the Internet and consider how teachers can actually make use of this technology in the classroom. We'll start with a look at the role of the Internet as a tool to enhance learning, showing you two teachers, Chris and Tina, who are both using the Internet in their classrooms, but in very different ways. We will then examine the ways we as teachers orient ourselves to this new tool. How can we make good decisions about how to use the Internet? Your conception of teaching and your ideas about what should go on in a classroom are crucial factors that you should be aware of. Finally, we will hear from four experienced teachers and Internet users about how the Internet helps them teach more effectively.

▲▲▲▲▲▲▲▲▲▲▲

CHAPTER 13

Using the Internet in your classroom

▼▼▼▼▼▼▼▼▼▼▼

MAKING THE CHOICE TO USE IT WELL

If you're considering adding the Internet to your teaching toolkit, then you should also be considering how your students learn. In this chapter, we compare the approach to learning and the use of the Internet in two imaginary classrooms, and offer tips on how to use this new technology more effectively.

▲▲▲▲▲▲▲▲▲▲▲▲

How do we learn?

The reason we teach is so that students will learn. This seems like a truism but its important to keep in mind as we consider the use of the Internet in the classroom. Whenever we consider a change in the way we do our jobs, one question that has to be addressed is: How will this affect my students' learning? If we are going to take this question seriously then we must know something not only about the change that's being considered—in this case, the introduction of the Internet into the classroom and curriculum—but also about *how children learn*.

In the next few pages we will take a brief look at how learning takes place, consider some of the necessary conditions for learning to occur and the ways in which the Internet can enhance the process.

Cognitive scientists tell us that we learn by rearranging what's in our heads—that is, by modifying, extending, and changing our knowledge, understandings, and beliefs. We all have connected webs of understanding that allow us to explain the things we perceive in the world and to deal more or less successfully with the problems that we encounter everyday. For example, when a child plays a typical video game for the first time, he or she probably has a very clear idea of the problem: How can I get the highest possible score? Depending on the child's level of experience and sophistication with similar games, he or she will be able to recognize cues provided by the experiences in the game that point to successful patterns of action and reaction. Some of the experiences will be visual, some will be auditory. The child will learn cognitive and affective lessons about the game. Through a cycle of perception, action, experience, and reflection, the child adjusts and extends what is known or assumed about the way the game works. Gradually, a complex web of understanding is constructed, and the child is able to solve the problems presented by the game.

Changing the way we teach

On a different level, when we as teachers are asked to change the way we teach, we are faced with the task of revising, adjusting, and extending what we understand about the way the classroom works. Currently, in the field of mathematics education, for example, there is a great deal of support for the idea that we should teach mathematics in an integrated fashion. That is, those subject areas that have traditionally been considered as separate and distinct—algebra and geometry, for example—should be taught together. This sounds reasonable; students should understand the connections between the algebraic and geometric interpretations of the Pythagorean Theorem. In reality, however, when we try to modify the curriculum so as to make these connections clear, we have to make significant changes in the ways we teach these concepts, the examples we give, the experiences we ask the students to engage in and the ways we evaluate the understanding the students construct. We have to rearrange many of the notions we have built up and internalized about how we should teach mathematics. This is learning on a large scale and it is no small undertaking.

As teachers we are forever trying to get our students to take part in the process of learning. If learning is to take place three things must happen.

 First, the student must ask or adopt a question. This is especially important in a classroom. With a video game, the motivation is supplied by the game itself, with a system of rewards and incentives. In a classroom, the rewards are generally not so obvious and the work is usually more difficult.

 If there is no interest in or commitment to a question on the part of the learner, there is little motivation to go on to the second step which is to seek information relevant to the question. Good teachers know how to inspire their students to ask questions; they are masters of motivation. If students are motivated there are many ways to gather information. They might try an experiment, read a paragraph in a book, go to the library, consult an appropriate site on the World Wide Web or talk to one another or to an expert.

 Third, students have to reflect on the information they have gathered. They have to think about what it means and make it part of the structure of knowledge, beliefs, and understandings they use to interpret the world they live in.

So, in short, we are saying that, in order to learn, students need to ask (or adopt) a question, get information, and then reflect on that information in relation to the question. How can the Internet help in this learning process?

Using the Net in the learning process

Teachers who allow and encourage their students to ask their own questions will find that the Internet can be a useful tool. The amount of information and the number of resources that are available make it possible for students to consider concepts and ideas that would otherwise be outside the realm of the typical classroom.

For example, Earth Viewer is a World Wide Web site (*http://www.fourmilab.ch/earthview/vplanet.html*) where students can view a map of the earth showing the regions where it is currently day or night. They can also see what the earth would look like at any given moment from a vantage point on the moon, the sun, or in a satellite situated at whatever latitude, longitude, and altitude the student chooses. This site can also generate an up-to-date image of the whole globe that includes the current cloud cover. A student who wonders why it gets dark so much earlier in November than it did in June will be able to see the path of the sun's light around the globe and the way the patterns (and the dominant weather phenomena) change as the earth moves through its orbit around the sun.

With this sort of capability, they can not only ask interesting questions, they can begin to generate some of the information they will need to answer these questions.

As you know from the preceding chapters of this book, students can also join a wide variety of mailing lists and newsgroups where there are ongoing conversations about any number of topics, ideas, and concepts (some of which are not appropriate for children; see *Perils of the Net* on page 57). Some examples of newsgroup that might be of use to secondary students include *sci.agriculture*, a newsgroup devoted to the discussion of the science of agriculture, *sci.physics.research*, or *alt.history.what_if*.

Likewise, there are a number of sites on gopher and the World Wide Web where students can submit questions for experts to consider. For example, at the Newton site (*http://www.newton.dep.anl.gov/*), students can leave questions in a variety of categories related to science. Scientists periodically check the questions and offer responses. Students can read their own questions and responses or peruse those left by other students.

Along the same lines, there are many sites offering up-to-the-moment weather information. Students can get not only the latest weather conditions for a given city or region, they can also get satellite images of the earth so that, for example, they can watch as a storm develops in the Pacific, gathers strength and then sweeps ashore, bringing rain to the Puget Sound and snow to the Cascade foothills of Washington state. Having done that, they can log in to the University of Michigans Weather Underground (*telnet madlab.sprl.umich.edu 3000*) where they will find the weather forecast, the forecasters notes, and the current conditions for any major city in the United States, and some abroad as well. Students can use these sites and the information available there in the important process of constructing their own understanding of how the worlds weather works on both a global and a local scale. Opportunities for gathering this and other kinds of information are becoming more and more common on the Internet.

Communicating with others

Finally, one of the most useful means for gathering information and for reflecting on this information is through communication with others. Our ability to communicate with a wide range of others is dramatically increased through the magic of the Internet. Of course telecommunication cannot and should not replace face-to-face contact. The Internet, however, can allow students to interact in some fashion with a much greater variety of people than they could ever hope to reach without it. And it is in this communication through the trading of ideas and understandings that students have the opportunity to check their own understanding with that of others and to refine and reflect on their growing ideas about the way the world works. You can read about several examples of classroom projects where this sort of process was successfully employed by teachers in the case studies near the end of the book. It seems clear then that the Internet can be used as a valuable tool to enhance students' abilities to ask their own questions, gather information and communicate with others in the process of reflection and learning. Now let's take a look at some of these ideas in the context of the classroom.

The following descriptions of two imaginary teachers and their classrooms will help set the stage for further discussion and for the case studies that will follow. While the classrooms are outwardly similar, the ways in which the Internet is being used are fundamentally different. As you read, ask yourself whether the process of learning is being served or not.

Chris and Tina

A cautionary tale in two parts

Chris Devore

Mrs. Devore directed her car into her customary parking slot at Selmar Elementary School. She cut the engine, but left the radio on. It was 7:15 a.m. on a beautiful sunny day in March and one of her favorite songs had just begun. She let the music wash over her as she relaxed in her seat and thought about what would happen that day in Room 12.

Selmar Elementary was a medium-sized school with 320 students in grades K-5. It was an older building on the edge of the downtown core of a large city in the Northwest. The students at Selmar came from a variety of neighborhoods and circumstances. If you had looked at a demographic profile of the school, you would have found that 30% of the students were from various minority groups, 40% qualified for free or reduced priced lunch, and for the first time in the schools history, the ESL population was in the double figures at 11%.

Chris Devore had been at Selmar for eight of her eleven years of teaching; she liked it there. She had friends among the staff and faculty. A few even lived close enough that her children and theirs were growing up together. Only a few of the schools employees lived near Selmar and Chris was not one of them. She commuted about 20 minutes each way from a neighborhood a bit farther out where the yards were larger and the sirens a little less strident.

A fresh approach

Chris was making a few changes that year in her fourth-fifth-grade split class. She had recently finished a masters degree in education (she was just getting used to the idea of having her nights free, and the prospect of a summer not filled with courses was a bit overwhelming) and had found some ideas that seemed at least harmless, maybe even useful. She switched off the radio, picked up her notebooks, her gradebook, and the stack of student papers she had worked on last night, and walked across the parking lot into Selmar Elementary.

The building was still quiet at this time in the morning. School didn't start until 8:30, but she was not the first one there. As usual, the principal, Mr. Belbo, was there. He began each day with a swim at the nearby high school and was generally in his office, wet and ready to greet the day, at 6:45 each morning.

He had come to Selmar five years ago and had brought with him some ideas that had stirred up some trouble. The portfolios, for example. At first they had seemed like a waste of time and effort, but Chris and some of the others had stuck with it and now thought they were beginning to make sense of them.

He had also introduced the multi-age classroom, and Chris was finding more and more that this was a good way to teach. She liked having the students for two years (well, most of them) and she liked the way they worked with one another. They taught themselves!

Mr. Belbo was also an advocate of educational technology. He had wrung some money out of the district in the form of a leadership grant and had encouraged teachers to propose projects and curriculum ideas. The upper-grade teachers had asked for and received seven new computers, including one in the library with a connection to the Internet. Chris had also been given a computer for her classroom and, along with the old Apple IIgs, it stood on a rolling table now pushed over to the side of the room. She found that access to this technology opened up some new options in teaching.

Connecting the curriculum

The project she was currently working on with the five other teachers who taught third, fourth and fifth grade at Selmar focused on the social studies curriculum, but new connections to other parts of the general curriculum seemed to appear each week. They had finally stopped trying to identify it as a social studies project and they worked on it whenever it seemed appropriate.

The project had begun a year and a half ago as a cross-cultural exchange, a kind of glorified pen-pals project in which a class at Selmar made contact with a class in Chiappas, Mexico. The fourth-grade class belonged to Mrs. Tuttle, a teacher down the hall from Chris, but the project had been initiated by Mrs. Tuttle's student teacher who was doing her internship. This student teacher ran the whole project through her laptop computer. The other teachers had heard about the project and had seen her sitting in the faculty lounge, always just a phone cord's length away from the phone jack. She would dial in to her account at the university and upload her students' work, sending it thousands of miles away. A day or two later she would chatter excitedly about the replies she was getting and what it was doing for her students' view of the world. Her cooperating teacher, Mrs. Tuttle, and the rest of the regular faculty watched with a mixture of disdain, envy, impatience, and interest. Most of what her students were doing at that time was simply trading information about their respective schools and neighborhoods. The exchange was conducted in English using e-mail.

When the student teacher graduated, Mrs. Tuttle had let the program lapse. Then, one day, one of the memos in the endless stream that seemed to flow from her mailbox had rung a bell. It advertised a three-hour seminar on the use of the Internet to enhance teaching. This was a bell that had been rung pretty continuously by her student teacher, and so Mrs. Tuttle had asked Chris if she wanted to attend. Ever on the lookout for new and unusual course credits, Chris had agreed. Mr. Belbo had come up with the registration fee on the condition that the two of them make some sort of report at the next faculty meeting.

On the appointed Saturday, the two of them had spent the morning learning about FTP, modems, Veronica, World Wide Web, e-mail and gophers. As part of their report to the faculty, they proposed a sketchy outline of a classroom project making use of the Internet. The project followed the same lines as the one conducted by the student teacher but incorporated a few more twists and turns and covered a lot more curricular ground, integrating—at least on paper—a variety of subjects, such as writing, social studies, science and mathematics. They thought of it mostly as an academic exercise, but after the meeting, another teacher, Mr. Tucker, had asked if he could get involved, and so they had decided to give it a real try.

Putting a plan in place

Mr. Tucker had an Internet account through a local service provider and knew a bit about e-mail and the Internet in general. They met on four Wednesday afternoons in May and assembled the specifics of a plan that involved the students in all three classrooms. Mr. Belbo found them a modem and they had hooked it up to the computer in the library (the only machine near a phone line). They used Mr. Tucker's account to access the Internet.

That fall the students in the three classrooms began the year with three virtual field trips to Chiappas, Mexico; Brisbane, Australia; and Århus, Denmark. They also hosted virtual delegations from classes in these three cities. In preparing for these exchanges, the students either wrote to, talked on the telephone with, or visited directly with a variety of people including civic leaders, police officers, the representatives of several local employers, a historian at a regional museum, some dock workers, and some homeless people in the shelter downtown. Using video cameras and tape recorders, they gathered information for a portrait of their city. They practiced their writing skills and learned a great deal about the way the city worked and some of the ways it didn't.

It took a lot of time, a lot of work, and some of the students learned more than others, but, in the end, the quality and depth of the information they sent to the classes in Mexico, Australia, and Denmark far surpassed what the three teachers had envisioned.

From gathering data to learning concepts

They were now engaged in a more quantitative project, and it was this project that Chris was thinking of as she walked into her empty classroom and checked the fish tank near the windows. Her students were working on a data-gathering project that would lead to an exchange of information with the other schools and would culminate in a live debate between the four schools near the end of April.

The data they were gathering for their own city involved a range of demographics, such as the population of the city, the number of public and private schools, churches, bars, hotel and hospital beds, movie theaters, golf courses, and so forth.

They were also finding out about the number of violent crimes committed the previous year, the average amount of rainfall that could be expected and the average range in temperature over the course of the year. The students in Mexico, Australia, and Denmark were gathering similar information and would share this via e-mail and IRC chat.

With all this information and a good deal more, the students were beginning to construct a statistical portrait of the city. They began with a simple statistic — like the number of cemeteries in the city — and asked via e-mail about similar figures in the other three cities. It soon became clear, however, that the numbers alone did not mean very much. They had to be compared to something. Four cemeteries might seem like a lot in a small town but not as much in a large city.

So the students began to construct ratios. When they looked at the number of cemeteries in the city, they compared this to the city's population. This lead them to enquire about the city's birth rate. And this raised questions about the average life-span and the average age of the city's residents. When they found that there were 21 murders committed in the city in the past year, they discovered that it was useful to express this number in terms of murders per 100,000 residents. Moreover, they had to explain these ratios to the other classes around the world, and the process of explaining had taught them these concepts in ways that Chris could not have hoped to approach by using textbook problems and worksheets.

Today they were going to continue working on constructing some new and different ratios. Two days ago, the students in Århus had sent a report in which they listed and discussed the ratio composed of the number of schools divided by the number of children under the age of 17. They had also reported the number of churches divided by the number of bars, and asked what this ratio was like for the other cities. Chris students had talked about these ratios and wondered just what they meant. What did they tell you about a city? What is the ideal ratio of museums to malls?

A motivating force

Of course, these questions could be addressed without the Internet, but for the students, comparing their city and their way of life with those of children around the world gave a motivation to the investigation that proved to be a powerful force. The immediacy and intimacy of the communications they shared with the students around the world had not just given them a context in which to study some social studies and mathematical concepts—it was changing their perceptions of geography, politics, and history.

School did not begin until 8:30 but Chris smiled as five of her fifth-graders entered the room at 7:45 and pulled up chairs around the big meeting table. They had volunteered to come early and begin talking about the home page they wanted to create to represent their class and their school on the World Wide Web.

▲▲▲▲▲▲▲▲▲▲▲▲

Tina Moore

The alarm was loud, deafeningly loud, and Tina Moore rolled out of bed, walked across the room and turned it off. She stood there for a moment, getting her bearings, then headed for the shower. It was 7 a.m. and she had a 25-minute drive from her home to Rivertown Elementary School. The students would be there at 8 a.m.

Tina didn't usually cut it so close. She had been teaching for 14 years and had developed a pretty successful approach to the profession. At Rivertown Elementary, where she had been teaching for the past seven years, she was one of three fifth-grade teachers in a school of about 420 students. The school, built in the rush of the 1960s, was set in a middle-class suburb of a large city in the Northwest. Like many schools and neighborhoods in the area, Rivertown Elementary was experiencing a rapid shift in its demographics. What had once been a predominantly white, middle-class, suburban environment was developing into a much more heterogeneous mix of ethnic and racial groups. The minority enrollment was 30%. Five percent of the students were classified as gifted and talented, and 40% qualified for free or reduced price lunch. Tina had three children in her class of 25 fifth-graders for whom English was a second language; two of these were recent immigrants from Southeast Asia and spoke virtually no English at all.

Scrambling to stay ahead

Tina parked the car at 7:45 a.m. and hurried into the school building, aware of the principal, Mr. Bailey, watching her disapprovingly behind the partially drawn shades in his office. She didn't like to be late but she had been up until nearly 2 a.m. the night before wandering through the endless labyrinth of the Internet, so she had adjusted her alarm from 6:00 to 7:00.

The first thing she did when she got to her classroom, after turning on the lights and dropping her book bag, was to go to her desk and turn on the computer, the monitor, the modem, and the speakers. There were a couple of sites she had not been able to get into the night before and she wanted to see if there was anything useful there before she turned the students loose with them. It took several minutes to retrace the wandering path she had followed last night, so that by the time she found the first of the sites she was looking for, the first students were coming in and sitting down at the two machines in the back of the room.

She sighed and reluctantly moved away from her computer screen, wondering, as she often did these days, how she had come to such a state of affairs. Up until a year and a half ago, she had thought that gophers and mice were rodents. Now she was surfing the Net until the wee hours.

Lots of technology, little expertise

The school district had passed a technology levy the year before, after two previously unsuccessful tries, and had spent a good deal of the money buying and upgrading computers for the elementary school teachers in the district. Every teacher at Rivertown Elementary was given a computer for his or her desk and two more for students to use. It had been an exciting day that last September when the truck had pulled up outside the library and the boxes had been unloaded. Two weeks later, the boxes were in the classrooms but the computers were still inside them.

Tina's sister, who lived nearby and worked for a software development company in the city, had volunteered to come over and set up Tina's computers and the modems that came with them. Tina had taken her sister out to lunch, and it had turned into quite a thriving little business for her sister as eight other teachers in the building prevailed upon her to set up their computers. The alternative was to take a place on the six-week waiting list for help from the district tech people.

All the teachers had also been provided with an Internet account and a connection to the state educational network. Tina had learned from her sister the basics of e-mail, gopher, and the World Wide Web. She had been surprised at how easy it was—much simpler than programming the VCR—and she had become the default guru of the Information Superhighway at Rivertown Elementary.

Tina would be the first to admit, however, that guru was a relative title, and at her school, it didn't take much to assume the position. Even now, eight months after the computers arrived, there was not a lot going on with technology in the building. While Mr. Bailey had insisted that all the machines be set up and plugged in, he had not gone so far as to require that they be turned on. Other than an optional two-hour session offered on a Saturday in December, and a flyer that came twice a year from the district office listing the software that could be checked out, no training had been provided. To Tina's knowledge, only four other teachers at Rivertown Elementary had activated their accounts and used e-mail or ventured out onto the Internet.

Finding the on-ramp

Tina, by contrast, had definitely found the on-ramp. She had spent many hours cruising the Information Superhighway. She felt that she had, in fact, been run over on several occasions by flames from crazy people in various newsgroups and by the occasional sites on the World Wide Web where the material presented was so universally offensive that she wondered if schools could ever sanction unrestricted access to the Internet in the classroom.

On the other hand, she had also found a number of sites that she thought might be useful for her fifth-graders. For example, there were several sites where students could get information about concepts Tina included or might manage to work into her curriculum: Volcano World was a World Wide Web site (*http://volcano.und.nodak.edu/*) containing dozens of images and a great deal of textual information about volcanoes. Virtual Tourist II (*http://wings.buffalo.edu/world/vt2//*) was another site that might prove useful. It contained links to pages of information and graphics about places like Hawaii. Tina was so impressed with this site that she was planning a mini-unit based on the resources students could gather there.

Beyond that, there was gopher access to sites such as the geographic name server (*http://www.mit.edu:8001/geo* or *telnet martini.eecs.umich.edu*) where students could get the elevation, latitude, longitude and population of most of the cities and towns in the United States. Tina was not sure how she would use this data, but it was certain to come in handy at some point.

Her immediate concern, however, was for that morning. Tina had met another teacher in the same city on an electronic bulletin board and the two had agreed to have their classes make some sort of collaborative contact. The new project they had developed required her students to work in teams of three and to make e-mail contact with the other class of fifth-graders across town. Having traded the usual basic information—name, age, favorite color, and fast-food preference—the teams proposed topics for investigation. For example, a group in Tina's class was interested in the process of recycling aluminum. Across town, there was a group interested in waste reduction.

The teachers had matched teams with similar interests and they were now writing collaborative reports. The teams were required to go through at least three drafts of the report, which was traded back and forth through e-mail, before it could be turned in for evaluation. The plan, hastily worked out over the phone the night before the project was initiated, specified that while one team was reviewing the latest draft of the report, making changes and suggesting improvements, the other team would be conducting research using traditional sources and at least two sites on the Internet.

A first for teacher and students

For many of the fifth-graders, this was their first experience with something that approached a formal report and Tina had expected them to struggle with the format. She also expected, however, that the added motivation of working electronically with another group of fifth-graders would help them to get through the project. She had *not* counted on the difficulties the students would have in dealing with the e-mail system as a medium for trading drafts of their reports. Several student teams lost substantial chunks — or, in some cases, all — of their reports to the rather primitive and unforgiving interface with the text. Tina made a mental note to herself that should they ever repeat this project, they would have to learn how to move the messages in and out of the e-mail system so that students could do their editing in a word-processing program with which they were more comfortable.

A more pressing problem was the students' difficulty in finding really useful information on the Internet. This was not a problem that Tina had anticipated. After all, the Internet was nothing *but* information. She and her partner had simply assumed that students would be able to find appropriate sources of information about their topics. But it wasn't working out that way.

Part of the problem was that the students were not able to make very effective use of the Internet's various search mechanisms, such as Veronica and the Web Crawler. They entered keywords that resulted in long lists of limited and often apparently unrelated sites. Most teams explored a few of these, found little or no useful information, and simply wandered away, up one or another of the thousands of graphical garden paths in the World Wide Web. Other teams simply disintegrated; their members found more engaging ways to occupy their time. Maybe they were just too young. The project was becoming a classroom management nightmare.

Tina's objective this morning was to salvage what she could of this project and move on. Today was the final research day for her class. Tomorrow the teams would receive the third drafts from the other class, make their final changes and print the results. She decided to give them one hour this morning instead of the planned two hours. That would make more room for her social studies unit. They needed it.

By 8:30 a.m. the classroom was awash with the disengaged fifth-graders. One team had found a reference to an online encyclopedia and many of those who hadn't found a useful source related specifically to their topic had asked if they could use this one. Tina agreed. But when they tried to log in, the connection was refused—too many users—and Tina was left in a big empty space. She called the schools librarian to find out if the students might use the encyclopedias on the shelves. There was an hour available, at 9:30. That left an hour to kill. Well, they had a spelling test coming up at the end of the week. ... She pulled out the lists and lined them up for spelling baseball.

Chris and Tina
Drawing conclusions

What are the differences between these two classrooms? What are some of the factors that make the work being done in Chris' class more productive than that being done in Tina's?

There are a number of factors to be considered. One is the way the Internet is being used: Is it used as a tool to support valid educational objectives or are the objectives being wrapped around the limited capabilities of the Internet? To answer this question, you have to know what you want to accomplish in your classroom.

In our work with teachers who are using the Internet in their classrooms, we have noticed a number of factors that seem to influence the likelihood of successful use—that is, use that leads to increased student learning. Many of these factors have been discussed by other authors, notably Judy Harris. In her article "Organizing and Facilitating Telecollaborative Projects,"[1] Harris gives us a list of steps to help ensure a successful telecollaborative project. The very first step is to choose the specific curricular goals of the project. These should spring directly from the larger framework of the curriculum. This connection, between valid, well-considered educational objectives and the use you make of the Internet is crucial. Without it, you and your students are likely to wander aimlessly in the vastness of cyberspace, concentrating more on the bells and whistles than the productive use of this powerful set of tools.

Another author, Margaret Riel,[2] education program manager with the AT&T Learning Network, has produced another set of general recommendations that should help prospective telecommunicating teachers to avoid the black hole into which so many classroom telecommunications projects (along with the teachers' planning time) so easily disappear. One of her recommendations is that teachers carefully consider the relationship between the big picture of the goals and objectives the teacher holds for the students in the course and the specifics of the project.

She points to a teacher in Australia who was working on a unit dealing with a local aboriginal tribe. His students were to read some of the legends that were part of the tribe's culture. The class entered a Learning Circle (facilitated by the AT&T Learning Network) with six other classroom groups around the world. Participants in this circle used the Internet to share similar stories from indigenous people in their states or countries. In this way, the students used the power of the Internet to extend their understanding of the indigenous people in the area where they lived. The role of stories and legends in the transmission and maintenance of the culture of pre-literate people could be generalized and extended beyond the local context; the students could share and develop their understanding with others in different cultures.

In this case, the telecommunications project was part of a larger unit that focused on learning about the local tribe. The role of the project was relatively well-defined and directly supported the larger goals established for the unit. The Internet

---

1   Harris, J. "Organizing and facilitating telecollaborative projects." *The Computing Teacher*. February 1995 pp. 66-69.

2   Riel, M. "Telecommunications: Avoiding the black hole." *The Computing Teacher*, December-January 1992, pp. 16-17.

was used simply and effectively as a means of achieving those goals.

Looking back at the classes described earlier in this chapter, one of the most telling distinctions between Chris' class and Tina's was the clear connection between the Internet project and the larger curricular goals in Chris' class. When Chris guided her students into the investigation of the various factors affecting the local community, she was clearly using the Internet as a tool to enhance understanding of an important set of integrated concepts. On the other hand, when Tina asked her students to write a collaborative report with the class across town, she did not build any substance into the assignment. The hidden agenda was to have the students explore the Internet and it did not appear to be working for Tina's students.

Some recommendations

What follows is a general set of recommendations for ways to use the Internet successfully in your classroom. This is not an exhaustive list; we are sure that you will be able to add some pointers of your own. They may not all seem applicable to you in your school. Nevertheless, we think that these constitute a sound set of suggestions and reminders.

Teachers who use the Internet successfully in their classrooms:

- **think of the Internet** as one of many tools at their disposal as a professional teacher;

- **explore the Internet broadly** and don't become transfixed by a single shiny object;

- **seek the help** of knowledgeable friends;

- **have reliable** (if limited) access to technical support;

- **are supported by** the schools administration;

- **involve their students** in the creation of the work they do on the Internet;

- **allow and encourage students** to teach them about new things on the Internet;

- **are not afraid** to try new things — to be a learner in front of the students.

More tips on how to use the Internet successfully in your classroom can be found at the end of each of the case studies in Chapter 16. In the next chapter we'll recommend ways of putting together collaborative projects on the Internet.

CHAPTER 14

Working with people on the Net

▼▼▼▼▼▼▼▼▼▼▼

TELECOLLABORATION

Conducting projects over the Internet has become a popular activity among schools that are connected. In this chapter, we look at why you'd choose to conduct a project this way and, if you did, how you could go about it. We also offer some strategies for making your telecollaboration as effective as possible.

▲▲▲▲▲▲▲▲▲▲▲

▼▼▼▼▼▼▼▼▼▼▼

Teacher on the Net

Creating projects on demand

Dr. Karl Sarnow
German coordinator of the European Schools Project
Gymnasium Grossburgwedel
Burgwedel, Germany
Teaching experience: 20 years
Internet experience: 7 years
E-mail address: karl@gygro.h.ni.schule.de

As the German coordinator of the European Schools Project, Dr. Karl Sarnow has been involved with a number of different Internet-based projects over the past several years. In the Memories project, for example, survivors of World War II answered students' questions about their experiences during the war. In the AquaData project, students recorded data about the water quality of a river or lake, then compared their findings with those of other students. Dr. Sarnow is currently involved in an ESP-statistics project, in which students gather data on extra-sensory perception. He describes the project like this:

❝I call this project a 'project on demand.' Using a mailing list, it is easy to cooperate on a long time scale, without the need for synchronous activity. Simply use the data in the project and send your own statistics data when your learning group is ready to do so. Sometimes there will be some contacts between students, but this is not the main reason for this activity. … If you are joining the statistics project, you get live data from students all over the world. You then can easily compare properties from different countries and continents.❞

In Dr. Sarnow's opinion, using the Internet this way gives teachers and students

❝… some kind of liberty from time. … You are free to join a discussion when you really need it. Students are able to get information when they want it. They are encouraged to start their own activity. And they learn that students across the world think alike·❞

▲▲▲▲▲▲▲▲▲▲▲▲

What is telecollaboration?

I t's not hard to guess what the word "telecollaboration" means, even though the term was coined only recently. In its broadest sense, telecollaboration is the act of working with people over long distances. In the context of this book, it means working over the Internet, mostly via e-mail or mailing lists. It also connotes a goal or project; just getting together on-line to chat or discuss issues isn't truly telecollaboration. The high-profile telecollaborative projects (like the ones mentioned in the preceding chapter) usually involve students collaborating with students. To set these projects up, however, teachers also telecollaborate.

There are many advantages to working on a project over the Internet. Using the Internet like this is commonplace for

---

NET FACTS

▼▼▼▼▼▼▼▼▼▼▼▼

Finding projects on the Web

Although mailing lists and newsgroups carry the bulk of teacher project information, there are also a number of World Wide Web sites at which you can find classroom project ideas and contacts. We've listed a few below:

Intercultrual E-mail Classroom Connections
http://www.stolaf.edu/network/iecc/

The Boundary Breakers Web Server
http://jasper.stark.k12.oh.us/

NCSA Education Program
http://www.ncsa.uiuc.edu/Edu/EduHome.html

EE-Link (Environmental Education information, including projects and contacts)
http://www.nceet.snre.umich.edu/index.html

Quest, NASA's K-12 Internet Initiative
http://quest.arc.nasa.gov./

▲▲▲▲▲▲▲▲▲▲▲▲

Net Facts

▼▼▼▼▼▼▼▼▼▼▼

Call for collaboration: An example

Heres an example of a good call for collaboration. *(This is not an idea for collaboration that weve actually seen; the name and address are made up, too. However, it might make an interesting project.)*

```
newsgroup: k12.teacher.chat, k12.ed.math
posted by: Emile Griffin (griff@dne.edu)
subject: Interested in exchanging inspira-
tional quotes?
```

I'm a high school math teacher (algebra mostly) who likes to adorn the cinder block walls of my classroom with inspirational quotes for my students. I've been through Bartletts and to other teachers in my school, and I've got some favorites, but I'd like to hear yours.

If you'd like to participate in such a project, send me a list of your favorite inspirational quotes (five or so would be good). They don't have to be for math or high schoolers in particular (though Id love to get some more math quotes), just be sure to include their source! I'll compile them into a list, e-mail that list to everyone who participated, and post the results to this newsgroup.

NOTE: Please do not post your list to this newsgroup (it's got enough messages already =). E-mail the list to me at griff@dne.edu and I'll make sure you get a copy of the final tabulation.

Thanks,

Skip Griffin

▲▲▲▲▲▲▲▲▲▲▲▲

university educators and researchers, who have long recognized the value of student collaboration over the Internet. It seems obvious that these same benefits apply to teachers who are working together. Teachers, like students, would learn from the experience of others who are struggling with similar problems. Like students, they would get to practice some important skills and spend time reflecting upon their own thinking processes. It seems reasonable to assume that we teachers—like our students—are more motivated to produce quality work when we know we will be presenting the work to peers.

How to get started with telecollaboration

In order for telecollaboration to work, you must first have a project, then a group interested in working together, and finally a medium for your collaboration. The third you have already: For small groups, electronic mail is an excellent collaboration tool; for large groups, mailing lists often work better. Either way, you have already mastered the Internet services you'll need.

Finding a project and a group can be a bit more problematic. There are two ways to get involved in a collaborative project on the Internet—join one or start your own. In either case, you'll want to begin by spending time in the electronic company of other teachers, and that means either newsgroups or mailing lists. If you frequent an electronic "hang-out" (such as a favorite teacher mailing list, or the k12.chat.teacher newsgroup) you are guaranteed to find messages from people who want to start a project.[1] Unfortunately, not all of these projects fit the criteria we have outlined for an effective classroom project.

The Internet is a new tool for teachers and most people aren't quite sure how to use it. When looking for collaborators, you may find that it helps to read for the teacher behind the message than the project within. Suppose you read a message

---

1   For other project-oriented newsgroups, see the description of the "channel" groups on page 272.

on your favorite mailing list from a teacher in Montreal, Canada, who would like to start a "keypal" project[2] with a sixth-grade class in the United States. You may not be interested in the keypal project, but here's a Canadian sixth-grade teacher who's online and wants to do something. Perhaps you could start talking to her about putting together the unit on language differences you wanted to try in the spring.

If you have a pet project, and you see another project on the Internet, you could also try a little I'll-do-your-project-if-you'll-do-mine. Or you can simply post your own idea and hope you get some favorable responses. If you choose the latter route, you should be aware of the guidelines for effective Internet messages.

☑ **Make your call for participation concise.** Describe what you want to do, but refrain from limiting yourself to teachers from one subject area or grade level; you can exchange any necessary details later.

☑ **It's probably a good idea to suggest** that interested teachers respond to you via e-mail (as opposed to sending a message to the newsgroup or mailing list); this is a general courtesy, but not all newsgroup and mailing list participants follow it.

☑ **Finally, make sure that the subject line** of your message is short and to the point. Experienced readers tend to skip long messages with vague subjects.

Even if you put together a picture-perfect message for a truly outstanding project idea, you may get no responses at all. This is one of the problems of working on the Internet—sometimes you feel as though you are shouting into empty space or, even worse, into a space crowded with people completely ignoring you.

---

2   Keypal projects are widely used, and some say even over-used, methods of getting students online. Many keypal projects are just pen-pal projects updated for the Internet, and their educational value is questionable.

If this happens to you, don't be discouraged. Perhaps you didn't describe your idea exactly right, or your subject line was too vague, or maybe you posted the message to the wrong newsgroup or mailing list. Perhaps the people who would be interested just weren't reading at the right time. One thing you can be sure of: a lack of response to your message is not meant as a slight to you. In fact, you'll find that much of the attention goes to users who send stupid or annoying messages (negative attention to be sure, but maybe that's what they're looking for). In any case, if you get no responses, try waiting a week or two, rewording your message, and sending it again.

Strategies for telecollaboration

An Internet collaboration project differs from other uses of the Internet in that it has a defined goal. This goal can be as simple as compiling a list of inspirational quotes (as we mentioned in the *Call for collaboration: An example* sidebar), or as complex as planning curricula on an international scale. People collaborating over the Internet face the same problems as those collaborating face to face — and more. Below are some suggestions for making sure your Internet collaboration project is as effective as it can be.[3]

 Start with an attainable goal. We recommend this for any group project, but it's particularly important when the collaborators are not meeting face to face. Since the written word is the unit of trade on the Internet, the goal in most Internet collaborations is a document of some kind. This document can be anything from a compiled list to a complete lesson plan to a research paper, but if you set up what you want at the outset of the project, you'll know what it is once you get it.

---

3   For more strategies of telecollaboration, see "Network-Based Instructional Interactions, Part 2: Interpersonal Strategies" by Waugh, Levin, and Smith, *The Computing Teacher*, March 1994.

Net Facts

▼▼▼▼▼▼▼▼▼▼▼

What happens when no one answers?

One of the biggest difficulties in working with a group over the Internet is that you can never really tell what it means when someone doesn't answer. Say, for instance, that you have something you want to run by the group. You send a message to everyone involved, asking their opinion on the matter. Most everyone writes back, perhaps with a few suggestions, but generally affirming your ideas. So far so good, right?

But what about those people who didn't answer? Do they agree with the majority and just not bother to say so? Or do they disagree, but don't feel as though their opinion would be heard? Did they even see the message? Perhaps some emergency situation has been keeping them from the Internet recently! If you don't get an answer, you just can't tell.

Unfortunately, there's no easy remedy for this problem. Your best solution is to save important questions for face-to-face meetings where you can judge even silent reactions. For less important issues, you may want to phrase your first message in an "unless I hear otherwise..." format, or make it clear from the beginning that you'd like them to R.S.V.P.

If someone else in the group asks a question, remember that they won't know your answer unless you tell them. A quick reply, ("I got your message, and am still thinking") goes a long way. Silence isn't golden when you're working online.

▲▲▲▲▲▲▲▲▲▲▲▲

Consider mixing methods. If the people in your project are close enough to meet in person occasionally, you might consider doing so. Although telecollaboration is often more efficient than face-to-face meetings, some decisions need to be made with full and often simultaneous input from everyone involved.

 Don't get hung up on deadlines. Chances are that most of the people working on your project will be fully employed with other projects (including their job!). It may be that days or weeks go by without hearing from someone. Although this can be frustrating, it's important to keep it in perspective: one of the advantages to an Internet collaboration is that it can be done in your "spare time" — and sometimes there isn't much time to spare. For this reason deadlines don't always work as well over the Internet as they do when meeting regularly face to face.

 You'll need a leader of sorts. Although the collegial atmosphere of the Internet often dissuades groups from choosing a leader outright, it's important to have someone "in charge" of a project if you actually expect it to go anywhere. This person doesn't have to declare him- or herself The Leader, or be elected by popular vote. He or she just has to be responsible for moving the group towards a result. This kind of person is necessary in any collaboration, but is even more important when the collaboration takes place over time and in separate places.

 Consensus decision-making doesn't always work. Another good reason for having a leader is that it can be difficult to make consensus decisions over the Internet. Unless you have the ability to talk to each other in "real time," the process of trying to get everyone to agree on a course of action can stretch out over days and weeks. You may want to consider handling decisions using the unless-somebody-has-an-objection method.

Work at keeping the project alive. Another essential personality in any collaborative effort is the "cheerleader," someone who'll encourage others to present their ideas and give support to those who need it. In a face-to-face collaboration, people nod and say "uh-huh" and support one another without much effort. Over the Internet this kind of psychological sustenance must be intentional. Here are a few ideas of the kind of messages you'll want to send:

"Ping" messages. Much like the way submarines "ping" objects with their sonar, sometimes it's necessary for Internet collaborators to send brief messages even when there's nothing new to report ("I'm still working hard on my piece. How's it going with you folks?"). Without these messages, it can feel as if the project has faded away and no one bothered to tell you.

Return receipt messages. Returning any message with a quick reply is a good habit to get into. This lets your fellow collaborators know you received and read their message.

Cheerleader messages. Recognize the efforts of your colleagues by sending acknowledgments of their work. Everyone likes to know that what they're doing is appreciated, especially when that appreciation can't be communicated using body language.

 Finish your project with publication. It's important to bring some sort of closure to your project. At the very least one person in the project should mail out a summary: what was proposed, what occurred, what was produced. The best kind of closure is publication. It motivates group members and may benefit a larger audience. Publication on the Internet is simple: You just send your summary to an educational mailing list or an appropriate newsgroup.

TELECOLLABORATION BALANCE SHEET

Reasons to telecollaborate	Reasons *not* to telecollaborate
✔ **To overcome distance.** There are times when telecollaboration is the only collaboration possible. If this is the case for your group, and you all have access to the Internet, you may want to set up an e-mail collaboration.	✘ **Lack of access.** If somebody you are working with doesn't have easy access to telecommunication, you might as well not bother. Access is one of the most important issues for telecollaborators, and if you don't have it, it's not going to work.
✔ **To combat isolation.** Researchers and reformers agree that shutting the door to the classroom doesn't do much to improve your professional development. Telecollaboration is yet another way to learn from others who may be struggling with the same problems you face.	✘ **Inexperience.** Just as lack of access can make things a real hassle, so can lack of experience. Usually this isn't such a big problem, since collaborators don't need much more than e-mail proficiency.
✔ **To get a breath of fresh ideas.** Although it may be argued that your most important professional community is your school community, there comes a time when everyone feels that their school colleagues are too much of a good thing. When that happens, it's nice to have some folks to work with that you don't see on a daily basis.	

Reasons to telecollaborate	Reasons not to telecollaborate
✔ **To work around busy schedules.** If your group is finding it hard to meet, telecollaboration can be an excellent addition to normal collaboration. You can use e-mail messages to resolve issues which don't need face-to-face discussion; then you can free up your meeting times for issues which do.	

CHAPTER 15

The goals of education

▼▼▼▼▼▼▼▼▼▼▼

PUTTING YOUR PHILOSOPHY FIRST

Before the Internet can become an effective classroom tool, it's important to establish what you hope to accomplish with your students. The learning goals you set are tied to your philosophy and approach to teaching. In this chapter, we examine various orientations to the curriculum and explore how the Internet might be incorporated to best support them.

▲▲▲▲▲▲▲▲▲▲▲▲

The role of goals

One of the ways in which this book differs from dozens of other Internet books is the emphasis we place on the importance of using the Internet as a tool in service of well-considered, valid educational goals. Further, these goals should spring from your commitment to a particular conception of what schools are all about; your philosophy of education should guide your thinking as you and your students venture online.

When this connection is loose or absent, the result is likely to be a haphazard collection of Internet experiences that may or may not lead to learning. Looking back at such a set of experiences messages sent and retrieved, sites visited, and files downloaded and deleted can remind you of looking at the transcript of your first year or two at college. If your experience was typical, you had little direction or guidance, either internal or external, in those early semesters. Your record shows a list of courses (sometimes with less than sterling grades) that cover the range from transcendental college algebra to Hegelian handball. But as you moved into your junior, senior, and senior-senior years a pattern became apparent. You became aware of your own commitment to a particular realm of the universe of knowledge. You found a major! The courses you selected thereafter were the means to achieve a well-defined end. Fortunately (or unfortunately), someone else had already designed the major, and established a sequence of appropriate educational experiences. The path you followed toward graduation was paved with courses meant to sequentially build the knowledge, skills, and understanding needed to enable you to claim some degree of mastery in that field.

Now, as a teacher, you are in charge of designing the experiences that will enable your students to move toward the educational goals that you see fit. The Internet can serve as a tool used deliberately to support these goals or as a distraction, pulling you in random directions, now toward, now away from the ends you seek. Likewise, your awareness of and commitment to a particular philosophy of education will serve as a kind of template, enabling you to decide on the kinds of experiences that are appropriate for your class.

With the number of options available as you enter the world of telecomputing and the Internet, this kind of logical internal guidance couldn't be more valuable. Coming to an understanding of your own philosophy of education and using this to craft appropriate educational goals is like selecting and pursuing a major. In this case, however, *you* design the program and *you* write the courses! In the next few pages we will consider some of the traditional goals for and approaches to the process of education.

The purpose of schooling

If you spend some time in the teachers lounge and ask teachers to tell you about the purpose of schools, you're likely to encounter a wide range of responses. Some will say that schools are there to facilitate the growth and development of the human spirit. Others will speak of the school's mission to transmit the highlights of the record of human knowledge developed across the centuries. Still others will tell you that schools serve to develop childrens critical thinking, reasoning, and problem-solving skills. Or they may simply say that schools are there to prepare kids for the world of work. And on a bad day, a teacher may say that teaching is mostly just a struggle to keep the kids in line and that school is little more than institutionalized baby-sitting. The answer we give is a product of our experiences and our subsequent understandings and beliefs about schools. Whether well-considered or ill, that answer is important because, consciously or unconsciously, it underlies the day-to-day decisions we make as teachers about how our classrooms are run.

If, for example, you believe that the purpose of schooling is to pass along the great ideas and the essential knowledge accumulated by the human race, then your approach to a senior literature course will probably include the study of classic works from Shakespeare, Twain, and Conrad. You might ask your students to analyze the writing in order to see how the author addressed some of the fundamental questions about our mortality, and what constitutes the good life.

If, on the other hand, you believe that the purpose of schools is to develop in each student the ability to learn the

content and processes that are important to that student as a developing individual, then you are more likely to stress individual choice, self-awareness, and reflection. While some students will choose to study William Shakespeare, others may select J. D. Salinger or Maya Angelou. Your job as a teacher will be to enable the students to recognize and capitalize on their own strengths and to address their weaknesses as learners. Mastery of content will take a back seat to the development of an understanding of the process of learning as it unfolds in each individual.

The goals and objectives you select with regard to content and process will differ as a result of your orientation to the curriculum. In both cases, the Internet can be used as a productive tool to enhance learning, but the kinds of applications selected will probably be quite different. In the next section, we'll discuss five different orientations to the curriculum and their implications for the purpose and process of schooling. As you read, consider your own commitments to and conception of the work that you do each day as a teacher.

Orientations to the curriculum

Elliot Eisner, in his book *The Educational Imagination: On the Design and Evaluation of School Programs*,[1] described five ori-

---

1   Eisner, Elliot W. (1985) *The Educational Imagination: On the Design and Education of School Programs*. Macmillan Publishing Company.

entations that teachers (and others concerned with schools) might take to the curriculum, and to schooling. We'll summarize them here so that you can think about how your commitments affect the decisions you make about the use of the Internet in your classroom.

Cognitive processes

The first orientation Eisner describes is one in which the purpose of schooling is seen as the development of cognitive processes. These processes may be conceived as relatively separate aptitudes or faculties, such as inference, analysis, speculation, and so on. These faculties must be exercised and developed so that students will be mentally fit and ready to solve the problems they encounter in life.

In this view, process is emphasized over content. If a student learns to reason, he or she will be able to apply this skill across the curricular board. The value of subjects like algebra and geometry lies as much, or more, in the mental exercise and discipline they impart as in the practical value of the theorems, postulates and facts that are memorized. This is the notion of transferability, the idea that if a student gets practice in reasoning in the course of learning mathematics, for example, he or she can transfer that skill in reasoning to more effectively analyze a philosophical argument.

Eisner points out that this notion of transferability has been criticized by educational psychologists since the beginning of the century. Nevertheless, curriculum and theory centered on this view of the purpose of school continues to be generated and widely employed.

A teacher whose view of schooling emphasizes the development of cognitive process would probably stress problem solving and might use the Internet as a source of information to aid in this process. For example, with the truck bombing of the federal building in Oklahoma City in April 1995, a great deal of information was immediately available on the Internet. Within hours of the tragic blast, virtual places where people online could write to one another were being set up by some of the major Internet service providers.

In these virtual meeting areas and on many bulletin boards and newsgroups that discuss and analyze social and political issues, arguments arose over the nationality of those responsible for the bombing. At first, there was widespread speculation that the bombers might be Islamic fundamentalists demonstrating that they could strike America's heartland. Comparisons were drawn between the Oklahoma attack and that on the World Trade Center three years earlier. Later, of course, these assumptions were discredited.

A teacher of twelfth-grade civics might ask her students to download and examine some of the statements and arguments that were posted. She would help them analyze the arguments, perhaps differentiating observation from inference. The emphasis would be not so much on the specifics of the case as on the generic ability to criticize and reformulate an argument, and to understand the workings of the democratic process.

This same teacher might also make good use of e-mail, asking her students to trade, edit, and critique the work of others with different cultural and/or ethnic backgrounds. The purpose would be to develop these component skills, and the Internet, combined with the magic of word processors, would make this project work in ways that wouldn't be possible otherwise.

Academic rationalism

The next orientation to the curriculum and schooling is labeled academic rationalism. From this point of view, the proper subjects of study are the great ideas and modes of thought handed down to us from the thinkers of  the past. Students should be enabled to deal with life's most fundamental questions: What is the nature of the good life? How is truth defined? What is justice? and so forth.

To bring learners to this point, they must be made aware of not only the great ideas that come to us from the classics, they must also be equipped with an understanding of the ways in which humans have addressed such questions. These ideas should be approached through dialectic discussion. In this way, reason, the key to understanding and critical analysis, can be developed. This is the essence of liberal education.

Despite the strong emphasis on the development of reason, academic rationalism differs from cognitive process in the emphasis that is placed on specific content. If they have not all been solved, the classic problems and questions have at least been identified and addressed by luminaries from the past. People like Einstein, Mozart, Curie, and Rousseau have provided us with starting points and we must understand their thoughts before we can proceed.

A teacher who fits the description of the academic rationalist might find that the Internet provides a fertile ground for the development and study of cases in which students can *apply* the understanding they are gathering of the great thinkers. She might also find that such established services and sites as Newton's Ask a Scientist (*telnet://newton.dep.anl.gov*) and Ask a Volcanologist (*http://volcano.und.nodak.edu/vwdocs/ask_a.html*) on the Volcano World Web page allow students to get acquainted not just with the *results* established or claimed by scientists but with the mode of inquiry and analysis that apply as well.

Beyond that, the academic rationalist might applaud the growing presence of e-classics, electronic copies of the great books, from *The Little Prince* to *Moby Dick* (see, for example, Project Guttenburg at *http://jg.cso.uiuc.edu/pg/lists/list.html*). Downloading a copy of *Crime and Punishment* to your screen may very well be a ridiculous waste of time and computing power when a printed copy of the book is available, and you simply intend to have the student read it. The ability to print and edit portions of this classic work, however, could suit some interesting curriculum inventions in ways that can't be accommodated by a book in its traditional format. For example, if the teacher downloaded a single copy to her machine and then asked teams of students to copy selected passages and print, read and then translate them into another context (say, Miami in the year 1995), students would have a chance not only to practice some crucial academic skills involved in inferring and transferring meaning, but would also have a chance to really come to understand what the author had to say.

Personal relevance

The third orientation to schooling is labeled personal relevance. Here the emphasis is on the individual students sincere commitment to learning and on the teacher's role as the facilitator of the process. Ideally, students decide what they're interested in knowing, and then work with other like-minded students to pursue those interests.

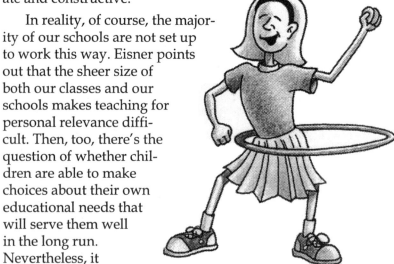

The reasoning, of course, is that while children will generally jump through the hoops we put before them, the development of true, useful, and lasting understanding is more likely when students make real choices about what they will learn. The teacher, then, is responsible for uncovering the real interests of each child and knowing enough about his or her abilities that the educational experiences that are offered are appropriate and constructive.

In reality, of course, the majority of our schools are not set up to work this way. Eisner points out that the sheer size of both our classes and our schools makes teaching for personal relevance difficult. Then, too, there's the question of whether children are able to make choices about their own educational needs that will serve them well in the long run. Nevertheless, it seems reasonable to say that students will be more likely to learn if they have a personal investment in the subject matter than if they are simply following a predetermined and seemingly irrelevant line of coursework.

The teacher who believes in the importance of personal relevance in the curriculum pays attention to the interest of the class and seizes the teachable moment in order to capitalize on the motivation and commitment of the learners. In the classroom, the Internet has a valuable role to play as one of the gateways to the information students will need as they investigate their own questions.

For example, the National Aeronautics and Space Administration (NASA) maintains a large presence on the Internet (*http://spacelink.msfc.nasa.gov/*). The agency provides a great deal of information that would be useful for a student interested in space travel generally or in the progress of a particular mission.

Another use of the Internet that will appeal to the teacher interested in a curriculum centered around personal relevance is as a means of distributing and publishing their students' work. If a teacher is working through a unit on Africa and a small group of students becomes interested in the carnivores of the African veldt, the teacher might help them to pursue their own questions and concerns. One source of information, standing alongside others such as the encyclopedia, African folk tales, people who have traveled to Africa, and programs aired on commercial and public television, will be the Internet.

Once students have constructed their own understanding, the teacher might ask the students to synthesize their knowledge in any number of ways. One time-honored way to accomplish this task is to have the students create a report. The ease with which these reports and other documents, including pictures and the students graphical creations, can be made available on the Internet has led hundreds of schools around the country to create their own home pages on the Word Wide Web (see *Creating your own Web page* on page 161).[2] On these pages, students (and teachers) can make their work available

2   For a list of schools with their own home pages, see Web66 at
    http://hillside.coled.umn.edu/others.html.

to the rest of the world. This wider audience will give some students extra motivation to create a meaningful product. Of course, this is true regardless of the curricular orientation held by the teacher. But the opportunity for students to publish work about any reasonable topic and, perhaps more importantly, to receive responses from others around the world may serve to facilitate this individualized approach to the curriculum.

Kidopedia (*http://rdz.stjohns.edu/kidopedia/index.html*) is a site created early in 1995 on the World Wide Web where students are gradually helping to create a sort of random encyclopedia. The entries are all submitted by children. A child or group of children in Dallas can decide that they would like to investigate giraffes. After consulting the usual sources and visiting the zoo for some first-hand experience, they could assemble and post an entry in Kidopedia. Their article describing their conception of a giraffe would stand alongside another written by children who had lived on an African game preserve and had lived in the presence of wild giraffes. The two entries would be quite different in content and in nature, but both would present a view of the animal we think of as a giraffe. The ease with which this sort of project proceeds and grows once its under way is impressive and is a reflection of the spectacular *availability* of the Internet.

Social adaptation and social reconstruction

The fourth orientation to schooling is known as social adaptation and social reconstruction.[3] In this case, school is seen as the institution where adjustments to the social, political and economic course of the nation can be made. These changes may support the status quo, or they may be aimed at fundamental change. This distinction is the basis for the dual nature of the label.

When the purpose of schooling is seen as social adaptation, changes in the school curriculum are designed to keep the nation moving more or less along the path that has been established. Eisner uses the example of the computer literacy movement that has impacted our curriculum in the past 20 years. He asserts that

---

3   Eisner's fifth orientation to the curriculum is centered around the concept of curriculum as technology and will not be discussed in this context.

the motivation for changes emphasizing the use of computers and technology in our schools is usually attributed to the need to maintain a competitive position in the world.

Industry is interested in students who can use the microcomputer. Because the future of high technology is said to require people who understand its use, it follows in the eyes of some that schools should offer, even require, programs of study in the computer, Eisner says.

"Like drug abuse education, tech prep programs are seen as ways to respond to the perceived ills of society. The objective is to address the forces that seem to be moving us away from the course accepted by the powers that be," he says.

Social reconstruction, on the other hand, involves an orientation that sees schools as the place where the critical consciousness of students can be raised. Successful graduates should be able to look at the strengths and weaknesses of our society, and then be able and inclined to respond to the problems they see. If this involves a significant change in the ways our lives are constituted then it is the job of the schools to prepare students to effect this change.

In either social adaptation or social reconstruction, one use of the Internet in the classroom is as a source of information and a mechanism for the exchange of information.

The teacher concerned with social adaptation might view the Internet as a way for students to obtain the latest information

about the shifting job market, the rise or fall of the value of the U.S. dollar as compared to the Japanese yen, or the spread of HIV in the United States. This teacher would make students aware of this information to give them access to the facts that indicate the direction and nature of the changes needed to maintain the status quo. Of course, this information is available from other sources, most commonly the newspaper. But the current direction of information technology seems to indicate that in the near future this sort of technical information, at least, will be best sought on the Internet. If students are to keep up with changes around the globe and enable the United States to maintain its position in the world, then they must learn to use this technology efficiently.

The teacher whose curriculum emphasizes social reconstruction would probably also be interested in the Internet's potential for enhancing the flow of information. The nature of the information, the way it's used, and the direction of the flow, however, would probably be quite different.

For this teacher, the democratic nature of the Internet (the fact that anyone with access to a computer and an Internet account can publish a document that is instantly accessible to millions of people the world over) is crucial. At present, there are few restrictions on the kind of information that can be placed on the Internet. The development of a critical consciousness is enhanced by access to a wide range of viewpoints and the Internet can be an ideal vehicle for such study. Likewise, the drive to social action can take place, in part, on the Internet as students seek to educate others or influence political policy through the dissemination of information.

Incorporating the Internet

As the examples we have given show, you can effectively incorporate the Internet into any curricular orientation. The important part is to bring the Internet in as a tool to enhance your teaching. Different teachers have different approaches to their curriculum, of course, and so different teachers should incorporate the Internet in different ways. We can't tell you what means of using the Internet will work best for you, but we can tell you how teachers experienced with using the Internet in their classroom go about it. In the next chapter, we'll do just that.

CHAPTER 16

Case studies

▼▼▼▼▼▼▼▼▼▼▼

VETERAN TEACHERS SHARE
THEIR EXPERIENCES

What does it take to use the Internet effectively in your classroom? Certainly you must be comfortable with the Internet yourself, and if your school supports its use and provides access, you're in good shape. As we described in the last chapter, a solid grasp of your particular orientation to the curriculum is also essential.

So, what if you've got all that? What then? In this chapter, Dr. Mark Roddy talks to four educators who have the will and the resources to use the Internet well. Although you may not be blessed with the same level of technology and support at your school, we hope that by presenting some of the teachers who are blazing new paths, we can make the journey safer for those who follow.

▲▲▲▲▲▲▲▲▲▲▲▲

Teacher on the Net

Bring people together on the Internet

I first met Jim Golubich early one morning in the parking lot of Echo Lake Elementary School in Shoreline, a Seattle suburb with a school district known for its high degree of involvement with and support for technology in education.

This was Jim's fourth year at Echo Lake. He had 13 additional years of experience in Washington and Ohio. In addition to his strong commitment to teaching, Jim was an inveterate student. He had a Master's degree in Elementary Administration. He had completed 2½ years of a graduate program at Kent State and was finishing his third year in a Ph.D. program in educational philosophy at the University of Washington. He was also a graduate of the Danforth program for school administration at the University of Washington.

Jim Golubich
4th-6th Grade
Echo Lake Elementary
Shoreline, Wash.

When asked why he was taking all these courses, Jim confessed his love for learning. "I enjoy it. I just do it sort of as a hobby. I find that studying the theory and philosophy of what I do here is very enriching. And my teaching here helps me make a lot more sense of what I do in my coursework."

He took me through the building, which was quiet at that hour in the morning, and we sat down near a computer in a room adjoining the school library. The room held a number of computer stations and was connected to a resource room with more Macintosh computers. We began to talk about technology and the Internet. Jim recalled an experience that illustrates his attitude toward the Internet and, more importantly, toward the use of the Internet as a tool to enhance good teaching.

"This fellow and this girl were exchanging questions and answers and, bless his heart, he was writing, in some cases, three-page summaries of things she could never have gotten from a book or any other source."

Investigating culture

It was Jim's first year at Echo Lake. He was teaching fourth-graders and he was out in the portables behind the school with a modem and one computer. His students were engaged in an investigative research project on different cultures. The class worked in small groups to develop an understanding of some culture different from their own. One group selected the Jewish culture.

"Just by serendipity, I got this little girl connected to a fellow in Israel who was a 60-year-old retired military person. He was actually a friend of somebody at (a nearby school). This fellow and this girl were exchanging questions and answers and, bless his heart, he was writing, in some cases, three-page summaries of things she could never have gotten from a book or any other source. It was a wonderful example of some of the primary resources that become available through the Net," Jim said.

The unit culminated in a presentation by the students to the whole class. They also had an evening exhibition at which students displayed and discussed their findings. Some had created video tapes, others had artifacts, while others had HyperCard stacks. Jim enthusiastically described the quality of learning that took place. He had been trying out some of the ideas that he'd been exposed to in his graduate studies regarding constructivism and project-based learning.

"I was trying to see if kids could actually go about making sense and meaning of this extended setting. And what was almost a religious experience for me was to watch these little fourth-graders who had investigated a particular aspect of culture demonstrate their ability to explain in depth everything that everybody else had studied, because of the interactions that were going on, and the fact that they collaborated on the videos, the HyperCard stacks and so on. They just picked up way more than anything I could have given them with a direct approach."

The Internet's role in this success story is that of a tool, one tool among many applied by an experienced professional in the service of quality education.

Jim also gave me a look at the World Wide Web page he was helping to create for the school. It was well-thought-out and executed with general information about the school, links to the district pages, and more useful information for teachers and students at Echo Lake. There was an extensive set of links to sites that students might use as resources for future projects. Jim was hoping that with the creation of a set of resources like this, he would be able to reduce some of the aimless wandering, dead-end searches, and subsequent frustration that can result when students look for information on the Internet. He had some of his sixth-graders help design and create the page which, of course, would not be complete without links to these students own home pages.

There was more to this project though. Jim was watching the way students work in a hyperlinked environment like the World Wide Web.

"I'm interested in how kids interact in a hyper-learning environment. With the Web, because of its looseness, they sort of tend to get lost. It's interesting to see if they can manage to create logical links instead of just having a series of projects where Billy's paper is linked to Jill's paper and so on," he explained.

"If, for instance, a group is talking about slavery and in the course of their report they mention Frederick Douglass, do they anchor that word? Does it connect to someone else's work, a biography or a graphic? But I don't want to be the one to suggest it to them. I want to see if they can interact enough that this occurs to them," he said.

> *"It's interesting to see if they can manage to create logical links instead of just having a series of projects where Billy's paper is linked to Jill's paper and so on."*

This is an important point for Jim. In line with his growing understanding of the constructivist theory of learning and some of the possible implications for teaching, he tries to help students take responsibility for their own learning.

Noting how students had to take control in their investigations into various cultures, he said, "I would not give them answers. I really held back. They would ask me, 'Is this what you want me to do?' I'd say, I don't care. You make that decision."

"I had parents calling me just about every night. They were frustrated because the kids would go home and say 'I don't know what I'm supposed to do.' I would say, 'It's your baby. You need to make sense of it yourself before you can help us understand it. How are you going to convey it to us?' It was a lot of sweat and blood."

But this doesn't mean that Jim abdicated his role as a teacher. He did offer guidance, assistance and coaching.

"You'll hear some instructors say its a sink-or-swim situation. 'Go out and whatever you do is fine.' I don't believe that at all. I think it behooves teachers to get in there and impart some of our experiences and help [students] structure their experiences so that they are more successful."

"I think it behooves teachers to get in there and impart some of our experiences and help [students] structure their experiences so that they are more successful."

This, of course, was no small task. He spent many hours planning, critiquing proposals, and conducting conferences with groups regarding the research process and the way the results were communicated.

Jim is fortunate to teach in a district widely recognized as a leader in the application of technology to enhance learning. This is a district which recently gave every teacher a Power Macintosh, software, an account on the Internet, and free or low-cost in-service training designed to enable teachers to make sense of the resources.

He's also an asset to the district. He has learned some valuable lessons about the Internet and spends a good deal of his time serving on various committees and task forces concerned with technology, the Internet, and the process of restructuring.

Jim underscores the importance of using the Internet as a tool rather than as the center point of the curriculum. He emphasizes the need for flexibility in the ways teachers approach the curriculum. They must be ready to seize the teachable moment and be aware of the ways in which the Internet can serve as a tool to facilitate the learning process.

What would he describe as a successful Internet project?

"[That's] hard for me. I haven't seen one of those. There are certain projects where some kids really cook with it and some don't find any direct use for it. To me, that's as it should be. … My philosophy is that we use the Internet when the Internet can be of service, not gratuitously, because it's there and it's slick."

Jim's tips for using the Internet in the classroom

 Try to make students initial experiences with the Internet successful and productive ones. There are many dead ends and distractions, and it's very easy for novice users to get disoriented and frustrated. A negative first impression can discourage students from viewing the Internet as a worthwhile resource. Do some advance searching to locate rich and relevant sites, and guide students toward them. Consider starting with fairly structured activities to develop competency with specific Internet skills.

 Question the value of surfing as a method of introducing students to the Internet. The aimless and random nature of surfing does little to encourage efficient and purposeful location of relevant information.

Teach students to critically evaluate the information they find on the Internet for commercial and/or political bias (there's plenty of both), accuracy and credibility. As with all resources, they should learn to examine the source of the information and to seek multiple perspectives.

 Keep a balance between the Internet and other resources. Some students (and adults) become so seduced by the technology that they scoff at using more traditional resources which may, in fact, be superior in both quality and quantity of information.

Teacher on the Net
Library without walls

Shorecrest High School sits on a rise, separated from the street by an extensive stretch of grass and a few pine trees. It's a setting that mirrors the relationship between the school and the community.

The school and, indeed, Shoreline School District, are widely regarded as being successful in a world in which that adjective is not often applied to institutions of public education. It was about 5:30 on a rainy afternoon when I arrived, but Shorecrest was still open for business.

LoAnne Larson
9th-12th grade
Librarian
Shorecrest High School
Shoreline, Wash.

I made my way to the library, a large and open room with tables and work spaces in the center and most of the stacks and resource areas around the periphery. I recognized an acquaintance, a mathematics teacher, who was part of a drop-in tutoring program available at the school in the evenings. When I explained I was there to see LoAnne Larson, the librarian, he smiled and said, "Ah, I'll bet it's about the Internet," and pointed me in the right direction.

Coordinating resources

LoAnne, like many teachers working with the Internet, is a relative newcomer. And, like most users of the Internet, she began with e-mail.

She started working with the Internet in 1992 when the Shoreline School District received a National Science Foundation grant that helped them get started. The grant allowed the district to give Internet accounts to the science teachers and a few librarians. Once she was familiar with e-mail, LoAnne branched out and joined a mailing list that supported her professional interests. She has found the work she does on the Internet surprisingly valuable.

"What hooked me on the Internet was the electronic mail. And what I found most valuable professionally was the discussion with my librarian colleagues about issues and resources. The LM_Net [mailing list] volume has gotten ahead of what I can handle and I no longer subscribe to that listserv, but I'm on other listservs that don't have that volume. I've found that professionally it's one of the most valuable experiences of my career," she said.

LoAnne is quick to praise her district and the voters in the community for the support that she and the rest of the faculty have received in accessing newer technology.

"This community has been very, very supportive of technology, and that's not always the case. We've always been able to pass our bonds here and so that's been a wonderful experience for our students and for this community in general."

She points to the computers stationed throughout the library. Some are set up as work stations with access to various reference programs. Others are connected to the Internet. In fact, there are four stations in the library where students and teachers can access the Internet, including one Macintosh Centris where students can work with the World Wide Web.

How do the students use these resources and how does LoAnne help them make sense of the vast potential represented by the Internet?

"I think it's important to get them used to the idea that they can go beyond the walls of this building to find information."

"I make sure that all of our freshman students coming into Shorecrest have a demonstration and an opportunity to go online. That way they will know what it is to access other resources, specifically, libraries.... I have a terminal open all the time and students can just telnet out to search," she explains.

"There are some resources that I can't afford in a high school library that are available at the [county library system]. For instance, there are indexes to some of the major newspapers. I often refer students to other libraries when they are doing research. I think it's important to get them used to the idea that they can go beyond the walls of this building to find information."

The library serves as a resource and a tool to support the students' academic work. Most of this stems from assignments given by the teachers and, so, the students' use of the Internet is largely determined by the teachers' familiarity with the Internet as a resource.

Most of this [work] stems from assignments given by the teachers and, so, the students' use of the Internet is largely determined by the teachers' familiarity with the Internet as a resource.

LoAnne recalls a social studies teacher in her school who was interested in having his students learn first-hand about the laws being made in the state capital. He helped his students access a site on the Internet where information about laws that are being made is available to the public. He also asked his students to conduct an online search of the Washington state code by accessing information stored on remote computers.

The students learned to use the Internet to take advantage of the detailed record that is created and archived, chronicling the legislative process. This fits with the mission LoAnne sees as appropriate for the electronic resources that have become part of the library.

"The bulk of the teaching I do has to do with accessing information that is free. Most of our students, of course, don't have accounts. ... I am concerned about these students and want to give them a place to come and access electronic information," she says.

LoAnne also wants to increase the abilities of her students to take advantage of the many and varied resources on the Internet. She thinks that students are getting better, class by class, at thinking about the Internet as a mainstream resource for information. She is concerned, however, that not enough of them are evaluating the information they are getting from the Internet. She wants them to think of the Internet as one tool in a range of tools.

One of the ways she tries to address this goal is through classes offered to incoming freshmen and to any student interested in working with the World Wide Web.

Classes are taught, under the supervision of LoAnne, Shorecrest's computer teacher and two students. These students have extensive experience with the Internet, particularly the World Wide Web. They offer an introductory class on the use of the Internet for the freshmen students. They offer four evening classes that are open to the community and focus on the World Wide Web.

The students created this course and teach it with support from a grant from the Shoreline Foundation, a private organization of parents who conduct fund-raising activities. The students played a large part in the grant-writing process and use the money to pay for their time and, in part, to maintain their own private account with a commercial Internet access provider.

"I think the most valuable resource are the students themselves who are interested in the field. With these two young men, I've done everything I can to provide them opportunities to teach and to use their expertise. That is how I see one of my jobs as a librarian: identifying students, supporting their abilities and skills, and broadening their experiences in high school," LoAnne says.

"I think that there needs to be more instruction for students and for faculty. No one uses the potential that exists there."

She realizes, however, that there's a long way to go and that, for the most part, neither teachers nor students have learned to take advantage of the benefits the Internet offers. She's particularly interested in the use of the Internet as a tool to enable and enhance communication.

"I think that there needs to be more instruction for students and for faculty. *No one* uses the potential that exists there. That's really true. The Internet is not an encyclopedia. Some people come in and say, 'I want to go to the Internet and find this bit of information.' I say, 'Wait a minute. You have to think this through again because it is not an encyclopedia. In fact, foremost, it's really a communication tool.' "

She has been trying to encourage teachers to use the Internet as a communications tool, but it's an uphill battle. High school teachers work with many students and have a lot of responsibilities. For them to leap into an area where they aren't necessarily comfortable and where they don't see the need, isn't a reasonable expectation. Before they can use this tool creatively, teachers need time to explore and to find ways they can use the Internet to do some of the simple things they see as useful in their curricula.

Before they can use this tool creatively, teachers need time to explore and to find ways they can use the Internet to do some of the simple things they see as useful in their curricula.

LoAnne also worries about the larger issues that surround the Internet and the process of electronic communication generally, and maintains a healthy level of skepticism.

"I wonder if computers will pose some of the same problems that television does for us as a society in terms of isolating people?" she asks. "When you are watching TV, you don't mix with the community. You stay home and watch your TV or work on your computer. And I question very seriously the value of some of the material that is available. I'm very conservative in that respect and I think that most of the programs on the television are absolutely a waste of time."

LoAnne continues: "If the computer gets to be an entertainment tool, then it has the potential for the same negative spin-offs that we have seen come out of television. ... I worry because we, as a society, tend to get caught up in glitzy kinds of entertainment as opposed to really knowing about something of substance and that concerns me personally."

"It makes our world much smaller because it enhances our ability to communicate; but how well it's done in terms of helping us *understand* that world is another question. It's not there yet, not by any stretch of the imagination."

LoAnne's tips for using the Net in the classroom

☑ **The Internet serves best** as a tool for communication. Start with e-mail and make connections with your colleagues.

☑ **The Internet can also** be used as one of many tools connecting you with the information and resources you need to teach more effectively. Rather than wandering all over the Net, find a few specific, reliable sites that will support the educational needs of your students and your curriculum.

☑ **Students are our best teachers.** Involve them in the effort to educate their peers as well as faculty members and administrators about the Internet.

☑ **The Internet is not an encyclopedia.** The ability to evaluate information gathered from the Net is crucial. We need to teach our students to be critical consumers, and—more important—to be thoughtful users of the information gathered from the Net.

☑ **The real value** of the Internet will become more apparent when you and your students begin to contribute to its resources.

Teacher on the Net

Students explore issues of importance

*I*t was the end of the school day at North City
Elementary. Lorrain Higgins met me in the hall and
we walked to her classroom through the library and an
adjoining computer lab where small groups of children
were gathered around the machines.

Lorrain's room was nearby. The
children, under the direction of a student teacher from Seattle University,
were seated in small groups and clus-
ters, quietly engaged in a writing task.
Lorrain directed me to a table in an activity room adjoining the classroom.

Lorrain teaches a fifth-sixth grade
split at North City Elementary. The
school has an enrollment of about 440 children and is set in a semi-suburban neighborhood north of Seattle. Most of the students
are middle class but there is the usual range
of backgrounds, races, interests, ethnicities,
and abilities.

Lorrain Higgins
5-6th grade teacher
North City Elementary
Shoreline, Wash.

Lorrain has been teaching at North City Elementary for two years but has been in this school district
for many more. Throughout her career, she has been involved with educational technology in one form or another and she is known as a resource for teachers
interested in finding out about and using technology.

The school district is known for its high level of
commitment to innovation and reform through the use
of technology. At the start of the 1994-95 school year,
teachers were invited to attend a three-hour training
seminar. At the end, each received a Power Macintosh
computer. Lorrain was one of four trainers for the 11
elementary schools in the district.

By normal standards, there is a good deal of technology available to the students in this school. Many of
the teachers elected to keep the personal computers

All classrooms have one or two additional computers, depending on the grade level, and two portable word processor keyboards that can be used in class or checked out to students overnight.

they were given in the classroom. In addition to these, a Macintosh 520 was placed in every classroom for the students' use and all of these machines were equipped with video cards that allow them to import and export images to and from VCRs, video cameras, and other digital image sources. These computers can also be hooked up to large-screen TV monitors so that the students can see what the teacher is doing on the computer.

All classrooms have one or two additional computers, depending on the grade level, and two portable word processor keyboards that can be used in class or checked out to students overnight. In every classroom there is one data port where teachers can plug their computers in, gaining full access to the Internet (including the World Wide Web) through the district's connection to the statewide network. More connections are planned for the coming year.

The water monitoring project

As I looked around the classroom, I could see more than half a dozen computers arranged in stations or at tables that would accommodate small groups. Lorrain has more than the usual number of machines because of the work she does with technology. This work is supported, in part, by a number of grants she has received over the years.

One of these involved her students in a water monitoring investigation. Lorrain and three other elementary teachers in the area had written a grant proposal that involved their classrooms in water monitoring programs designed to examine the impact people are having on our ponds, lakes, streams, and so forth. Participating students in several locations around the country were assigned bodies of water.

They spent time on the Internet, trading ideas with other groups about the questions they would like to answer and the variables they would need to investigate.

They gathered and analyzed these data, for example, temperature, pH, and vegetation. The information was then traded and compared via networks established for this purpose. Students were able to compare the conditions in their area with those experienced and described by others around the country. The project will continue next year.

This [video-conferencing technology] allows a student or group of students in Seattle to share images as well as text and numerical data with their research counterparts in Florida, Australia, or Bosnia-Herzegovina.

Video conferencing

Lorrain is just beginning to take advantage of a new technology that allows quick, easy, and relatively inexpensive video conferencing. This exchange takes place over the Net as well. The students use video recorders to capture and transmit black-and-white (grayscale) video images to other classrooms. The CU-SeeMe software is available free on the Internet and can be downloaded from a number of FTP sites.

The images can also be saved and brought into graphics or word processing programs. This allows a student or group of students in Seattle to share images as well as text and numerical data with their research counterparts in Florida, Australia, or Bosnia-Herzegovina.

Speaking of the potential of this technology, Lorrain said: "[It's] really quick and easy. You just plug [the cameras] into the modem port and you are ready to go. You don't need any fancy graphics cards. We figure that the kids can do some in-class and independent conferencing back and forth on how its going and what they did. Being able to see a face and talk at the same time makes it a little more real."

Issues investigation

In yet another project, Lorrain's students investigated and reported on a series of issues revolving around current events. The entire project took about three months and allowed the students, working in pairs or alone, to investigate an issue that was important to them. Lorrain took care to allow them the time to select the issues they cared about.

"We took about a week and a half or two weeks talking about current issues in the world and in our own community. They have been doing current events all year long in different ways. So they were able to come up with a master list of possible issues that they could focus on or research. Then, through their preferences, they kind of had a couple of days to think about it to see if they could find any information and just explore the Internet, look in the newspapers, listen to the radio and decide what they wanted to do. They ended up selecting topics such as 'Should the media be allowed in the courtroom?' ' Should gardeners be allowed to use pesticides?' 'Should we preserve old growth forests?'" Lorrain explained.

"Then they used, predominantly, the Internet and interviews to find information because with these topics, you don't find information in the regular elementary school library. For the interviews they would get on the phone and call associations that were connected with these issues and do interviews either on the phone or in person. Several of them set up interviews and then we found a parent to drive them over."

"Then [the students] used, predominantly, the Internet and interviews to find information because with these topics, you don't find information in the regular elementary school library."

During this issues investigation, National Public Radio did a weeklong series of reports on educational technology in public schools. The network learned of the work being done in the Shoreline School District and interviewed Lorrain and her students.

"One of the little girls was investigating the question of whether DNA testing should be allowed as evidence in court trials. Our class happened to be interviewed by National Public Radio and she was on one of those segments and a lawyer from Boston who specializes in that heard it and contacted us and he sent some information to her and they went back and forth a little bit. Not a whole lot of contact there but they did have a connection."

The students put together a 10-15-minute presentation. Each team (or individual) had to present the background—some historical information—the pros and cons, as well as their analysis of the issue. Their presentations had to have a strong oral component but many of the students supplemented this with various forms of multimedia. Some downloaded images from the net and assembled slide shows using Kid Pix or HyperCard. Others assembled short video segments to illustrate their arguments. The presentation took place on one of the visitation days. These take place every few weeks and different grade levels take charge of the days. Lorrain scheduled the issues presentations for one of the visitation days when the sixth grade was in charge.

Lorrain's students were using the Internet as a tool to broaden and lend power to an investigation that allowed them to explore issues which had personal significance to them.

Lorrain's students were using the Internet as a tool to broaden and lend power to an investigation that allowed them to explore issues which had personal significance to them. In such a project, students are engaged in experiences that will prepare them for the work they will do beyond the protective walls of their school. Lorrain stressed the importance of communication and working with people to solve problems. "Just having connections with people is important. The more addresses we got, the more we were able to trade information back and forth. It really starts to build up."

Lorrain described how her students used the Internet to support more traditional sorts of investigations. She has helped support pen-pal projects in her class and in others in which students correspond with scientists or other classes at the same grade level. Another activity involves the use of the Internet strictly as a tool to gather information. Students investigate and report on people they are interested in, such as Michael Jackson, Larry Byrd and Michael Jordan. They have been fairly successful in finding information. They use this information to supplement the information they get by reading biographies, magazine articles, and other publications at the library.

Lorrain is also part of a district team putting together components of the Shoreline School District home page. This effort will result in pages of information about resources in various content or subject areas suitable for various grade levels. These resources might include references to appropriate books, films, CD-ROMs, Internet sites, and video discs. Teachers and students will be able to use these to support the various units that are part of their curricula.

If a teacher, for example, finds that she wants to plan a unit on the rain forests, she might open the district's home page and click on a link to her grade level. From there, she could click on a link to specific content areas, and select rain forests from among a list of possible topics. Clicking on this word would connect her to a page citing appropriate resources. Students doing independent research could use these as well. Perhaps at the bottom of the page, the teacher would find another link to a repository of unit plans and specific lesson plans used by teachers who had already worked with this topic. Most of the details are still being worked out, but this is the direction in which the project is heading.

But the work done by the fifth- and sixth-graders in her class went well beyond giving the younger students Internet addresses to try.

Games

Lorrain's class also helped second-graders in an investigation they were doing on games from other countries, part of a larger unit on other cultures. The assignment for this particular component was to find out about a game played in another country by another culture, and then re-create that game and write directions so that classmates would be able to play the game without assistance. Lorrain's fifth- and sixth-graders helped the second-graders navigate the Internet in search of the information they required.

But the work done by the fifth- and sixth-graders in her class went well beyond giving the younger students Internet addresses to try. They helped them do the searches and really hunted together for information that was not always easy to find. Not all of the students used the Internet; many used more traditional sources. But for some the Internet became a useful tool.

After hearing about this work, I remarked that this seemed to be a very appropriate use of the Internet. She smiled and agreed that the Internet is an important tool to be used thoughtfully in the educational process. It shouldn't just be glitz and glamour without purpose.

Lorrain's tips for using the Internet in the classroom

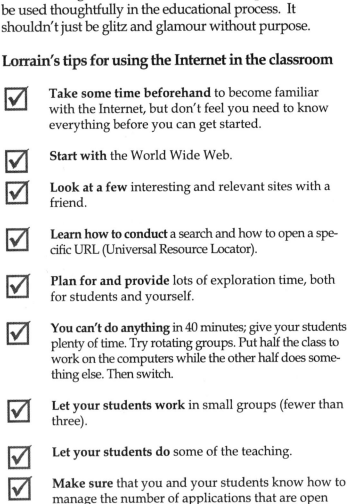

☑ **Take some time beforehand** to become familiar with the Internet, but don't feel you need to know everything before you can get started.

☑ **Start with** the World Wide Web.

☑ **Look at a few** interesting and relevant sites with a friend.

☑ **Learn how to conduct** a search and how to open a specific URL (Universal Resource Locator).

☑ **Plan for and provide** lots of exploration time, both for students and yourself.

☑ **You can't do anything** in 40 minutes; give your students plenty of time. Try rotating groups. Put half the class to work on the computers while the other half does something else. Then switch.

☑ **Let your students work** in small groups (fewer than three).

☑ **Let your students do** some of the teaching.

☑ **Make sure** that you and your students know how to manage the number of applications that are open (and taking up your machine's memory).

Teacher on the Net

Teaching the teachers

When I caught up with Mike McMann in the summer of 1995, he was between meetings with small groups of teachers. He was helping them work on projects centered on the use of educational technology as a tool to enhance student learning.

Mike McMann
7th- 8th Grade
Kellogg Middle School
Shoreline, Wash.

We sat down at a table in a large airy classroom. There were half a dozen or more Apple Macintosh computers around the room. The white board was covered with notes on pedagogy and curriculum associated with instructional change and educational technology.

Mike is one of those individuals who becomes such an effective teacher that he gets moved out of the classroom. In this case it seems to have worked out well for all concerned. Mike is still working with students but now he reaches them primarily through the medium of their teachers, helping educators think about the issues surrounding instructional reform and the ways that educational technology can be used to support positive change in the classroom.

While Mike works on staff development with teachers from all over his district, he is still based at Kellogg Middle School where, until just last year, he had a regular teaching assignment. Kellogg has just over 800 students in grades 7 and 8. It sits a few hundred yards from Shorecrest High where LoAnne Larson (see earlier case study) is the librarian. Shoreline is a suburb of Seattle and a relatively affluent community.

"We are still a pretty cloistered bedroom community. That has changed a lot in the seven years that I've been here but still the large majority of our students come from a fairly homogeneous middle to upper-middle class Caucasian background. But our diversity is growing," Mike says. The ethnic mix is becoming more noticeable with an influx of eastern European and south Asian immigrants.

Mike has been teaching for nearly 10 years in a variety of situations, including a year at a high school and another at a private school specializing in work with dysfunctional students. The majority of his time, however, has been spent at Kellogg. His current position allows him to take some of what he has learned and pass it along to others looking for ways to restructure their approach to education.

Mike works with teachers in a variety of settings but, the common goal is a brand of instructional reform that emphasizes project-based learning, student-centered instruction, and constructivist pedagogy. To make this more tangible, Mike employs a set of questions teachers can ask about their curriculum in order to move toward productive change:

"We strive for tasks where learning occurs beyond the school, and we emphasize the idea that there is a wealth of knowledge that exists beyond the texts, classrooms, and libraries. It's out in the family, neighborhood, community, workplace"

 In what ways does the work in schools connect with the world outside the classroom?

 In what ways are we providing opportunities for multiple approaches and multiple solutions to problems?

 In what ways are the tasks and problems high stakes?

"We strive for tasks where learning occurs beyond the school, and we emphasize the idea that there is a wealth of knowledge that exists beyond the texts, classrooms, and libraries. Its out in the family, neighborhood, community, workplace," he explains.

"We try to provide the students with a valid audience so that they know that their work is for a real purpose. When you can provide positive answers to this list of questions, there's a good chance that meaning is being made by the students," Mike says.

He also firmly believes that modern educational technology can help teachers do a better job in the classroom. The Internet in particular, with its strong potential as a means to enhance communication, can help students and teachers in all three areas.

I asked Mike to describe the room he taught in before he moved into professional development. He pointed across the hall and asked if I would like to take a look.

The classroom was really two rooms with a retractable wall pulled back and tables distributed throughout. There was an impressive array of educational computer equipment spread about the room, including a scanner, a laser disk player, and many Apple Macintosh computers equipped with CD-ROM drives. All the computers were networked, connected to the Internet, printers and other peripherals. It was not much like the ordinary classroom I am used to seeing. Mike explained that the room was currently set up for a summer computer camp. That explained some of it.

Seeing that my jaw was still pretty near the floor, he added that his was an Apple Classroom of Tomorrow (ACOT), which receives equipment and support from Apple Computer. This allowed him to maintain a 7 to 1 student-to-computer ratio during the regular school year with an up-to-date set of Macs. Students also had access to two computer labs — one equipped with LCs and one with Classics — for those occasions when everyone needed his or her own workstation.

He also firmly believes that modern educational technology can help teachers do a better job in the classroom.

But he had more surprises in store. Mike explained that during the school year he team-taught with another teacher. They shared 60 seventh-graders for four hours each day. While the remainder of the school ran on traditional 50-minute periods, his class operated under a special arrangement. He emphasized that this sort of adjustment was central to the kind of work he was doing.

"Frankly, I see traditional scheduling as a real deterrent to the depth of learning that we are striving for. Having a segmented school day that is subject-centric, broken by department, broken by hour, where kids are flying between six or seven different adults is counter-productive in many ways."

Along one wall, near the window, was what looked like a long aquarium, about three feet tall, two feet wide and eight feet long. It appeared to be filled with soil, grass, water and ... was something moving in there? Mike smiled and asked if I had ever heard of an Internet project called Global Lab.

All the information was shared via the Internet. ... "It made it so much more real for them to actually be doing science and to be doing science with a purpose."

Global Lab

Global Lab is an online project involving about 150 classrooms around the world. Teachers and their students sign on to the project and agree to gather and share information regarding an environment and the changes that take place in that environment over time. For some, it's a local wetland. For others, it's their classroom or the roof of the school building. Still others monitor a true piece of wilderness.

In each case, once that environment is selected, participants agree to work within a loose structure to share and analyze common information. They agree, for example, to conduct a set of benchmark experiments.

"On a given day, at a given time, everybody would do, for example, ozone measurements. That would give us some consistent information to share across sites. Then each site would generate research questions that were relevant to the site," Mike explains.

The people coordinating the project help to match group sites that have similar research questions—questions dealing, for example, with water quality or biodiversity.

"Then we would link with a smaller subset of schools that were studying similar questions. We would share results and deliberate and so forth," he says.

Mike's class did water-quality measurements and biodiversity assessments along a stretch of creek and in a small pond nearby. They monitored the stream condition, watched the animals and insects, did some night photography, took paw imprints, made sketches, and conducted native speciation studies. They were matched with schools in the Ukraine, Mexico City, San Antonio, Texas, and Cambridge, Massachusetts. All the information was shared via the Internet. They sent verbal descriptions as well as graphics: digitized photos, scanned reproductions of charcoal drawings, video, and the like.

"It was really exciting to put the kids in a direct field experience of science. It made it so much more real for them to actually be doing science and to be doing science with a purpose. They actually had an audience and a reason to communicate what they found," Mike says.

"The fact that they had to communicate with others around the world and then explain their results and interpret the results of others, I think, also gave them a deeper understanding."

"What's more is the fact that the questions really came out of their experience rather than from a curriculum. There was more ownership and more connections made with the questions they pursued. The fact that they had to communicate with others around the world and then explain their results and interpret the results of others, I think, also gave them a deeper understanding."

The students were quite enthusiastic and wanted to spend more time at the field site. But transportation logistics prevented them from doing as much as they would have liked. They decided to apply for a grant and create a stream tank in the classroom. That was the tank I was now looking at.

In it were frogs, salamanders, fish, and other creatures. When they began to stock the tank, the students knew that the stakes were high. Only if they were able to accurately re-create the environment they had been study-ing would the animals live. This was an opportunity for truly authentic assessment of what the students had learned during the pro-ject.

"[The In-ternet] made it possible to place ourselves within a com-munity of learners and it gave us the perspective of being one voice amongst many"

In Mike's view, the role of the Internet was crucial to the project. First, it increased the scope of the community with which the stu-dents could interact. Second, it gave them greater access to experts. Third, it enabled the students to look at results from a wide variety of environments.

The ease with which the information could be transferred was also greatly increased. Even if they had been simply trading data with another class down the hall, the logistics of gathering, analyzing, storing and transferring the information would have been much more challenging.

"That made it possible to place ourselves within a community of learners and it gave us the perspective of being one voice amongst many. That would have been very difficult to achieve otherwise," Mike says.

"The kids got, I think, a greater sense both of the nature of communicating scientific results and of cul-tural peculiarities, their own and those of other places. You learn a lot of interesting things just writing and saying what seem to be common sense things to you and finding out that it doesn't come through that way. The way it was communicated had a local nuance that everybody here was familiar with. That wasn't neces-sarily true at the other end."

Through interactions such as these, the students in these classrooms built a wider understanding of cul-ture and its effects on communication and on society in general.

"As a teacher, you seize those times. That's a teach-able moment. We would play on that when it would come up in other curricular areas. It became an important, first-hand experience that kids could refer to. My subjective sense is that this group of students got a more vivid and useful experience of their cultural place in the world."

A student's guide to the community

Another project culminated in the publication of an 80-page guide called *The Seattleite—A youth's guide to the North Seattle/Shoreline area*. It was designed for children new to that area and describes the school, the broader community, and some of the recreational and educational opportunities available to children. The chapters of the publication, each containing several articles, focus on entertainment, sports, clubs and organizations, restaurants, fashion and shopping, education, the neighborhood, downtown Seattle, and places to go. Students picked the content area they wanted to work on, making each person part of a team within the larger group. Individuals then wrote and illustrated their articles and also contributed to the production of their chapter.

The students took on a variety of jobs that needed to be done, such as those of art manager, editor, and so forth. They worked with a desktop publishing program, learned to use a scanner, and discussed layout, format and the myriad tasks that are part of assembling a full-scale publication. The guide, now in its third printing, is available at the Shoreline Chamber of Commerce, local schools, and real estate agencies.

Mike points out that it's important to move beyond the notion that the Internet has to dominate any project where it's used.

Mike was enthusiastic about the way the duties and the learning were distributed. There was a real jigsawing of the tasks and skills that had to be learned.

In the course of this project, the students were able to integrate learning from a wide variety of subject areas. They did an environmental education unit of study on recycling and non-toxic inks. They did a mathematics unit on budgeting and another on ratio and proportion. They did social studies units on community and market.

While the Internet could be considered one of the stars, or at least a co-star in the Global Lab project, it was more of a supporting player in the production of *The Seattleite*. The Internet was used as an online resource facilitating research for writing some articles and allowing some of the students to contact experts in various fields.

Mike points out that its important to move beyond the notion that the Internet has to dominate any project where it's used. The Internet is best conceived as just one more tool to be employed by the resourceful educator in the service of good education.

The class plans to translate the guide into a hypertext document so that anyone, anywhere, with access to the World Wide Web can browse through the information they have assembled.

Mike points out three general ways in which the Internet was used in his classroom:

☑ **As a means** of putting kids in a larger community of learners, as in the Global Lab project.

☑ **As a tool** to conduct research, as in the production *The Seattleite*.

☑ **As an arena** for thoughts and ideas. Internet facilities like Kidsphere and Kidlink allow students to post their ideas, to consider others posted there, and to enter a free-flowing dialog about ideas and topics of interest.

"I really believe that the Internet is a tool that's too important for teachers not to use. I liken it to the advent of the printing press. I think that we are entering an era of redefinition of what it means to be literate. Those who have the capacity and have the skills — who know how to access and navigate the Internet and how to discriminate between good information and not so good information are going—to have a market advantage over those who don't.

"Our job as educators is to try to maintain equity and provide for everyone, making sure that all of our children grow up with that capacity. It's really opening doors for us in terms of teaching thinking skills and life-long learning skills. It's such a natural match with what I think will be the needs of learners in the 21st century that we need to pay attention to it and we need to find ways to make it more a part of what we do in the classroom."

Mike's tips for using the Internet in the classroom

☑ **Develop your own short list** of bookmarks (shortcuts to sites you visit often). Most of the things you'll use in the classroom can be accessed from a few sites.

☑ **Avoid the heavily used sites.** They are often difficult to access during peak hours.

☑ **Find some backwater search engines** (ways to search the Internet). The more popular programs used to search for information are sometimes hard to get into.

☑ **Pay attention** to the ways you can help students learn to judge the value of the information they are getting and use it wisely.

☑ **Think carefully about how** you view your students and the curriculum before you decide how you want to use the Internet in your classroom.

☑ **The Internet is not** a good encyclopedia. If your students are consumers of information, the Internet is not going to be seen as a very valuable resource. If you see your students as producers of information, then it's extremely valuable.

 Ask yourself what outcomes you're seeking for your students. Once you've answered this question, then you can look at the Internet and think about how it can be used as a tool to serve these objectives.

CHAPTER 17

A final word

▲▲▲▲▲▲▲▲▲▲▲▲

This book began as a question: How can we use the Internet most effectively as teachers? While searching for the answer, we found that there's much more to learning how to use the Internet effectively than simply learning how to use the Internet. Like any educational tool, the Internet is used best when its use is justified; bringing the Internet into education for the sake of the Internet rarely produces worthwhile results.

We also discovered that the Internet is best used when teachers use it for themselves before bringing it to their students. Teachers can start by using the Internet in their personal lives: writing electronic mail to friends, joining discussions with people who have similar interests, browsing the World Wide Web for movie listings or traffic reports. As teachers use it personally, they begin to use it professionally as well: finding lesson plans, continuing to learn about their subject area, debating educational theory, and so on. After a while these teachers become comfortable with the Internet, able to use it efficiently and effectively.

The first sections of this book were designed to take you through the different Internet services, describing how they work, and more importantly, how you can best use them. We hope that these chapters gave you an understanding of the Internet and what it can do. We also hope that by pointing out the good and the bad aspects of the Internet, we have given you the opportunity to decide if the Internet is the right tool for you.

The last sections of this book showed you how you might bring the Internet into your classroom. When you make the choice to use the Internet in your classroom, and you integrate it into your educational objectives and philosophy, you can make a visible difference in your students' learning. We brought you the stories of teachers who have done so and the tips they would share with you.

In researching this book, talking to teachers, and using the Internet in and out of our own classrooms, we have come closer to an understanding of how best to use the Internet as a teacher. We hope that this book has conveyed some of what we've learned. As long as it's not viewed as another cure-all for education, the Internet can be a valuable tool. By using it efficiently in places where it is justified and goals are set, we believe your teaching can be enhanced. Oh yes, one more thing: Don't forget to have fun!

SECTION 5

Appendices

▼▼▼▼▼▼▼▼▼▼▼▼

▲▲▲▲▲▲▲▲▲▲▲▲

Appendix A

Internet resources

▼▼▼▼▼▼▼▼▼▼▼▼▼

▲▲▲▲▲▲▲▲▲▲▲▲

Mailing list resources

There are three parts to each of the resources listed below. The first, the descriptive name, will give you an idea as to what topic the mailing list covers. The second and third, the list title and subscription address, give you the necessary information needed to subscribe. For instance, if you wished to subscribe to the Alternative Approaches to Learning mailing list, you would send an e-mail message to the subscription address, i.e. *listserv@sjuvm.stjohns.edu*

Leave the subject line blank. In the body of the message, type in the word subscribe, the name of the list, and your name. For instance, if someone named Ima Teacher wanted to subscribe to the Alternative Approaches list, she would send a message containing the following information:

Address:	listserv@sjuvm.stjohns.edu
Subject line:	(leave bank)
Body of message:	subscribe ALTLEARN Ima Teacher

We have tried all of the mailing lists shown, and they are currently working. Of course, this does not mean they will still be working by the time you read this. If you can't get through to a certain list, try sending an e-mail to the subscription address, The body of the message should only contain the word "help" (again, no subject line is necessary). If this doesn't work either, then try another list.

For a more up-to-date list of mailing lists, see one of the following sites:

http://www.neosoft.com/internet/paml/
http://www.tile.net/tile/listserv/index.html
gopher://dewey.lib.ncsu.edu/11/library/stacks/acadlist

Discussion lists

Descriptive name	List name	Subscription address
Alternative approaches to learning discussion list	ALTLEARN	listserv@sjuvm.stjohns.edu
Association for direct instruction	EFFSCHPRAC	mailserv@oregon.uoregon.edu
Children Accessing Controversial Information	CACI	caci-request@media.mit.edu
Computer applications in science and education	APPL-L	listserv@vm.cc.torun.edu.pl
Creative writing in education for teachers and students	CREWRT-L	listserv@mizzou1.missouri.edu
Discussion group for children	TALKBACK	listserv@sjuvm.stjohns.edu
Distance education online symposium	DEOS-L	listserv@psuvm.bitnet
Early Childhood education/young children (0-8)	ECENET-L	listserv@uiucvmd.bitnet
Education and technology	EDTECH	listserv@msu.edu
Educational administration discussion list	EDAD-L	listserv@wvnvm.wvnet.edu
Educational media	MEMO-NET	listserv@vax1.mankato.msus.edu
Elementary education	ELED-L	listserv@ksuvm.ksu.edu
High school scholastic journalism	HSJOURN	listserv@vm.cc.latech.edu
Hypertext in education	HYPEREDU	listserv@itocsivm.bitnet
Information and technology for the disabled	ITD-TOC	listserv@sjuvm.stjohns.edu
International e-mail classroom connection	IECC	iecc-request@stolaf.edu
International network for children and teachers	KIDSPHERE	kidsphere@vms.cis.pitt.edu
International society for education through art	INSEA-L	listserv@unbvm1.csd.unb.ca
Issues and resources in education	EDNET	listserv@lists.umass.edu
Journal of technology in education	JTE-L	listserv@vtvm1.cc.vt.edu
Kidcafe: Youth dialog	KIDCAFE	listserv@vm1.nodak.edu
Law and education	EDLAW	listserv@ukcc.uky.edu

Descriptive name	List name	Subscription address
Learning styles theory and research list	EDSTYLE	listserv@sjuvm.stjohns.edu
Middle level education/early adolescence (10-14)	MIDDLE-L	listserv@vmd.cso.uiuc.edu
Multi-lingual education	MULTI-L	listserv@barilvm.bitnet
Multicultural education discussion	MULTC-ED	listserv@umdd.umd.edu
Music education	MUSIC-ED	listserv@vm1.spcs.umn.edu
Reform discussion list for science education	NCPRSE-L	listserv@ecuvm1.bitnet
Secondary biology teacher enhancement PI	BIOPI-L	listserv@ksuvm.ksu.edu
Special interest group/telecommunications.	SIGTEL-L	listserv@unmvma.unm.edu
St. Johns University chatback planning group	CHATBACK	listserv@sjuvm.stjohns.edu
Talented and gifted education	TAG-L	listserv@vm1.nodak.edu
Teachers applying whole language	TAWL	listserv@listserv.arizona.edu
Teaching in the mathematical sciences with spreadsheets	SUSIG	listserv@miamiu.bitnet
Technology in math education	MATHEDCC	listserv@vm1.mcgill.ca
UC Berkeley Vocational Education Discussion List	VOCNET	listserv@cmsa.berkeley.edu
World Wide Web in Education	WWWEDU	listproc@kudzu.cnidr.org

Announcement lists

Descriptive name	List name	Subscription address
National Update on Americas Education Goals	RPTCRD	listserv@gwuvm.gwu.edu
Teachers Networking for the Future	NOVAE	majordomo@uidaho.edu
A Word A Day		wsmith@wordsmith.org Note: Rather than sending a message with a blank subject line for this mailing list, send a blank message with a subject line which reads: subscribe *your name*

Descriptive name	List name	Subscription address
David Letterman's Top Ten List	TOPTEN	listserv@clark.net Note: This is currently the largest mailing list on the Internet. It has over 60,000 subscribers.

K-12 newsgroups

These are the names (and brief descriptions) of the newsgroups in the K-12 hierarchy. If your Internet service provider does not carry these newsgroups, you may want to request them.

Newsgroup	Discussion area
k12.lang.francais	French Conversation
k12.lang.esp-eng	Spanish Conversation
k12.lang.deutsch-eng	German Conversation
k12.lang.russian	Russian Conversation
k12.lang.japanese	Japanese Conversation
k12.lang.art	Language Arts Education
k12.ed.tag	Talented and Gifted
k12.ed.art	Art Education
k12.ed.music	Performing Arts Education
k12.ed.business	Business Education
k12.ed.health-pe	Health & Physical Education
k12.ed.life-skills	School Counselling
k12.ed.soc-studies	Social Studies Education
k12.ed.tech	Technical/Vocational Education
k12.ed.science	Science Education
k12.ed.math	Math Education
k12.ed.comp.literacy	Curricular Computing
k12.ed.special	Special Education
k12.chat.teacher	Teacher Chat

Newsgroup	Discussion area
k12.lang.francais	French Conversation
k12.chat.elementary	Elementary Student Chat
k12.chat.junior	Junior High Student Chat
k12.chat.senior	Senior High Student Chat

The Channel newsgroups are reserved for short term projects, activities, or discussions conducted over the Internet. Their primary purpose is to provide a vehicle for teacher-designed and/or implemented classroom projects utilizing international telecommunications. Teachers propose projects and find collaborators in the k12.sys.projects newsgroup. A listing of the projects currently in progress is also posted regularly there.

k12.sys.projects	Project Channel Coordination
k12.channel.*	Project Channels

World Wide Web resources

Many of the resources contained in this section were taken from *Internet for Parents*, available from the publisher of this book. Please see page 282 for details.

Art and music

African Art
http://www.lib.virginia.edu/dic/exhib/93.ray.aa/African.html
This online catalog is based on an exhibition of African art at the University of Virginia's Bayly Art Museum. It combines images and explanatory text discussing the aesthetics and meaning of the displays.

ArtsEdge Resources Center
http://artsedge.kennedy-center.org/disclaim.html
A quickly growing Web site clearinghouse cataloging new visual and performing arts resources for students, teachers, and parents. This is a joint project between The Kennedy Center and the National Endowment for the Arts (with support from the U.S. Department of Education). The home page is well organized, easy to navigate and provides quick access to the most recent additions for fun, curious

browsing. A comprehensive and reliable list of music, art, theater, and visual art sites.

ArtServe
http://rubens.anu.edu.au/
Based at the Australian National University, this Web server offers thousands of images of art and architecture, both thumbnails and full pictures as well as a few texts related to art history. The image archives include prints from 15th- to 19th-century Europe; classical, medieval, and Renaissance architecture and sculpture; and miscellaneous works from other periods and regions.

Krannert Art Museum
http://www.ncsa.uiuc.edu/General/UIUC/KrannertArtMuseum/KrannertArtHome.html
This art museum at the University of Illinois at Urbana-Champaign offers images of many of its more than 8,000 art objects. It also offers virtual visitors an electronic tour of its halls.

Resources for Music Educators
http://www.ed.uiuc.edu/EdPsy-387/Tina-Scott/project/home.html
Tina Scott, a music educator at University of Illinois, has put together a very thorough collection of music resources for teachers and music lovers. There are links to both educational materials as well as commercially oriented sites.

WebMuseum network
http://sunsite.unc.edu/wm/
This site began as the personal project of Nicholas Pioch and has expanded into one of the most successful collaborative sites on the Internet. Once known as the WebLouvre, this site won the Best of the Web '94 award for Best Use of Multiple Media. As of this writing the site is delivering links to over 5 million documents!

The big picture

Academy One
http://www.nptn.org/cyber.serv/AOneP/
Academy One attempts to do what this section of this book does: provide a topical list of educational resources. It is not comprehensive, but definitely worth looking at.

APPLICATIONS Education
http://www.rpi.edu/Internet/Guides/decemj/icmc/applications-education.html
An excellent collection of educational resources available on the Internet; this list is being published by John December, a very familiar

name when it comes to individuals making a difference in cyber-space.

AskERIC Home Page
http://ericir.syr.edu

Trust us, just spend a little time at this site and you'll be coming back again and again! A blessing for the first-year teacher! The federally funded Education Resources Information Center (ERIC) offers lesson plans, digests, publications, reference tools, Internet guides and directories, information from government agencies, AskERIC InfoGuides, archives of education-related mailing lists (listservs), and access to other library catalogs and Internet sites.

Best of the K-12 Internet Resources, InforMNs
gopher://informns.k12.mn.us:70/11/best-k12

Some of the best K-12 resources available on the Internet have been pulled together in one place by Internet for Minnesota Schools (InforMNs), a partnership of educational services. You will find links to an assortment of organizations, such as NASA and various school districts, with online educational materials and projects on topics ranging from ecology to government studies. Lessons, images and even sound files can be downloaded. While many of the projects are now over, the information they provide can still be adapted.

Classroom Connect
http://www.wentworth.com

Brought to us by the same folks as the monthly printed publication, this is an online collection of resources organized for educators. It includes everything from lesson plans, to information on conferences and seminars, to links with the businesses that are influencing the direction of the Internet today.

Educational Online Sources
http://netspace.students.brown.edu/eos/main_image.html

Starting with the belief that we should all be working together, this site has the worthy, collaborative mission of building a clearinghouse for educational information.

EdWeb Home Page
http://k12.cnidr.org:90/

The purpose of this hyperbook is to present the world of educational computing and networking in a single, easy-to-use guide; maintained by Andy Carvin at the Corporation of Public Broadcasting, this site has an extensive collection of resources.

Global Schoolhouse Project
http://k12.cnidr.org/gsh/gshwelcome.html
Funded in part by the National Science Foundation, Global School-
house (GSH) is an experiment in the use of the Internet in K-12 education. Each year GSH sponsors several interactive learning projects,
such as e-mail discussions and video conferences linking schools in
different cities. Several mailing lists allow teachers to share ideas
about integrating GSH projects into classroom activities. On GSH's
server, you can learn about current projects and the schools participating in them.

HPCC K-12 Home Page
http://www.lerc.nasa.gov/Other_Groups/K-12/K-12_homepage.html
This site includes teacher resources, a what's new feature, various
search methods, and lots of general references.

Jon's Home-School Resource Page
http://www.armory.com/~jon/hs/HomeSchool.html
A nice collection of resources on Home Schooling; includes information on newsgroups, Web pages, and a variety of educational resources of interest to Home Schooling.

The Montessori Education Page
http://www.seattleu.edu/~jcm/montessori/menu_link.html
Everything you ever wanted to know about Montessori education,
including an annotated bibliography of books by and about Montessori, research into Montessori techniques, and more.

Northwest Regional Ed Lab
http://www.nwrel.org/
The Northwest Regional Educational Laboratorys (NWREL) evolving server provides a means for educators and researchers in the Pacific Northwest to share information about promising practices and
resources. Offers an evolving source of information on educational issues, networking. Much of the content has been developed by
NWREL and the national network of Regional Educational Laborato-
ries and Research Centers. For example, there are links to materials
and resources dealing with family issues, drug-free schools and communities, education and work, Indian education, and regional services.

PBS Learning Services
http://www.pbs.org
Whether you're simply trying to find program listings or searching
for ways to reinforce what your child learns through PBS instructional TV shows, this is where to look. This Web site provides information about the networks various services that support the use of

educational television in K-12 curriculum (as well as preschool and adult learning), plus pointers to curriculum resources, electronic field trips and interactive projects.

U.S. Department of Education
http://www.ed.gov/

The U.S. Department of Education (ED) offers a variety of information for parents, teachers, and researchers. You can read about ED's programs and goals, or browse and download a variety of publications, including ED's *Helping Your Child* series and an article that suggests actions which parents, schools, and communities can take to improve the educational experience for their children. The site also offers statistics, research results, calendars of events, and links to state departments of education and other educational resources. Users can order and receive documents by subscribing through an electronic mail server to the departments catalog, and search some of ED's databases to find a particular document.

Web66
http://web66.coled.umn.edu/

This site is brought to us courtesy of The University of Minnesota College of Education. The site has a goal to help facilitate the introduction of technology into K-12 schools. If you are trying to set up a Web server in your school, this is the place to look for how-to resources and tips .

Web66: WWW School Registry
http://hillside.coled.umn.edu/others.html

Part of the Web66 Project, this is an ongoing list of schools that have a Web presence. It is a wonderful way to visit other school sites around the world. It could be very helpful when your school is trying to decide what sort of a home page would you like to create and what would you like others to know about you.

Welcome to the DeweyWeb
http://ics.soe.umich.edu/ed712/DeweyHome.html

Named after John Dewey, one of the founders of public education in America. Thus, it is no surprise that this page provides computer-mediated communication between students and scientists in an attempt to extend classroom walls.

Foreign language

Ecuanet
gopher://ecua.net.ec
EcuaNet, the gopher maintained by the Equatorial Information Corp., offers news and information, in Spanish, about Ecuador and other Latin American countries.

French Connection
http://ausarts.anu.edu.au/french/french.html
Designed for students of French, as well as francophiles, the French Connection offers direct links to museums, art galleries, libraries, maps, news bulletins and other items with a French theme. Web pages, gophers and Usenet newsgroup pointers allow you to tap into French art, culture, current affairs, language and Canadiana, in French.

Human Languages Page
http://www.willamette.edu/~tjones/Language-Page.html
The Human Languages Page, based at Willamette University, offers an extensive variety of materials for students of languages, from Aboriginal languages to Vietnamese. Its language and literature resources include a series of Spanish lessons, a German-English dictionary, Japanese lessons for travelers, an introduction to the Slovene alphabet, and audio clips of news in Greek. It also offers links to multilingual resources, language labs, vendors of language-learning software, and commercial translation services.

Languages and ESL Literature
gopher://goober.mbhs.edu:70/11/languages
This site offers a mixed bag of materials for teachers and students of foreign languages and English as a second language (ESL). You'll find links to gophers and intercultural mailing lists in French, German, Italian, and Spanish, as well as ESL course outlines.

Serbian Language Web
http://www.umiacs.umd.edu/research/lpv/YU/HTML/jezik.html
This Web page, based at the University of Maryland, teaches the alphabet and simple phrases of the Serbian language. It includes sound files, so you can listen as you learn (with the aid of appropriate software).

Traveler's Japanese with Voice
http://www.ntt.jp/japan/japanese/
This Web page, presented by Takada Toshihiro of the Information Science Research Lab at Japans Nippon Telegraph and Telephone Corp., offers a brief introduction to the Japanese language for travel-

ers. It includes a pronunciation guide and essential expressions for getting around, eating, and shopping. Downloadable sound files are also included, if you have the necessary software to listen to them. You'll also need a World Wide Web Japanese browser to read the kanji and kana characters.

Universal Survey of Languages
http://www.teleport.com:80/~napoleon/

The Universal Survey of Languages is a project aimed at developing a comprehensive online reference point for linguists and laypeople alike, created by users of the Internet with expertise in this field. Currently, you not only can read a brief general description of various languages, but listen to sound clips of each. Eventually, more detailed information on morphological and phonological features, examples of written language, and links to further resources on a particular language are expected to be available here. The survey hopes to cover everything from modern languages, such as Arabic and Armenian, to ancient and invented languages, such as Latin and Esperanto.

University of Guadalajara
http://www.udg.mx

Information on the university, Mexican art and culture, local news plus connections to other servers in Mexico.

VCU Trail Guide to International Sites and Language Resources
http://www.fln.vcu.edu/

Using the theme of the rugged traveler, this site takes you around the world without leaving your seat. It is a wonderful collection of resources including Russian, Spanish, French, Latin, Italian, German and Chinese links. The small graphics make the page visually fun as well as fast loading.

Geography

Great Lakes Information Network (GLIN)
http://www.great-lakes.net:2200/0/glinhome.html

The Great Lakes Information Network (GLIN) is a binational data and information service covering the Great Lakes region of the United States and Canada, including the states of Illinois, Indiana, Michigan, Minnesota, New York, Ohio, Pennsylvania, and Wisconsin, and the provinces of Ontario and Quebec. Students will find fact sheets, calendars, newsletters, directories, and other resources that may be useful for projects in science, history, geography, civics, and related subjects. Materials are provided by a variety of federal, state, and provincial agencies as well as universities and private organizations.

Journey North
http://ics.soe.umich.edu/ed712/IAPIntro.html
The Journey North focuses on life in the Arctic: the various cultures, the environment, and wildlife migration. Arctic Bites is a section of excerpts from newspaper articles, poetry, and Inuit writings about issues in the north. Another section of this Web site provides explanations and reports on the training exercises carried out by researchers from the 1994 International Arctic Project in the Canadian Arctic. Yet another area provides students' observations of wildlife migration. This project is an experiment in using the Web to deliver multimedia education to students, and is part of the University of Michigan School of Education's DeweyWeb.

National SchoolNet Atlas (Canada)
http://www-nais.ccm.emr.ca/schoolnet/
This online atlas of Canada includes political, econonic, and environmental maps. It also features a teacher's guide.

Perry-Castaneda Library Map Collection
http://www.lib.utexas.edu/Libs/PCL/Map_collection/Map_collection.html
An extensive collection of electronic maps is available from the University of Texas at Austin map server. It includes maps of cities in the United States and around the world as well as maps of most countries. The maps originate from a variety of government sources including the U.S. Army, CIA and U.S. Geological Survey. A word of caution: These maps tend to be large graphic images and can be slow to download.

Road Trip USA
http://www.moon.com:7000/1h/rt.usa
The paperback edition of *Road Trip USA*, from Moon Travel Handbooks, may not be available in time for your crosscountry expedition but don't let that stop you. The publisher offers the rough drafts of each route online, and invites readers to comment. You may even win a free copy of a travel book! The guide, being written by a team of travel writers, will describe the secondary highways, such as U.S. 50, that traverse the United States.

U.S. Geological Survey
http://info.er.usgs.gov
The USGS is proud to be the largest earth-science resource in the country! Science teachers will find an abundant supply of information ready for classroom use. Be sure to check out the Education link on USGS's home page for lesson plans and available publications.

The Virtual Tourist
http://wings.buffalo.edu/world/
This site adds a whole new meaning to the term mental traveler by allowing you to see images from around the world and read about any part of the globe.

Volcano World Home Page
http://volcano.und.nodak.edu

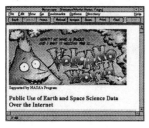

A wonderful classroom resource! This site is attempting to bring us as much information about volcanoes as we could possibly want without asking for field trip permission slips. They have put together factual information along with numerous graphical images for students to see the power and wonder of volcanoes come alive.

Government

CapWeb: A Guide to the U.S. Congress
http://policy.net/capweb/congress.html
CapWeb offers an unauthorized hypertext guide to the U.S. Congress that is searchable and contains links to related resources. For senators and members of the House of Representatives, it gives full addresses, including e-mail (if they exist); information about state delegations; and committee assignments. Images include inline graphics of members of Congress and thumbnails that link to larger originals on the C-SPAN server. CapWeb plans to post party rosters, party leadership, and pointers to state government Internet resources. CapWeb is an independent project of PolicyNet, a service of Issue Dynamics, Inc.

Congressional Quarterly
gopher://gopher.cqalert.com
*CQ*s server gives you access to the data files of *Congressional Quarterly*, the nation's leading nonpartisan authority on Congress and American politics. You'll find current feature stories and news briefs, an archive of past stories, information about pending legislation, election updates, contact information for members of Congress, and promotional material for *CQ*.

C-SPAN
gopher://c-span.org
The gopher of the C-SPAN cable television network offers the text of historical documents such as the U.S. Constitution and Lincoln's Gettysburg Address. Students will also find companion materials to C-

SPAN programming, such as the popular *Close Up* programs, which feature citizens discussing topics with national leaders.

Fedworld Information Network
http://www.fedworld.gov/
Do you have a question about the U.S. Government? This site attempts to provide answers to questions concerning topics ranging from agriculture to veterans' affairs.

LEGI-SLATE
gopher://gopher.legislate.com
LEGI-SLATE is a commercial gopher service that offers the texts of thousands of recent documents pertaining to the U.S. Congress and federal regulatory services. Some data is publicly available to all Internet users, such as information about recent bills and regulations. You can search the legislative information by title, status, number, data, sponsor, chamber, and type. Other free information includes bill cosponsors, a bill digest, and committee reports. Certain areas of LEGI-SLATE (such as Federal Register documents from regulatory agencies) require a subscription.

OpenNet
http://www.doe.gov/html/osti/opennet/opennet1.html
OpenNet is a searchable bibliographic database of more than 250,000 U.S. Department of Energy documents covering human radiation experiments, nuclear testing, radiation releases, fallout and historical records. Periodically updated, it includes references to all documents declassified and made publicly available since October 1, 1994. You also will find here sanitized copies of department documents as well as those that were never classified but are of historical significance. To get a copy of a document, you must contact the department directly.

Stockholm International Peace Research Institute
http://www.sipri.se/
This institute founded by the Swedish government conducts scientific research on the issue of conflict and cooperation among nations. The Web site includes chapter summaries of the organizations yearbook.

THOMAS: Legislative Information on the Internet
http://thomas.loc.gov/
For those who missed educational cartoons explaining how laws are made, this site fits the bill! Also, it provides updated legislative information including congressional records and full text versions of bills currently in legislation.

U.S. Census Bureau Data
http://www.census.gov/

The U.S. Census Bureau offers a variety of statistics about the nation's people and economy. You'll also find Census Bureau news releases, news and analysis of census data from the Center for Economic Studies, and statistical briefs (summary articles). Of special interest is a data extraction system, available via TELNET, that lets you download data from the Census Bureaus huge databases to your own site.

Welcome to the White House
http://www.whitehouse.gov/

You don't need a plane ticket to visit the nation's capital anymore! The Whitehouse is online and you can even sign the guestbook when you finish your tour. Welcome to the White House: An Interactive Citizens' Guide provides a single entry point to all government information on the Internet, plus a glimpse into the lives of those at the White House.

Internet directories

The Internet Educational Resources Guide
http://www.dcs.aber.ac.uk/~jjw0/index_ht.html

From the Computer Science Department at the University of Wales, Aberystwyth, this site provides a growing index of resources intended to aid educators in exploring the Internet.

Kids and Parents on the Web
http://www.halcyon.com/ResPress/

This Web site contains over 700 education-related Internet resources for parents and kids. Many of these are contained in *Internet for Parents*, a book published by Resolution Business Press, Inc.

McKinley Internet Directory
http:www.mckinley.com

At the time of this writing, this World Wide Web index was only a few weeks old, but it already showed much promise. Full-time employees were scrounging the Internet for World Wide Web pages, creating links, writing descriptions, and even rating the sites on a four-star basis for clarity, organization, and regular maintenance. These site descriptions are categorized, and can be searched by concept as well as keyword. Because of the newness of the directory, it was hard to say how busy it would be, but such an impressive service was likely to be well-used.

Uncle Bob's Kids Page
http://gagme.wwa.com/~boba/kids.html
This site is supported by Bob Allison. It is a fascinating collection of resources for the young and young at heart. It is quickly apparent that the site represents an incredible amount of time spent online collecting information and creating a forum for sharing with others. Our experience has been that the site is almost overwhelming for kids to try navigating through on their own. We suggest that you preview the site, find something of interest that your class can further examine and go from there.

The World-Wide Web Virtual Library: Subject Catalogue
http://www.w3.org/hypertext/DataSources/bySubject/Overview.html
Just follow the subject headings, this is the site that shook my bones and made me a true Web devotee.

Yahoo
http://www.yahoo.com

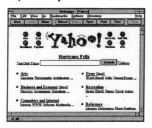

Originally maintained at Stanford University, this site has proven itself a favorite for both research and recreational browsing. It is considered to be one of the premier starting points on the World Wide Web, offering a searchable and regularly updated index to more than 30,000 sites.

Yanoff's Special Internet Connections
http://www.uwm.edu/Mirror/inet.services.html
Scott Yanoff began compiling a list of Internet resources back in 1991, the current size and extent of the list requires that it be broken up into segments; very overwhelming.

Language arts

Big Sky Language Arts Lesson Plans
gopher://bvsd.k12.co.us:70/11/Educational_Resources/Lesson_Plans/Big%20Sky/language_arts
The server of Big Sky Telegraph, an educational network based in Montana, contains this folder of lesson plans, classroom activities and games, and other materials for language arts teachers (prekindergarten through grade 12). Lessons address such topics as elementary reading, vocabulary, grammar, comprehension, and creative and expository writing.

Electronic Books at Virginia Tech
gopher://gopher.vt.edu:10010/10/25

Virginia Tech's Electronic Books gopher provides the full text of more than 130 books, speeches, and other works by great philosophers, political figures, historians, poets, and novelists. You can download texts by such diverse authors as Sophocles, Geoffrey Chaucer, Benjamin Franklin, W.B. Yeats, Eudora Welty and John F. Kennedy.

International Students Newswire (ISN) KidsNews
http://www.umassd.edu/SpecialPrograms/ISN/KidNews.html

ISN KidNews is a news service for students and teachers around the world. Anyone can electronically submit stories: news, features, profiles, how-to descriptions, reviews, and sports. The stories, with appropriate credit, may be used by anyone. Teachers and students each have their own forums for discussing news gathering, teaching, and computer-related issues, including the nitty-gritty of conducting interviews and publishing a student newspaper. The page was developed by Dr. Peter Owens of the English Department at the University of Massachusetts, Dartmouth, who hopes ISN will eventually publish an electronic newspaper highlighting the most interesting stories it receives.

IoQtns: The Quotations Web Page
http://pubweb.ucdavis.edu/Documents/Quotations/homepage.html

The loQtus Web page offers thousands of quotations from the staunchly literary to the humorous. The site includes quotation archives as well as recent postings.

Kidopedia
http://rdz.stjohns.edu/kidopedia/

A Global Children's Encyclopedia, written BY Kids, and FOR Kids!

A Kidopedia is an encyclopedia written by children. Schools across the world are making their own Kidopedia's, and the best articles from each are collected here, at the "Best of Kidopedia".

Now, lets move on to the Kidopedia CONTROL CENTER: Click here for *English* or click here to *Change Languages.*

Kidopedia is an ongoing global online encyclopedia being written by and for kids. Some schools have begun writing entries for their own local Kidopedias, from which the best will be chosen for the global encyclopedia. Organizers expect the global Kidopedia to include entries, links to local sites, links to resource people worldwide and a suggestion page.

MidLink Magazine
http://longwood.cs.ucf.edu:80/~MidLink/
A collaborative Middle School electronic magazine published bimonthly.

Online Writing Lab
http://owl.trc.purdue.edu/
The Online Writing Lab at Purdue University provides more than 100 searchable online documents filled with writing tips ranging from the use of grammar, to how to write research papers, resumes, and business letters. High school students also may find it helpful to e-mail specific questions to the labs tutors.

Web page on Children's Literature
http://www.ucalgary.ca/~dkbrown/index.html
University of Calgary has put together a collection of recommendations, resources for both parents and teachers, as well as a nice sampling of children's writings.

Word Games and Puzzles
http://syndicate.com/
A good way to expand your vocabulary is by playing with words. This publisher offers several interactive word puzzles and games to help you learn new words. There's also a monthly crossword puzzle to be solved. Syndicate also provides information about the educational software it sells.

Mathematics

Ask Dr. Math
http://forum.swarthmore.edu/
K-12 students who have a math problem or simply want to talk to someone who loves math can contact Dr. Math (actually a group of math students and professors at Swarthmore College). Ask Dr. Math is a project of Swarthmore's Geometry Forum, a program of the National Science Foundation.

Big Sky Math Lesson Plans
gopher://bvsd.k12.co.us:70/11/Educational_Resources/Lesson_Plans/Big%20Sky/math
Part of Montana's Big Sky Telegraph educational network, this server offers a collection of more than 40 K-12 mathematics lesson plans. Each plan includes an objective, overview, activities and procedures, and examples. The lessons were prepared at summer workshops held by the Columbia Education Center, an association of teachers from 14 western states.

CSC Mathematical Topics
http://www.csc.fi/math_topics/General.html
The Center for Scientific Computing (CSC), the Finnish national supercomputer center, includes a page of math-related materials, including animations. You may also contact specialists in math at the center.

Explorer Home Page
http://server2.greatlakes.k12.mi.us/
The Explorer resource database offers a collection of resources including lesson plans for teachers of mathematics and science.

Fun Math
http://www.uni.uiuc.edu/departments/math/glazer/fun_math.html
Puzzles, problems and pictures can help students learn and laugh about math. This assortment contains paradoxes, logic puzzles, and images of fractals, crystals, hyberbolics, and knots. They were collected by Kumar Das, George Petrov, Bren Halfwassen, and Douglas Sohn of University Laboratory High School at the University of Illinois

The Geometry Center
http://www.geom.umn.edu
The Geometry Center is hosted at the University of Minnesota. It has a lot to offer to educators; be sure to check out the Interactive Web Applications link!

MathMagic
http://forum.swarthmore.edu/mathmagic/
A wonderful telecommunications project integrating use of technology, problem solving and collaborative learning with fun!

MegaMath
http://www.c3.lanl.gov/mega-math
Elementary school students are intrigued by the size of infinity and the fact that the simplest-sounding math problems can challenge even the biggest computers. Through hands-on activities involving graphs, stories, games and other hypertext materials, the MegaMath project tries to show these youngsters that the study of math can be exciting. The project, involving teachers, students and mathematicians, is led by Los Alamos National Laboratory.

Project Athena
http://inspire.ospi.wednet.edu:8001/
Project Athena includes a growing collection of K-12 curriculum modules and information on such topics as observing the weather, viewing storms from space, Space Shuttle missions, Pacific Rim

earthquakes and planetary orbit. This is a three-year collaboration to develop science, math and technology educational materials using the resources of the Internet. Funded by NASA, it involves school districts in the metropolitan Seattle area, the Washington education department, and Science Applications International Corp.

SciEd: Science and Math Education Resources on the Web
http://www.halcyon.com/cairns/science.html
Alan Cairns, of Bellevue High School in Washington, has taken a stab at cataloging all the useful Web resources for teaching and learning science and math. The page of resources for chemistry, for example, links to tutorials, journals, reviews, images, databases and safety sheets, among other instructional materials. The SciEd home page also contains many links and pointers to material on other subjects, from art and literature to current evens and travel.

Science

Ask Mr. Science
gopher://gopher.cic.net:3005/00/classroom/dr.sci
This award-winning project encourages K-12 students to e-mail questions related to astronomy, biology, chemistry, geology, or physics to Mr. Science (actually a group of Advanced Placement students at Christianburg, Va., High School). The students research and formulate a reply within 48 hours.

Big Sky Science Lesson Plans
gopher://bvsd.k12.co.us:70/11/Educational_Resources/Lesson_Plans/Big%20Sky/science
On the server of Montanas Big Sky Telegraph, an educational network, you'll find more than 200 science lesson plans (and mini-lessons) for K-12. Each plan includes an objective, overview, activities and procedures, and examples. The lessons were prepared at summer workshops of the Columbia Education Center, an association of teachers from 14 western states.

Daily Planet/Weather World/Weather Machine
http://www.atmos.uiuc.edu/
The Daily Planet Web server is being used to test and demonstrate Web client/server technology to improve public access to earth sciences data. It is part of a joint project between NASA and the Atmospheric Science Department at the University of Illinois. The departments Weather World Web server and Weather Machine gopher server operate under this umbrella. These two sites will captivate kids (and adults) interested in weather patterns and forecasting:

- *Weather Machine:* This gopher provides directories of weather facts, mostly from the National Weather Service. It includes current weather summaries, forecasts, radar summaries, and some climatological information, all organized geographically. Other offerings include frequently asked questions and answers about weather, a list of weather newsgroups, phone numbers for road conditions around the United States, and links to related gophers.

● *Weather World:* The Web server emphasizes visual information, with hundreds of current and archived images and 60 MPEG animations. You'll find satellite photos, surface maps, upper air maps and plots, and forecast maps. This server also offers many of the text-based resources available on the gopher.

EarthViewer
http://www.fourmilab.ch/earthview/vplanet.html
John Walkers *Earth Viewer* is an interactive server that lets you see on a map where it is day or night around the world at the time of your request. You can also choose to look at the earth from a variety of perspectives: from the sun; the moon; the night side of the earth; above any location on the planet specified by latitude, longitude and altitude; or from a satellite in earth orbit. The server can generate images based on a topographical map of the earth, current weather satellite imagery, or a composite image of cloud cover superimposed on a map of the earth. Walker also offers public-domain space simulation software at this site.

Exploratorium
http://www.exploratorium.edu/
San Franciscos Exploratorium is a museum of science, art, and human perception. You'll find information about the museums exhibits and educational programs, scientific images and sounds, software, and a selection of educational publications. The museums quarterly magazine includes an Ask Us column inviting readers to post their own science questions.

Field Museum of Natural History
http://rs6000.bvis.uic.edu:80/museum/
Chicagos Field Museum takes virtual visitors on interactive tours of its exhibitions. Children will particularly enjoy the online sampling from *DNA to Dinosaurs*. Sounds, animations, 3-D images and explanatory text reveal where and when dinosaurs lived, what they ate and how they moved.

Green Disk Paperless Environment Journal
ftp://info.umd.edu@infoM/ReadingRoom/Environment/GreenDisk
GreenDisk offers information on environmental issues scanned from hundreds of sources. You'll find articles on such topics as renewable energy, waste disposal, and endangered species. The journal also publishes research reports, press releases, action alerts, and news summaries from environmental groups and government agencies around the world. According to *GreenDisks* publishers, much of this information is unavailable or hard to find in libraries.

Guide to NASA On-line Resources
http://naic.nasa.gov/naic/guide/
The Guide to NASA Online Resources showcases NASA and NASA-related scientific, educational and government resources. It includes NASA databases and archives, research announcements, a Space Shuttle launch schedule, pointers to image databases, software archives, and links to other NASA information servers.

Interactive Frog Dissection on the Web
http://curry.edschool.virginia.edu/~insttech/frog
The Interactive Frog Dissection is an online tutorial, combining text with 60 inline images and 17 QuickTime movies. Not only does it show a frog's organs and how to dissect them, but by using clickable images, it lets you practice these procedures on your computer screen. A possible substitute for school lab work, it was developed by students in the Instructional Technology Program at the University of Virginias Curry School of Education.

JASON Project
http://seawifs.gsfc.nasa.gov/JASON.html
The JASON Project is a series of interactive field trips in which K-12 students spend about two weeks following the adventures and experiments of a team of scientists. Its Web site provides, for example, continually updated footage of a volcanic eruption on one of Jupiters moons as part of a project studying the solar system. Past expeditions have visited the Sea of Cortez and the Hawaiian volcanoes. The JASON curriculum includes both printed materials (available for a fee) and a free online service in which the JASON scientists provide daily e-mail reports on their expeditions, along with answers to selected student questions. The projects are organized by the JASON Foundation for Education, established in 1989 by Dr. Robert Ballard, who discovered and explored the remains of the Titanic.

NASA's Welcome to the Planets
http://stardust.jpl.nasa.gov/planets/
Some 200 of the best images from NASAs planetary exploration program are presented here. These captioned images show major planets, small bodies in space and various spacecraft. The online exhibition is drawn from NASAs interactive CD-ROM program *Welcome to the Planets*.

NOAA
http://www.noaa.gov/
This is the home page of the National Oceanic and Atmospheric Administration (NOAA). It provides an index of links to data on weather, the earth sciences, and oceanography from NOAA Data Center and other organizations.

Periodic Table of the Elements
http://www-c8.lanl.gov/map/infosys/html/periodic/periodic.map?169,45
Los Alamos National Lab has created a very graphical and searchable representation of the chemical elements. By clicking on the name of an element in the table, you can read a page of information about it, including its atomic number, symbol, weight, electron configuration and history. This site also links to other periodic tables on the Internet.

Puget Sound Green Gopher
gopher://futureinfo.com
The Puget Sound Green Gopher is sponsored primarily by People for Puget Sound, an organization dedicated to protecting and restoring the Puget Sound region of Washington state. On it you'll find environmental information about that region, including pollution reports, growth management and watershed databases, and a newsletter. Also available are details about Kids for Puget Sound (the junior arm of People for Puget Sound), such as copies of *Kids Sound,* a newsletter containing poetry, letters, and short articles contributed by kids. The gopher also offers links to other environmental information on the Internet.

Rainforest Workshop Home Page
http://mh.osd.wednet.edu/
This sites purpose is to provide information and lesson plans for classrooms studying rainforests. While the site began with a focus on tropical rainforests, they are now expanding to include temperate rainforests.

Space Calendar
http://newproducts.jpl.nasa.gov/calendar/calendar.html
The calendar covers NASA activities and anniversaries that are coming up in the next year, full of interesting links and historical information on NASAs space program.

Weather
http://www.mit.edu:8001/usa.html
The Weather page offers an interactive weather map of the United States. You just point and click on a location to learn its current and extended forecasts, including temperature, humidity, wind speed, barometric pressure, and actual conditions (fog, snow, and so on). The map is located on the Massachusetts Institute of Technologys Student Information Processing Board World-Wide Web, and it draws its information from the University of Michigans Weather Underground project. From here, you can connect to popular online weather sites, such as the Weather Underground TELNET site and maps, satellite images, forecasts, and animations from the University of Illinois, Urbana-Champaign.

Weather Underground Homepage
http://cirrus.sprl.umich.edu/Weather_Underground.html
Located at the University of Michigan, the Underground Weather site provides a wide variety of resources for earth science; high degree of emphasis on the interactive classroom.

Search engines

The Lycos Home Page: Hunting WWW Information
http://lycos.cs.cmu.edu/
Served by Carnegie Mellon University, Lycos will allow you to search on document titles and content. The word lycos is derived from the Latin word for spider; who better to serve your Web searching needs?

Search the World-Wide Web
http://galaxy.einet.net/www/www.html
Search the Web via the ElNet Galaxy search engine.

WWWW(The World Wide Web Worm)
http://www.cs.colorado.edu/home/mcbryan/WWWW.html
Best of the Web 94 — Best Navigational Aid.

Social studies

Asia Pacific Region Information
gopher://emailhost.ait.ac.th:70/11/AsiaInfo
Thailands Asian Institute of Technology is building this wide-ranging site covering the nations of the Asia Pacific region. you'll find materials about Brunei, Cambodia, China, Indonesia, Korea, Laos, Malaysia, Myanmar (Burma), the Philippines, Singapore, Thailand, and Vietnam. The server, which links to several others, provides information on such topics as tourist attractions, business practices, currency, criminal justice, human rights, and national economies. The resources are gathered from a variety of sources, both inside and outside the region.

Big Sky Social Studies Lesson Plans
gopher://bvsd.k12.co.us:70/11/Educational_Resources/Lesson_Plans/Big%20Sky/social_studies
The server of Montanas Big Sky Telegraph educational network includes this collection of more than 180 K-12 social studies lesson plans and mini-lessons on topics ranging from the Civil War and the Oregon Trail to the criminal justice system and resolving conflict. Each plan includes an objective, overview, activities and procedures, and examples. The lessons were prepared at summer workshops of the Columbia Education Center, an association of teachers from 14 western states.

Library of Congress World Wide Web Home Page
http://lcweb.loc.gov
The Library of Congress is using the Web to present exhibits from its vast collection; basically, a history teachers dream site.

Pathfinder from Time Warner
http://www.pathfinder.com

The Web server for several Time-Warner publications includes *Time Magazine, Sports Illustrated* and *People*. All or part of the magazines are available electronically before they reach the newsstands. The contents of back issues can be searched and articles retrieved. This server is extremely popular and access can be very slow.

Youth Music/Youth Culture
http://www.drake.edu/univannounce/thomas/honors123.html
Drake University's Jean-Paul Davis and Thomas Swiss compiled the
Youth Music/Youth Culture home page as part of their study of music and its effect on culture. Direct links take you to electronic magazines, academic sites for music and culture (such as the study of
punk rocks roots), listings organized by type of music, song lyrics,
audio clips, and Usenet newsgroups that focus on these topics. You
can also connect to home pages created by a range of performers
(from Nirvana to Janet Jackson) and their fans.

Special education

Cornucopia of Disability Info
gopher://val-dor.cc.buffalo.edu
Based at the State University of New York (SUNY) at Buffalo, the
Cornucopia of Disability Information (CODI) server offers resources
for local and international audiences alike. It provides medical information about a variety of disabilities, government documents, information about technology for the disabled, sources of legal assistance,
employment information, a TDD phone directory, lists of services for
the disabled in the Buffalo area, and lists of other Internet resources
on disabilities. You can search all CODI resources by keyword.

Deaf Education
gopher://gopher.educ.kent.edu:70/11/edgophers/special/deafed
Based at Kent State University, the Deaf Education gopher focuses
on the learning needs of children who are deaf or hard of hearing. It
includes resources and instructional strategies for teachers and parents, materials for deaf people, news, a list of addresses and contacts
in the field of deaf education, a list of students who want to correspond with the deaf, and links to related servers and mailing lists.

Disability Resources, Products, Services, and Communication
http://disability.com
Still in its infancy, this site hopes to offer a comprehensive listing of
and direct links to disability-related resources on the Internet. Currently you can get free disability tips and a free copy of a disability
magazine. A link to the Disability Mall lets you view images of products and request further information by e-mail about disability services. Disability Resources, Products, Services and Communication is
sponsored by Evan Kemp Associates, a company managed by people with disabilities which provides information, products and services to people with disabilities.

World Wide Web tools

A Beginner's Guide to HTML
http://www.ncsa.uiuc.edu/General/Internet/WWW/HTMLPrimer.html
An easy-to-navigate primer for creating Web pages.

The Best of WWW Contest
http://wings.buffalo.edu/contest
This page highlights the flashiest, most visual places in the WWW for the purpose of promotion and also to show users what can be achieved if you're willing to stay up all night!

Yale C/AIM WWW Style Manual
http://info.med.yale.edu/caim/StyleManual_Top.HTML
Not how to create a home page on the Web, but a superb style guide of do's and dont's once you're able to author your own page.

Directory of /pub/packages/infosystems/WWW/tools
ftp://sunsite.unc.edu/pub/packages/infosystems/WWW/tools
An extensive source for WWW tools and helper applications.

Stanfords Info-Mac Digest
http://www.mid.net/INFO-MAC
An extensive archive of Apple Machintosh resources.

Sample acceptable use policy

From the Bellevue (Wash.) Public Schools

*Here is an example of a K-12 public school policy
on acceptable use of its computer network system.
It is contained in the network user registration form
that all users of the Bellevue, Wash., School District's
system must complete to gain Internet access.
While policies vary from district to district, this will
give you an idea of the types of restrictions a school
system may impose on network users.*

Reprinted with the permission of the Bellevue Public Schools.

Bellevue Public Schools Belnet User Registration Form

Educators wishing to use the Belnet System must complete this registration form
and follow the Belnet guidelines of conduct (on back of form) while online. Users
must agree to hold harmless the Bellevue School District etc., and understand
that the district may terminate system use at any time.

Personal Data

Name_____ Phone Number_____

School_____ Home Phone_____

Position_____

School Address_____ (Out of district only)

District_____

Computer Access In order to participate on Belnet, you must have access to a
computer with a modem or have access to a local area network.

How will you connect to Belnet? (School/Home/Both) What equipment will you
use?_____

Modem users will understand that the system will automatically disconnect after
15 minutes of no activity.

Account Purpose What job related need do you have to connect to Belnet? If you
are associated with a work-group, please specify which group. Indicate also how
long you wish to have access.

_____
_____
_____

Acceptable Use Network use is for collaboration and research. Use privileges are non- transferable. Unauthorized use may result in loss of privileges and or prosecution. Account theft, file theft, violations of informational privacy and/or penetration of harm to the operating system are prohibited. If complaints are made or we notice inappropriate behavior we may suspend your account.

Agreement I have the necessary equipment described above. I agree to use my account for purposes consistent with acceptable uses indicated above, and the guidelines for conduct described below. I will provide reports of my use when requested.

Signed_____Date_____

I support this request and verify that it is a job-related need.

Signed_____Date_____ (Supervisor or Online Moderator)

Belnet Guidelines of Conduct

Ethical

1. The Belnet user respects the confidentiality of information on Belnet, and refrains from sharing conference text outside membership without permission of conference members.

2. The Belnet user respects the intellectual property rights of ideas and information shared on Belnet.

3. The Belnet user practices effective and professional communication while on-line, and shows respect for the ideas, comments and opinions of others.

4. The Belnet user understands that use of the Bellnet system is a professional privilege and refrains from using the system for personal profit or gain.

5. The Belnet user refrains from discussion of student/staff issues of a personal nature online.

Practical

1. The Belnet user minimizes connect time by uploading and downloading text, and composing long responses off line, particularly during telephone line and long distance access.

2. The Belnet user manages mail efficiently by deleting or downloading messages after reading.

3. The Belnet user makes sure that the computer used for connecting to Belnet is virus free.

Effective uses of the Internet for K-12 teachers

▼▼▼▼▼▼▼▼▼▼▼

The idea for Teacing with the Internet: Putting teachers before technology was sparked by a report, written in 1994 by Douglas Steen and two other students in the Masters in Teaching program—Mari Andonian and Deborah Wilson—at Seattle University. Here is a portion of that report.

▲▲▲▲▲▲▲▲▲▲▲▲

Mari Andonian
Douglas Steen
Deborah Wilson

Seattle University

Abstract

As the Internet expands daily and provides more and better access to people and resources around the world, more and more teachers are finding it to be a useful tool both in and out of the classroom. The authors of this paper surveyed educators over the Internet in order to determine what common elements can be found in what they consider effective uses of the Internet for a K-12 teacher. They present the results of two Internet surveys and a review of projects from the Internet, as well as many suggestions from experienced Internet educators.

Introduction

This research project is of special value to its authors; we undertook this research in order to improve our own teaching. Although we were already somewhat proficient with the Internet, we had little to no idea of how to use it in our teaching. Our goal for this research was to discover how teachers who are similarly proficient with the Internet are using it to improve their teaching. How do these teachers use the Internet? What elements of use make the Internet an effective tool for K-12 educators?

We believe the Internet, and telecommunications in general, will play an increasingly greater role in society as people become more globally aware and as they grasp the advantages of having a vast amount of information at their fingertips. It is therefore important that we, as K-12 teachers, become more proficient at using the Internet and adept at teaching our students to use it effectively as well.

The Internet is also a versatile tool, whose use has yet to be fully exploited by educators. We foresee the Internet being used extensively by educators in the near future, and we know that it is already being used in and out of the classroom to a large extent. Students use the Internet to converse with people around the world, to conduct science experiments, and to improve reading and writing skills. Teachers use the Internet to do educational research, to find lesson plans and software, and to collaborate with colleagues. Teachers are also finding that the Internet can enhance their everyday lessons and take their students where they could not go otherwise.

In the future, we hope to see an expanded role for the Internet in the K-12 classroom. Rather than only being available to a few fortunate students and teachers, we hope the Internet will become available to all in K-12 education. As educators are made aware of the advantages of using the Internet, its importance as an instructional tool will become evident.

Although educators have been using the Internet for a number of years, analysis of its effective uses is still scarce. Although it appears that there are many works in progress in this field of study, there are very few published documents. The Internet itself holds a wealth of information, but it is scattered and difficult to access. It is our hope, then, that this study will be useful in aiding other teachers who wish to use the Internet effectively.

It is not our intent to provide the reader with a rigorous statistical study, but rather a guide reflecting a sampling of opinions from educators who have experience using the Internet in a K-12 environment. It is our opinion that this is the most helpful way to provide an accurate account of these educators' perspectives.

We plan to use this research to guide our own uses of the Internet as teachers. We hope that other educators who are at least familiar with the Internet will find this research useful as well.

Literature review

Over one million people use the Internet everyday (Bievenue et al, 1993), and it is not surprising many of them are teachers. In fact, some have estimated that there are approximately 50,000 teachers worldwide who use the Internet (Andres, 1993; Dyrli, 1993). Despite the large number of teachers on-line, there was very little literature available on its use in the classroom. What was available generally covered one or more of the following topics: why teachers should use the Internet, how teachers used the Internet for professional development, how teachers used the Internet in their classrooms, and what kinds of supports teachers needed if they were to use the Internet effectively.

For the purposes of this paper we were not concerned with the first topic, why teachers should use the Internet. We were concerned with the second and third topics—how teachers used the Internet for professional development and how teachers used the Internet in the classroom—and our research built upon the literature that we found by surveying and analyzing these uses. We were also interested in the fourth topic, what kinds of supports teachers needed if they were to use the Internet effectively, but only because the literature in this area helped us determine why certain uses were effective and other uses were not.

Professional development

The literature available on how teachers used the Internet for professional development was primarily concerned with how and why the Internet was used. A national survey on telecommunications and K-12 educators (Honey and Henriquez) published in 1993 found that sending e-mail to colleagues, exchanging information, and accessing databases containing information relevant to students were the most widely used professional development activities. Other forms of correspondence and information retrieval, such as participating in discussion forums, conducting online exchanges with researchers, accessing educational research, and researching subject specific databases were also cited in the literature (Honey and Henriquez, 1993; Andres, 1993). This information helped us to write our survey in that it made apparent the usefulness of dividing professional development activities into two sections: correspondence and information retrieval. It also gave us an idea of what kinds of answers to expect from survey recipients and the knowledge that if we did not receive similar answers on our survey we needed to do additional analysis to determine why our survey recipients answered differently.

The reasons educators used the Internet for professional development were often related to the fact that educators tend to be professionally isolated. Honey and Henriquez (1993) found in a survey of K-12 educators that communicating with other educators to share ideas, obtain information, and get feedback was the most highly rated incentive for using telecommunications as a professional resource. Combating professional isolation and accessing information were also highly rated incentives. This information gives us some insight into what types of professional development activities have been effective in the past.

Classroom use

The literature available on how teachers used the Internet in the classroom was primarily concerned with how and why the Internet was used and what made certain types of projects successful. In a survey of 550 K-12 educators who use telecommunications for student learning activities, Honey and Henriquez (1993) found that the most common uses involved information retrieval; specifically, accessing encyclopedias, news services, weather information, ERIC and other educational databases were the most common classroom activities. The second most popular type of student learning activities, according to Honey and Henriquez (1993), involved classroom exchange projects. Examples of such projects included penpal exchanges, conversations with experts, story-writing exchanges, and national cultural exchanges. Classroom exchange projects were also the easiest type of telecommunication project to find articles on—although most of the articles were of the how-to nature with few insights into the factors that make these projects successful (Butler and Jobe, 1987; Riel, 1987; Stall and Lawson, 1991; Reissman, 1992; Roblyer, 1992; Andres, 1993). This information, like the information on which types of professional development activities were most common, gave us an idea of what kinds of answers to expect from survey recipients. It also gave us the knowledge that if we did not receive similar answers on our survey we needed to do additional analysis to determine why our survey recipients were different from those educators surveyed and contacted by other researchers.

Many articles give reasons why the Internet should be used for student learning activities and what makes such activities successful. The most common reasons for using telecommunications and the Internet in the classroom include the feeling that it actively engages students in the learning process, it opens up the world for students, it allows students to get information they could not otherwise get, and it increases students' inquiry based analytical skills (Stall and Lawson, 1991; Honey and Henriquez, 1993; Ross.) Most teachers attribute the success of their student learning activities on advance planning, the full cooperation of participating teachers, well-defined project goals, the relevance of the activity to the curriculum and ongoing technical support. The goal of our research is to discover how educators used the Internet to improve their teaching and what made their projects successful. The above information helped us to design our survey and gave us ideas on how to analyze projects for effectiveness.

Teacher supports

The fourth topic available literature covered, what kinds of supports teachers needed if they were to use the Internet effectively, was important to our research only because the literature in this area helped us determine why certain projects failed. The lack of various teacher supports was a problem mentioned by numerous researchers. The most commonly mentioned problems related to a lack of support included the following: shortage of funds (Leslie, 1993; Honey and Henriquez, 1993), lack of time in the school schedule (Leslie, 1993; Honey and Henriquez, 1993), and access problems (Leslie, 1993; Ross; Honey and Henriquez, 1993).

Methodology

Our purpose in collecting data was to gather information on the ways educators use the Internet in order to help teachers implement Internet use. As a result our study was both qualitative and quantitative. Our goal was to collect descriptions, ideas and opinions, and this goal was reflected in our open-ended survey questions (see appendix B) and general methodology.

Data collection—Survey design

We approached data collection in two ways: we surveyed educators and we reviewed published literature. We sent out two surveys. Survey A, the first survey we sent out, was, in a sense, a pre-survey. It consisted of five yes or no questions designed to determine whether the respondent was a teacher in a K-12 classroom, whether the respondent used the Internet as part of her/his curriculum and/or professional development, and whether she/he would be willing to answer a longer survey. (See appendix A for a copy of the survey.)

The second survey, survey B, consisted of four sets of questions. Most of the questions were open-ended—the respondent could write as much or as little as she/he wanted. The first set of questions, personal information, asked about the respondent's connection to K-12 education, experience, access to the Internet, and frequency of use. The second set of questions focused on Internet use for professional development. These questions were designed to determine how the respondent was using the Internet and whether she/he thought this was an effective use. The third set of questions focused on using the Internet for student activities. These questions were also designed to determine how the Internet was being used and whether the respondent thought the use was effective. The last set of questions asked the educators for suggestions and comments regarding Internet use in general. (See appendix B for a copy of this survey.)

Data collection—Survey distribution

Survey A was distributed in four ways. 1) It was posted on relevant k12. USENET groups. 2) It was distributed via the k12wa@u.washington.edu listserv. 3) We combed educational gophers, especially the CICNet gopher, for the names and e-mail addresses of educators who use the Internet. We added these names to a list of educators who we personally knew used the Internet and e-mailed surveys to all of the people on the list. 4) Educators and other people who had received the survey forwarded it to other potential respondents. All replies were sent to us through e-mail. We had an Internet account set up through Seattle University for sending out surveys and receiving replies.

If a respondent to Survey A (page 312) indicated that she/he would not mind completing a longer survey, we e-mailed Survey B (page 312 , 313) to them. We had to receive answers to survey A before sending Survey B, and some people replied to the first survey very quickly while others took up to two weeks.

We sent out a total of 197 Survey A's and received 107 replies. For each reply, we sent out a Survey B from which we received 40 responses.

Data collection—Document review

In addition to surveying educators, we also used data that had already been collected. We examined a descriptive listing of Internet projects compiled by Jeanne Baugh and archived on the CICNet. This set contained fifty-two (52) projects which involved the Internet in a K-12 classroom.

Results and analysis

Because of the qualitative nature of the survey, we will not be tied to exact percentages when describing our results. By using descriptors such as "over half" or "only a few" instead of "51.6%" and "2 out of 40," we hope to provide a more intuitive sense of our results. This ambiguity also reflects the nature of our study, which was not designed for rigorous statistical validity.

The qualitative nature of our survey also creates a certain subjectivity. Even the more straight-forward questions produced answers which were difficult to classify. This sort of system creates a wide margin of error, and it is entirely likely that some respondents would feel that we misrepresented their responses. However, we did our best to retain our perceptions of the individuals' intent in the group results, and we will explain our categorizations as clearly as possible and provide examples directly from the surveys so that the reader may make her own decisions.

Survey population

Because of the nature of our methodology, we have two sets of survey populations, one from the pre-survey (Survey A) and one from the main survey (Survey B), and these two populations overlap. We had one-hundred seven (107) respondents to Survey A, most of whom (over 80%) are currently teaching in a K-12 classroom.

The more extended nature of Survey B allowed us to compile a better description of the respondents. We received forty (40) responses from a wide range of locales, including every major region of the continental US. and several other countries. Of these respondents, 70% indicated that they were currently teaching in a K-12 classroom. Half indicated they were involved with secondary education (grades 9-12), and the other half were split between elementary (grades K-6) and middle school (grades 7-8).

Over half of the Survey B respondents taught (or helped teach) math, science, computer-related subjects[1], or some combination of these and other subjects. Of the remaining respondents, a few taught all subjects (at the elementary level), a few taught foreign languages, and a few taught English, social studies, or history.

Less than one third of the respondents were new educators with less than five years of experience with K-12 education, and more than half had over ten years of experience. This even holds true for those respondents who had been using the Internet for three years or more. Almost half of the respondents had been using the Internet for more than one year, but less than three years, and the remainder are split between those with less than one year of experience and those with three or more years of experience. This distribution is almost the same for respondents who had more than ten years of experience with K-12 education.

More than half of the respondents used the Internet on a daily basis, another quarter used it even more often. All but five of the respondents had Internet access from their home *and* their workplace.

---

1   Including keyboarding, computer science, and business math.

Survey population analysis

Our survey methods produced the respondent population we were looking for: mostly classroom teachers experienced both as teachers and as Internet users (this can be seen both from their years of experience, and from their daily usage). Although the respondents represented a wide range of geographical locations, grade levels, and subject areas, as we had hoped they would, they were concentrated in the high school math/science/computer fields. This is surprising considering the number of Internet projects aimed specifically at elementary classrooms.

It should be noted that some characteristics of our survey population are most likely a result of our survey methods. The fact that most of our respondents were frequent Internet users connected at home and at their workplace may be because those Internet users who use the Internet frequently were more likely to come across our initial survey (Survey A) and respond, and therefore more likely to receive and respond to Survey B. In this way, our survey methodology may have skewed our respondent population.

However, our survey methodology worked to our advantage as well. We were interested in finding experienced Internet users, and by spreading Survey A over the USENET, which has, in the authors' opinion, a relatively complicated interface, we were able to do just that. We were surprised and pleased that our respondents were also experienced educators; this runs contrary to the popular belief that more experienced Internet users are likely to be younger, and therefore less experienced educators. Also, it was gratifying to receive responses from such a wide range of geographical regions. Our research was designed with the belief that as the Internet spreads around the world, effective uses of the Internet will depend less on geographical region than on other factors such as a teacher's experience with the Internet, or the ease of Internet access at a school. This seems to be borne out by the commonalty of responses we received from all over the United States and world.

Survey results—Professional development

Because "professional development" can encompass a wide range of Internet uses, it is easiest to define it negatively: using the Internet for professional development means using it in a way which does not directly involve the classroom. We chose to investigate two major ways of using the Internet for professional development: correspondence and information gathering. We also gave respondents a chance to identify their own uses of the Internet for professional development.

In Survey A, we asked about using the Internet for professional development directly and described it as "(i.e. to communicate with other teachers, to find lesson plans, etc.)". In Survey B we did not ask a general question about using the Internet for professional development, but instead identified the major uses (correspondence, information gathering, and other) and asked about them specifically.

Over 90% of all those who responded to Survey A indicated they used the Internet for professional development; only two-thirds used it in the classroom. The same percentages hold true for the subset of respondents who were currently teaching in a K-12 classroom. Everyone who responded to Survey B used the Internet for professional development in some way (either for correspondence, information gathering, or some other way), but over one quarter did not use it in the classroom. The numbers are similar for those who had used the Internet for at least a year and those who used it daily.

Only three Survey B respondents did not use Internet correspondence for professional development. Two of these three indicated that they plan to in the future. The most common methods of correspondence were email (almost all respondents) and USENET newsgroupss (well over half of the respondents). A smaller, but still significant number (over one quarter) used mailing lists, and a handful mentioned some form of real-time chat (e.g. ytalk or IRC).

Of those who used Internet correspondence for professional development, over 90% found it effective, and the rest felt that it has the potential to be so. Just over half cited reasons which indicate such correspondence broadens their perspective. Almost one quarter said that it provides immediate feedback at little to no cost and is therefore an efficient method of communication, and several mentioned that this kind of correspondence is generally motivating and uplifting.

Is this use of the Internet [correspondence] effective for you as a teacher? Why?[2]

> "I find that I am keeping abreast of my field of study and also about changes that are taking place in education reform throughout the US."

> "It broadens my perspectives tremendously and it allows me to be exposed to ideas and projects that I would otherwise never have access to."

> "I find new ideas and ways of solving old problems. I enjoy reading about others trials and tribulations — it creates a sense of belonging in a larger world."

All but three of our respondents also indicated that they gathered information from the Internet for professional development. The two most common ways they gathered information on the Internet were doing online research and downloading lesson plans; almost 80% of the respondents gave one of those two responses. Less than a quarter of the respondents indicated that they download software from the Internet.

Many found that gathering information on the Internet was an effective professional development tool (again, broadening perspective and efficiency were cited as important reasons). However, almost a quarter found that it was ineffective or not yet effective for some reason. Most of these respondents simply felt they were too inexperienced too fully appreciate the effectiveness, but a full third felt that it took too much time, and 10% thought it just too difficult.

Is this use of the Internet [gathering information] effective for you as a teacher? Why?

> "I am not sure that effective is the appropriate term, but it is certainly useful. Certainly, I glean a lot of useful information and ideas — it is like going to a conference without the cost"

> "I think the net requires a great deal of time to beneficially tap its resources. You can spend only so much time playing before you have to do the work of a classroom teacher"

Many respondents used the Internet in other ways, including for personal correspondence, gathering information not specifically job-related, hobbies, business transactions, and planning meetings. Most felt these uses were generally effective for the same reasons.

---

2   We wanted to present the quotes from our respondents as accurately as possible, so we did not make any changes unless they were absolutely necessary. Misspellings and incorrect grammar are common on the Internet and are more often the result of rapid typing than ignorance.

Is this use of the Internet [other uses] effective for you as a teacher? Why?

"If I need to reach 6 teachers at other schools, I no longer have to play telephone tag — instead, I send them a message, they read and respond, usually quicker than if we were doing it by phone. ... As a glorified answering machine it is wonderful."

"I reach a larger number of people. It's free so expenses are nil. I meet and make new friends."

"as I explore more on my own I find new sources that are classroom related."

Survey results - Professional development analysis

There are three key elements to the professional development results: 1) respondents were more likely to use the Internet for professional development than they are to use it in their classrooms, 2) respondents found correspondence to be a highly effective use of the Internet, whereas other uses (such as gathering information) were thought to be less effective, 3) the primary reasons for the effectiveness of these uses were broadening of perspective, efficiency and affordability, and motivation.

Although we did not intend our results to be generalizable, the first of these elements may be particularly dependent on our methodology. We specifically asked people who received Survey A to send it on to teachers who were using the Internet in their classrooms, but we were much more likely to receive responses from teachers who use the Internet for email and USENET than for classroom projects alone. Also, since we offered to send the results of this survey to anyone who participated (and almost all respondents indicated that they would like to see the results), the act of responding to this survey could itself be considered a way of using the Internet for professional development.

On the other hand it is instructive that our respondents were also enthusiastic about using the Internet, especially Internet correspondence, for professional development. The respondents were not as excited about gathering information on the Internet, and some complained that they did not have enough time or found it difficult to use. This is not surprising considering the complexity of the Internet and its lack of a comprehensive index. But it does show that our respondents, though they are all Internet users, are not all Internet evangelists. Though they appreciate certain uses of the Internet for professional development, they are more critical of other uses.

Survey results - Classroom use

We considered two sets of data to investigate classroom use of the Internet. First, we asked our respondents to describe a project in which they participated which involved the Internet in a K-12 classroom. Twenty-four (24) respondents gave examples of such projects. Next, we examined a descriptive listing of Internet projects compiled by Jeanne Baugh and archived on the CICNet. This set contained fifty-two (52) projects which involved the Internet in a K-12 classroom. By analyzing the projects in both sets we distinguished fifteen common elements of use. The graph below gives an idea of the frequency of each element in either data set. The elements are described below the graph for ease of reference.

Common elements of Internet use

Term	Definition
access	students access outside resources such as experts or powerful supercomputers which could be accessed without using the Internet (e.g. via field trip or letter)
collaborate	students work with other students to create a single project over the Internet
compete	students compete with each other over the Internet, either by submitting work for competition or by sharing results of athletic achievements
correspond	students correspond with other individuals (usually other students)
create	students create Internet resources (usually World Wide Web pages)
discuss	students discuss issues with other groups (usually groups of students)
exchange	students from different schools exchange their work, often grading or critiquing each other's work
explore	students simply explore the Internet to find what it holds
observe	students read regular bulletins about an event, such as the Iditarod, essentially observing the event from a distance
participate	students join others in an inter-school planned activity
publish	students publish their own work on the Internet
research	students use the Internet to research a topic
simulate	students use the Internet to simulate an activity, such as a space shuttle mission
survey	students survey others (usually other students) on the Internet
use	students use resources specific to the Internet, such as the Geographic Name Server or the World Factbook

Although many of the projects contained more than one of these elements, no one element was present in more than a quarter of the seventy-six projects included in both data sets. This gives an indication of the incredible variety of Internet projects available to the K-12 classroom teacher.

Several elements were more common to projects in our data sets than others. "Exchange" and "research" projects were common in both our survey data set and the CICNet data set. "Publish" projects were more common in the CICNet data set, and "correspond," "access," "participate," and "survey" projects were more common in the survey data set. "Correspond" projects were particularly common in the survey data set, one quarter of all respondents' projects included some element of correspondence, as did two-thirds of the projects from respondents who had been Internet users for two years or less. Other elements were mostly uncommon or common to one data set and nonexistent in the other. "Simulate" and "collaborate" projects were especially rare.

Other questions we asked of our respondents gave us a deeper insight into the projects in the survey data set. For example, more than 90% of these projects had students working individually at least some of the time, and almost three-quarters had them working in groups some of the time. Only a third were entire class projects.

Over half of our respondents who considered their project successful cited elements of student motivation for the success. This motivation was derived from a variety of sources, which are best described in the quotes below. Teacher commitment, organization and preparation, and various logistical factors (such as funding and equipment) were also cited by many of the respondents as elements which contributed to their project's success.

What elements contributed to [your project's] success?

> "The excitement of the Net itself, most of the students had no idea something like that was out there."

> "Publicly available data caused the feeling of being needed."

> "Exchanging and comparing data with students from other areas added authenticity and some sense of excitement."

> "Involvement by students, real information, real-time communication, student-generated questions"

> "I think that serendipity of the experience is an important element for student use of the Internet. It serves as a powerful motivator. I would not like to see student use so tightly controlled that they never get to find things on their own. The Internet is one of the last frontiers they can explore."

> "The students felt a tremendous sense of accomplishment that they had used their language skills to communicate with native German speakers to get information. Many now use these resources on an everyday basis on their own."

> "Careful planning!! KIDLINK offer projects about once per month, and these are always planned and moderated so they are very successful."

> "The organization of the projects were great. The small groups were purposely arranged as I wanted the students to experience success the first time they participated. ... The projects were not real difficult for the students either which led to their success and their desire to do more things with computers."

When asked what they might do to improve their project, a full 10% of the respondents explicitly stated "not much" or "nothing," which speaks to the high degree of success of these projects (or, possibly, the weariness of our respondents). However, better access to the Internet, more time for the projects, and the teacher or students having more familiarity with the Internet were each cited by a quarter of the respondents as ways of making their project more successful.

What would you change to the make the project or lesson more successful?

> "I would arrange to have greater accessibility to online services. ... As well, I would start the projects earlier in the year so that students could see the value in using the net for projects that they are doing later on in the year."

> "I needed more time. I would have liked to of had time for the students to add some of the changes that people suggested to them."

> "I needed to do more preparation. Specific to the Internet, access ... was not always available, or often required many tries. This

frustrated the kids (although it isn't a bad lesson - things don't always go smoothly.)"

"Sorry I am not more advanced. For many teachers, I think that the learning curve of the Internet is daunting. An educator's friendly format would be a real plus."

"Have a more comprehensive list of resources with topics that are good for students to use."

"I need to learn more about resources available on the Internet, how to use Internet search tools, and how to make contact with people who can provide meaningful information for students."

"I would use a text editor that is easier for the students to work with. They made more errors than normal because they were not completely comfortable with the technology and the editor."

Survey results - Classroom use analysis

There are many, many different ways to use the Internet in the classroom and a plethora of suggestions for use and ongoing projects teachers may take advantage of right now. Most of these involve students contacting students in some way: by corresponding with other students, discussing issues with groups, exchanging work, competing for prizes, surveying each other, or a host of other ways. When students aren't contacting students, they are usually doing research, either directly on the Internet or by contacting experts.

It is interesting to note the differences between our two data sets. From their descriptions, it is obvious that many of the projects from the CICNet data set were placed on the Internet as a call for participants. It was impossible for us to judge how successful they were. On the other hand, our survey data set was compiled from respondents who were, for the most part, active K-12 teachers who found their projects to be successful. The fact that "correspond" projects were the most common among our survey data set, and especially that two-thirds of the new Internet users had some element of correspondence in their projects, may arise from the relative ease of implementation of projects involving correspondence. It may also arise from the fact that our respondents are generally proficient email and USENET users.

From what we can tell the successful projects our respondents described were successful for many of the same reasons any project is successful in a K-12 classroom. Teacher commitment, preparation, and organization are essential. However, there are some extra benefits of involving the Internet in these projects. The Internet allows contact with other students, often provides "real-world" relevance for the project, and creates the general excitement of using a new technology.

Unfortunately, the newness of this technology also creates difficulties for teachers attempting to implement Internet projects in their classroom. Many respondents cited problems with access or a lack of familiarity with the Internet when asked how they might improve their projects. Lack of time, that bane of the teaching profession, may be aggravated by the Internet.

Survey results - General use

The variety of responses to our question about the best uses of the Internet for a K-12 teacher made it very difficult to categorize the results. Several respondents mentioned specific Internet projects, but many described general uses. We first divided the latter responses into those who suggested teacher uses and those who suggested student uses, and then redivided those responses into those who suggested some sort of interaction with peers (either correspondence or sharing/exchanging information) and those who suggested using the Internet to do research or gather information.

In general, respondents suggested students and teachers use the Internet to interact with their peers more often than they suggested using the Internet to do research. Also, respondents were more likely to suggest having teachers use the Internet over having students use the Internet. However, categorizing these responses was difficult enough to make any results tentative. Again, specific quotes from our respondents are probably more instructive in this case than generalities.

What would you suggest as the best use of the Internet for a K-12 teacher?

"I would suggest that it is the teaching of effective writing (this is an English teacher speaking remember). When students can connect with real audiences and the communication of real information for critical research or simply honest curiosity becomes the focus, we will find that student writing will improve."

"World Wide Web. Mosaic motivates the students. It is easy and has pictures. The Internet needs to be a resource."

"Getting involved in projects, like Ask Prof. Maths, Mathemagic, the Santa Letters, the geography projects, penpals with other countries, recipe projects..."

"It is very early to tell. Inter-teacher communication and support are important. Collaborations and consultations. Obtaining up-to-date, authentic information for use in classes is a very valuable ability. ... I'm positive that all kinds of new uses will be developed - ones we can't predict yet."

"Prepare students for the 21st Century ... Increase school connections to community and public"

"Depends on the teacher and her or his orientation. I especially like the Internet for a tool necessary to do research."

"Resource for themselves [teachers] and for their students. The key is for teachers to develop the comfort to empower the kids to go on-line and do their own exploring."

"Internet is an avenue for broadening personal and professional skills. Use will depend on the user's level of interest and need. I start most people with e-mail. On the other hand one teacher needed information available from ERIC which I obtained for her. She will probably not use Internet again for some time."

Responses to the "What should teachers avoid?" question were much more clear than the responses to the "What do you suggest?" question. Internet chat, MUD games, and some inappropriate USENET groups (especially those in the alt. category) were the most common responses. These respondents suggested that educators beware the adult nature of some areas of the Internet. Another common suggestion was avoiding the incredible time drain which the Internet causes. One eighth of the respondents suggested that there was nothing teachers should avoid on the Internet.

What would you suggest K-12 teachers avoid on the Internet?

"I have reservations about the mud games and chat lines. In theory they seem harmless, but I have had a couple of students get hooked on them (one was playing mud games an average of 7 hours a day, another met a kook through the chat lines that wouldn't leave her alone)."

"Open access! It HAS to be a moderated environment."

"Right now, I'd say it is important to avoid the "time swamp"; it is easy to spend huge amounts of time cruising the net. While it is fun, and stimulating, the amount of directly useful information which results is still small in proportion to the time spent."

"K-12 teachers should realize that the Internet is not a secure system. E-mail is not necessarily private, and responses to a posting on a listserv will reach a very wide audience. I think K-12 teachers should avoid flaming and otherwise inconsiderate behavior and should be very careful with the e-mail they send and receive."

"Getting discouraged by the disorganization and apparent confusion. Watch out for information overload."

At the very end of Survey B we asked our respondents for comments. Since many of the respondents used this opportunity to summarize their opinions and feelings about the use of the Internet in K-12 education, we thought it would be appropriate to conclude our research with their observations.

If you have any other comments, please include them here.

"The increased use of the Internet in the classroom will undoubtedly produce some very exciting teaching ideas. It needs to be easily accessible, not limited to the computer literate-elite (as my school's current system seems to be). When it is simply a classroom resource rather than a fad or gadget the truly creative applications will show up (and have already started showing up, of course)."

"I suspect that those of us who work and live in relatively isolated areas (I'm from Yellowknife, Northwest Territories) find the benefits of Internet far greater than someone who works in a large city. We simply do not have access to a number of the agencies and organizations that teachers in a large city do. As a result the opportunity that the Internet provides is quite important."

"A bonus to the program would be that my students have made incredible strides in their research and writing skills. They have developed a thirst for knowledge like I have never seen before in a group of sixth graders. One student explained his experience as, 'For once in my life I feel like there are adults who feel like I have something important to share. They actually want to carry on a conversation with me about a topic that I am interested in! The neat thing is that these people are not just anybody, they are professionals like from NASA or universities. Now I think I understand what it must be like to be an adult, and why it is important to keep current on the things that are happening around me.' That statement in itself tells all."

"It seems that because it is virtually anonymous, people feel free to be rude on Internet. I believe that it takes a great deal of talk, discussion, policy making to help guide students and teachers to properly use Internet offerings. Communication through the written format is not easy."

"Somehow we have to help teachers know where the appropriate resources for themselves and their kids are located. as a former librarian I fear too much censorship however there are places on the net kids do NOT need to go. We also have to make sure students know how to cite materials they use from the net... plagiarism is still an issue and one needs to know how to give credit to those who have provided the data."

"It's fun! Playing around on the Internet for professional or personal purposes is just plain fun!"

"If we are trying to decide how to fit the Internet into existing curriculum, we are missing the point. We need to change our curriculum to adapt to the possibilities that information and communication technologies present."

"I have not had any formal training so my knowledge is limited. I love what I do know and my students are fighting over who gets on Internet in the classroom. They love it."

"ALL TEACHERS NEED INTERNET ACCESS!!!!!!!!!!!!!!!!!!!!!!!!!!"

Conclusion

Because we plan to use the Internet as K-12 teachers, we used this action research project to identify common elements of effective Internet use. We surveyed educators over the Internet, thereby ensuring that we would reach educators who were at least marginally proficient with the Internet.

We did, in fact, reach a wide variety of such educators from all over the continental United States and from several other countries. They ranged in experience from new Internet users and new educators to veterans in either or both areas, and most, but not all were active classroom teachers. They were enthusiastic about the possibilities for the Internet in K-12 education, and they described effective professional development uses as well as successful classroom projects. By categorizing their responses we were able to identify key suggestions for effective Internet use.

The educators who responded to our survey were more likely to use the Internet for professional development than to use it in their classrooms directly. They indicated that this use of the Internet broadens one's perspectives, that it is efficient, affordable, and highly motivating. Although this result may be a consequence of our methodology, there was some indication that this type of use was less problematic. ·

When using the Internet for professional development, our respondents generally preferred using it to correspond with other educators and keep up-to-date in their field via email, mailing lists, and the USENET over doing research or gathering information on the Internet. The latter requires more experience and a greater time commitment.

We found a wide variety of classrooms uses for the Internet in our survey responses and on the Internet itself. Most of these uses involved students contacting students in some way.

The elements of successful Internet projects identified by our respondents were similar to those found in any successful classroom project: teacher commitment, preparation, and organization are essential. However, our respondents also indicated that the Internet itself provides students with extra motivation, not only because of its newness, but because it connects them with the outside world.

Our respondents' biggest problems with the Internet in classroom projects were mainly technical. They cited problems accessing the Internet, finding resources, and spending too much time for the results. The newness of the technology makes for a steep learning curve for many educators.

There were no prevailing suggestions for educators using the Internet in the responses to our survey. However, many of our respondents expressed a concern for the adult nature of some areas of the Internet, and suggested that student access be restricted.

The Internet is still a new technology for educators, and as such it can be difficult to incorporate into a teacher's work schedule. However, our research indicates that it can be quite useful for K-12 educators. Many of those who responded to our survey indicated at some point or another that it is, in fact, indispensable to them. With the wisdom we have gleaned from their responses, we believe it will become indispensable to us as well.

Survey A

The Masters in Teaching department of Seattle University is conducting
a research survey on effective teaching methods using the Internet. The
results of this survey will be used to improve Internet use in
Seattle-area classrooms. If you are a K-12 teacher or are working with
K-12 teachers, please take a moment to respond to these questions:

(Please type "Y" or "N" at the end of each line, then return this mail
to:mit-rsch@seattleu.edu)

Are you currently teaching in a K-12 classroom?

Do you use the Internet as part of your curriculum?

Do you use the Internet for professional development?(i.e. to
communicate with other teachers, to find lesson plans, etc.)

Would you be willing to respond to a longer email survey about your use
of the Internet?

If so, would you like to receive the results of this survey via e-mail?

If you know of anyone who is using the Internet in a K-12 classroom,
please forward this mail to them.

Thank you for your assistance in this project.

Deborah Wilson, chair
MIT Research Group
mit-rsch@seattleu.edu

Survey B

Thank you for agreeing to participate in a survey of effective
educational uses of the Internet. As the Internet grows at an
astounding rate, more and more teachers are trying to find ways of
incorporating it into their work. We would like to know how you use the
Internet, so that we may compare your experiences with those of other
educators and find common elements which make the Internet an effective
tool for K-12 teachers.

Please use the following form to tell us about your experiences. We
know that you don't have a lot of time to fill out surveys, but if you
could be as detailed as possible in your responses it will help us pick
out the essential elements of successful (or unsuccessful) projects. If
you have so indicated, we will send you our results this summer. Also,
be aware that we plan to post the results on the Internet, so if you
include any information which should remain confidential, please mark
it as such (personal information—your name, your e-mail address,
etc.-will not be used unless you have given us permission to do so).

Thank you again for your time.

Sincerely,

Deborah Wilson
Douglas Steen
Mari Andonian

***

Helpful Hint: Many of our questions require yes/no responses. For those
questions, you can simply type Y or N before or after the question to
indicate your answer.

Personal Information

Name:
E-mail Address (if not replying from your own account):
May we include your name and e-mail address in our report?

Are you currently teaching in a K-12 classroom?

If not, how are you involved in K-12 education?

What is your primary teaching assignment (i.e. grade level, subject area)?

How long have you been involved in K-12 education?

How long have you been using the Internet?

How often do you use the Internet (# of times per week)?

Do you have access to the Internet at home?

Do you have access to the Internet at school/your workplace?

Internet uses - Professional development

Do you use the Internet to correspond with other educators?

If so, please describe how (e.g. e-mail colleagues, USENET discussions,...)

Is this use of the Internet effective for you as a teacher?

Why?

Do you use the Internet to gather information for your professional use?

If so, please describe how (e.g. download lesson plans, online research,...)

Is this use of the Internet effective for you as a teacher?

Why?

Do you use the Internet in other ways that do not directly affect the classroom? If so, please describe how (e.g. plan meetings, obtain district info,...)

Is this use of the Internet effective for you as a teacher?

Why?

Internet uses - Student activities

Do your students use the Internet for class projects/lessons? If so, please describe a project or lesson in which your students used the Internet.

The following questions refer to the project or lesson you have described: Please describe the class involved (i.e. grade level, subject, gifted/special ed.,...).

Did your students use the Internet individually, in groups, or as a class?

Did your students communicate with others over the Internet?

If so, with whom did they communicate?

Did your students access information over the Internet?

If so, where (e.g. electronic libraries, encyclopedias, news services,..)?

Was this project successful?

What elements contributed to its success?

What would you change to the make the project or lesson more successful?

Internet uses - General

What would you suggest as the best use of the Internet for a K-12 teacher?

What would you suggest K-12 teachers avoid on the Internet?

If you have any other comments, please include them here.

Glossary

▼▼▼▼▼▼▼▼▼▼▼▼

Like the field of education, the Internet has a parlance all its own.Here are some of the terms you're likely tto encounter as you read this book and surf the Internet.

Adapted from The Internet Users' Dictionary, by William H. Holt and Rockie J. Morgan (Resolution Business Press, 1995)—©William H. Holt, 1995.

▲▲▲▲▲▲▲▲▲▲▲▲

academic rationalism   A theory of teaching which emphasizes use of the "great works." Teachers basing their work on academic rationalism often use the work of famous thinkers and artists to inspire their students.

acceptable use policy   A contract from an Internet service provider which defines appropriate and inappropriate use of an Internet account. Most Internet service providers, whether commercial or school-run, will ask you to sign an acceptable use policy statement before providing your account.

American Standard Code for Information Interchange (ASCII)   Defines a standard set of characters. Computers send files to one another in ASCII to avoid conflicting file formats. E-mail messages are composed of ASCII text, so you can't use bold, italic, underlined or other fancy format.

anonymous ftp   A means of transferring files from a host computer on the Internet to your Internet service provider's computer. When asked for your name, you enter "anonymous;" when asked for your password, you enter your electronic mail address. This gives you access to the files on the host computer and allows the host computer administrators to contact you if necessary.

article   A message posted to a Usenet newsgroup.

bits per second (bps)   A measurement of the speed at which data is transferred over a modem. To determine the number of characters a modem is capable of transferring per second, divide the bps rating by 10, e.g. a 4,800 bps modem is capable of transferring 480 characters per second.

body   The section of an e-mail message that contains the actual information your are receiving or sending (the message itself).

bookmarks   Also called hotlists in some World Wide Web browsers. These electronic pointers let you store the addresses of Web sites you plan to use frequently.

case sensitivity   The ability of a software program or programming language to distinguish between upper and lower case. E-mail addresses are case-insensitive, meaning that Internet.For.Teachers@POBox.com will be treated exactly like internet.for.teachers@pobox.com. World Wide Web pages have case-sensitive addresses (URLs). It is therefore essential that you type a URL exactly as it is written.

catch-up   To mark all of the articles in a certain newsgroup as already read. This is normally done at the end of a newsgroup session, so that the next time you read the newsgroup, these articles will not appear.

cognitive processes   A theory of teaching which emphasizes the development of thinking skills, with the intent of transferring these skills to other subjects. Teachers working from cognitive process theory will look for activities which stretch their students' cognitive abilities.

commercial networks   Companies such as Compuserve, America Online, and Prodigy, which support their own, private networks. These networks offer added services, such as online stock trading, as well as access to the Internet, and are usually more expensive than a simple Internet account.

cruising   Cruising the Net has several possible meanings, such as: sending an e-mail message directly to one person; browsing a newsgroup and posting a message to everyone who browses that group; or tapping into an informational server via the World Wide Web or gopher.

cyberspace   The online world. Cyberspace encompasses anything you can find over networked computers.

default home page   The first page that appears on your screen when you load your World Wide Web browser.

dial-up access   Describes a temporary connection to a computer or network using a modem and phone line. It's cheaper, and slower, than direct access.

direct access   Describes a permanent connection to a computer or network. Direct access is faster than dial-up access, but it is also more expensive and rarely used in homes.

discussion group   A type of electronic mailing list or Usenet forum.

discussion list   A type of electronic mailing list that encourages subscribers to exchange ideas and information. It may be monitored by the person or persons who administer the list so that discussions stay on track.

distribution list   A type of electronic mailing list that acts more like a newsletter or bulletin. It compiles and edits notices and news items from subscribers and others about a particular subject, and then e-mails this information to subscribers.

domain name   The mnemonic address used to make the Internet (or IP) addresses used by most computers more intelligible to humans. For instance, when you write to the White House computer, you use the domain name "whitehouse.gov." Your computer, however, sees this as 198.137.240.100.

domain type   Refers to the type of organization (in the United States, government, military, educational, commercial, non-profit or network). It is shown as the three letters at the far right of a domain name (whitehouse.gov).

download   Moving data or software packages from one computer to another, usually from a host computer to a client (your computer).

electronic mail (e-mail)   The oldest and most widely used form of communication on the Internet. Using an e-mail program, you can send messages, documents, even pictures, to other computer users around the globe.

File Transfer Protocol (FTP)   A protocol that lets you transfer files from a host computer on the Internet to your computer, using an FTP program. You can download software, images, sound files, and electronic texts from several FTP archives around the Internet. Certain FTP archives are now wrapped in World Wide Web pages, letting you download files just by pointing and clicking.

finger   An Internet service designed to let you find information about a person given a portion of their name or electronic mail address. For this service to work, you must already know the name of the person's host computer (which is part of their electronic mail address), and that host computer must run the finger software. For this reason, it is best used to determine a person's real name from their e-mail address, rather than the other way around.

flame   An inflammatory or insulting message sent over the Internet. Sending such files is known as "flaming," and when two people begin flaming each other it is called a "flame war."

follow-up   To post an article to a newsgroup in reply to another article. Usually the follow-up article contains relevant portions of the original article.

forms   Electronic questionnaires that are found on home pages on the World Wide Web, including those that help you search for information. They also are found at Web sites that have some kind of interactive feature so that you can set parameters or choose items, like building a wildlife migratory map or coloring a picture. Forms are graphical, so you need a Web browser like Mosaic or Netscape to view them

freeware   Software written by people for their own use and then distributed free of charge to others.

Frequently Asked Questions (FAQs)   A list of common questions and their answers. Most newsgroups and some mailing lists have FAQs which new users are encouraged to read.

globe   The icon in the upper right corner of the screen in Mosaic and some other browsers. (Netscape Navigator uses a capital N instead.) When the globe is turning, it indicates that the program is either retrieving or waiting for data.

gopher   A software program developed at the University of Minnesota (and named for that schools mascot). When you run gopher, you can burrow to thousands of informational servers just by clicking on folders and file namesyour screen resembles Windows File Manager and the Macintosh Finder. Gopher files contain only plain text, with no graphics or sound. Many World Wide Web browsers now also give you gopher access.

graphical connection An Internet hook-up which allows you to point and click your way around the Internet, instead of being restricted to a text-only interface. Graphical connections are also known as SLIP or PPP connections.

Graphics Interchange Format (GIF) A graphic file format, developed by the CompuServe online service, that is widely used on the World Wide Web because it reduces the amount of time required to transmit an image over phone lines.

hacker A computer-oriented hooligan.

header The part of an e-mail message similar to the address on the front of an envelope. It contains information mainly for the computer, such as where the message came from, where its going and its format.

home page The opening page of a Web site. When you enter a site, you usually start at the home page, which may branch off to other pages.

host address Commonly called an Internet Protocol (or IP) address The numbered address used to identify computers on the Internet. Your computer is usually assigned an IP address when you log on to your Internet service providers computer. For home accounts, the address generally changes every time you connect. When you try to access another computer, such as the one at the White House, you enter a domain name (whitehouse.gov) which the computers helping you translate into its IP addresses (198.137.240.100).

hotlist Another name for what are called bookmarks in some World Wide Web browsers. A list of Internet resources you plan to use frequently. By selecting a resource from a hotlist, you can go directly to it without entering an address.

hotspot Underlined text or an images surrounded by blue or green borders on the World Wide Web. By clicking on the text or image, you are linked to another page on the same server or to a different server entirely.

hyperlink A link between two related pieces of information. By clicking the link, which is usually displayed as underlined text by a World Wide Web browser, you can move electronically to another document that may be located anywhere in the world.

hypermedia Also called hypertext. A document that contains links to other documents or media, including sound, graphics, and video files. Links can point to items within the same document or anywhere else in the world on the Internet.

HyperText Markup Language (HTML) The language used to create documents for the World Wide Web. HTML lets an author lay out a Web pageplace graphics, set the size of text elements, install links to other documents, and so on. Web browsers take arriving HTML information and build the page onscreen.

HyperText Transfer Protocol (HTTP) The language computers speak to each other to transfer World Wide Web data.

Information Superhighway The term used by Vice President Al Gore for the National Information Infrastructure (NII), the U.S. Administration's vision of a huge, high-speed, interactive data network that would encompass even the Internet.

inline graphic   An image that is embedded in text or appears on a line beside text.

Integrated Services Digital Network (ISDN)   A means of connecting to the Internet which allows fast, dedicated service. Most often used for direct access only.

interactive   Describes any electronic resource that allows you to do more than passively read information. More and more home pages on the World Wide Web are creating interactive features to allow users to play games, create maps, color pictures, ask questions, and so on.

Internet (or Net)   A worldwide network of computer networks that enables people who connect to it to do research and to communicate online.

Internet access   The right to use software programs on a host computer which is connected to the Internet. These software programs provide Internet services, such as file transfer (FTP), remote computer access (TELNET) and newsgroups (Usenet).

Internet account   Personal space on a host computer, which is connected to the Internet through the organization that provides your Internet access. Having your own Internet account means that you can browse or search the Internet using various software programs and services, send and receive e-mail, as well as store personal files.

Internet Protocol (or IP) address   Also called a host address. The numbered address used to identify computers on the Internet. Your computer is usually assigned an IP address when you log on to your Internet service providers computer. For home accounts, the address generally changes every time you connect. When you try to access another computer, such as the one at the White House, you enter a domain name (whitehouse.gov) which the computers helping you translate into its IP addresses (198.137.240.100).

Internet service   A means of communicating and/or accessing the information resources of the Internet. Services include e-mail, the World Wide Web, gopher, FTP, TELNET and Usenet newsgroups. To use a service you need a specific type of software program, such as a browser for the World Wide Web. With the Webs rapidly growing popularity, many Web browsers are beginning to build in access to some other services as well, eliminating the need for multiple programs.

Internet service provider   The organization that provides you access to the Internet. For home computer users, this is usually a commercial entity.

Joint Photographic Experts Group (JPEG)   A standard for compressing graphic images, named for the committee that developed it. JPEG is typically used to compress photographs. Not all Web browsers can directly display JPEG imagesyou may need a second software application.

keyword   The particular word or phrase you enter in a questionnaire-type form onscreen to tell a search tool, such as Lycos, what you want it to look for on the Internet.

kill file   A list of newsgroup users whose articles you do not want to read. When you read a newsgroup, any article from a person in the kill file will not appear. Individual users can then ignore a rude or unpleasant participant.

link A connection from one World Wide Web page to another. Clicking on a link in your Web browser will open a new Web page. Usually links are highlighted in a different color, and underlined.

listserv An electronic mailing list, especially one that uses one of the LISTSERV mailing list management programs.

log on (or log in) : Generally, to establish a connection with a computer system. Specifically, to give a command that identifies the user to the computer and starts a process of validating the user's password.

log on name The name given by a user to a computer to establish a connection with the system.

lurking Monitoring a mailing list or Usenet newsgroup, but never posting a message or article.

mailing list A group of people with a common interest who sign up to regularly exchange messages by e-mail or receive a periodic summary of the messages. Some mailing lists serve as discussion forums for a particular topic; they may be moderated, but most are not. Other lists serve more as bulletins or newsletters that compile messages submitted by subscribers. Lists are founded and often maintained and moderated by listowners. Each develops its own customs and rules, and its often a good idea to monitor a list before posting a message. Mailing lists usually have a smaller but more focused following than Usenet newsgroups.

megabyte (MB) A measurement of storage (of a storage device, such as a hard drive or diskette), memory (of a computer) or communications transmission capacity. It actually equals 1,048,576 bytes.

modem A device used for data communications over telephone lines. It converts analog (telephone) signals to digital (computer) signals, and vice versa. Modems come packaged internally with most new computers, but can be added either internally or externally to older computers.

moderated A newsgroup or mailing list run by a human being. This person moderates the newsgroup or mailing list by screening each message which comes through.

Mosaic The first World Wide Web browser, developed by the National Center for Supercomputing Applications (NCSA) at the University of Illinois. Released in 1993, Mosaic has become the standard tool for browsing the Web. NCSA continues to develop free versions of Mosaic, but several commercial software developers have licensed the program and sell modified versions of it.

Moving Picture Experts Group (MPEG) A method of digitizing video and audio, named for the committee that developed it. MPEG allows computers to store and display motion pictures or animations. Most Web browsers dont include built-in MPEG viewer programs. While MPEG movies tend to be jerky, the technology will improve, and many expect MPEG to prevail over competing standards, such as QuickTime and AVI.

netiquette   Etiquette on the Internet. Rules of netiquette have been written by Internet veterans who are attempting to perpetuate the open, communal atmosphere of the Internet.

Netscape Navigator   A popular World Wide Web browser developed by Netscape Communications Corp., the company that hired many of the NCSA programmers who developed Mosaic.

network   A group of computers that are interconnected to allow data to be exchanged.

newsgroup   A forum on Usenet to which people with a common interest post messages (or articles) containing questions and comments. There are more than 10,000 Usenet newsgroups.

newsreader   A software program that enables you to read and post articles (or messages) to Usenet newsgroups.

online service   A commercial entity, such as CompuServe, America Online and Prodigy, which offers various online services to its paid subscribers, such as e-mail, discussion forums, information resources, and, to varying degrees, access to the Internet.

packet switching   A method of transmitting data over telephone lines on a communications network. The data is bundled and sent in packets, or envelopes, over multiple routes. The data can be switched from one path to another if a traffic jam occurs or a more direct route becomes available.

personal relevance   A theory of teaching which emphasizes the importance of allowing the student to determine her own path of learning. Teachers who believe in using personal relevance will act as guides on the learner's journey to understanding.

Point-to-Point Protocol (PPP)   A means of connecting to the Internet so that point-and-click interaction is possible. See graphical connection.

post   To send a message or article to an electronic mailing list or newsgroup.

query   The request that you send through your computer to an online database. By setting parameters, you can specify the type of information you want the database to find and display.

QuickTime   A standard for digitizing video and sound developed by Apple Computer, Inc.

real time   Synchronous communication.For instance, a phone conversation happens in real time; mail correspondence does not.

remote access   See Teletype Network (telnet).

reply   An electronic mail message written in response to an original message. Most electronic mail readers will allow you to reply automatically by clicking a button or pressing a key. The text of the original message may also be included automatically, so that you can comment upon it in your reply.

robot-generated index   A search tool used to search the World Wide Web for files containing specific words or phrases.

search tools   Internet services which help you find information on the Internet. Most search tools are designed to search for a specific kind of information. Archie, for instance, searches for files available via FTP, and

322 APPENDIX D—Glossary

Veronica searches for items in a gopher system. World Wide Web search engines allow you to search for Web pages, as well as files and gopher menus.

Serial Line Protocol (SLIP)   A means of connecting to the Internet so that point-and-click interaction is possible. See graphical connection.

server   A computer system that provides service, such as a database sharing, e-mail routing and file transfer, or controls the devices which it makes available for use by client computers (like yours).

shareware   Software made available for general use without charge. The developer may ask those who use it to pay a nominal fee

signature file (sig file)   A file that you may create, store, and automatically attach at the end of your outgoing e-mail messages. It can contain your job title, postal address, Internet addresses (such as e-mail and home page addresses), phone and fax numbers, and even a quotation or ASCII drawing that sums up your personal philosophy of life.

smiley   A means of expressing humor within a limited character set. To read a smiley, tilt your head to the left. =)

snail mail   Describes letters delivered relatively slowly by the U.S. Postal Service and the post offices of other countries, as opposed to the rapid delivery of electronic-mail messages.

social adaptation   A theory of teaching which emphasizes the role of schooling in preparing the learner for a role in society. Teachers who subscribe to the social adaptation theory will often emphasize civic responsibility and vocational education.

social reconstruction   A theory of teaching which emphasizes preparing the student to critique and help improve their society. Teachers who believe in social reconstruction may also emphasize civic responsibility, but with an eye towards improving, rather than maintaining, the status quo.

source code   The instructions, written in the original programming language, underlying any computer software. In the case of the World Wide Web, source code is written in HTML (HyperText Markup Language) and can be examined from your World Wide Web browser.

spider   A type of search tool that you can use to find information on the Internet.

subject   The line in the header of an e-mail message that indicates what the message is about.

subscribe   To join a mailing list or newsgroup with the intent of reading the messages there or posting your own.

surfing   Another for cruising, or using any or all of the multiple services of the Internet.

tag   A series of ASCII characters which denote a specific style or effect. Used to create World Wide Web pages in HTML (HyperText Markup Language).

Teletype Network (TELNET)   A protocol developed by the Defense Advanced Research Projects Agency that allows you to connect to a computer at another location. That computer (the remote host) lets your computer act like a terminal, or part of its own system. This enables you to access library catalogs. electronic bulletin boards and other information files that some organizations, such as universities, normally only make available to their staff. students and users in their local area. TELNET, a text-based technology, was a forerunner of Internet services like gopher. It is rapidly losing ground to faster and more graphical services like the World Wide Web.

text-only connection An Internet connection which allows only text transfers. All interaction on a text-only connection is restricted to reading and writing ASCII text.

thread A series of articles in a newsgroup, all pertaining to a certain topic. If one person posts an article, and another posts a follow-up article, and still another person posts a follow-up to that follow-up, then these articles constitute a thread.

thumbnail graphic A small image used on World Wide Web home pages that represents and hyperlinks to a larger image. The thumbnail can be a miniature, a portion, or simply something symbolic of the larger image. It gives you an idea of what the larger image will show without forcing you to spend time downloading that graphic. If you do want to view the larger image, just click on the thumbnail with your mouse.

Transmission Control Protocol/Internet Protocol (TCP/IP) The common language spoken by the millions of computers that make up the Internet. It is the program that you run first, before you can load programs to read your e-mail or access the World Wide Web.

Uniform Resource Locator (URL) An identification system that provides the protocol and address of any Internet resource. Every page on the Internet has a unique URL. The basic syntax of URL consists of the protocol, host name, port number and directory path, e.g. the URL for NFSnet backbone statistics is gopher://nic.merit.edu:7043/11/statistics/nsfnet.

unmoderated A newsgroup or mailing list run entirely by computer. Any message sent to such a newsgroup or mailing list will be posted to all subscribers without human intervention.

UNIX The operating system used by most of the large computer systems connected to the Internet. A registered trademark of X/Open Co. Ltd.

Users Network (Usenet) Also called Netnews. A worldwide bulletin-board system that includes more than 10,000 forums (or newsgroups) focusing on different topics. You can use a newsreader program to read other peoples messages (or articles), and post questions and comments.

user name The name given to identify an account on an Internet host computer. Usually a person's user name is constructed from their real name (first initial and last name, for instance), and can be found to the left of the @ sign in an electronic mail address.

V.32bis A data compression standard for 14,400-bps modems.

Web browser Also called a browsing program. A program for navigating and downloading information from the World Wide Web. A browser translates information coming from a Web server so that you can view it on your computer. Popular browsers include Mosaic and Netscape Navigator.

Web page   A file accessible by the World Wide Web. Web pages can contain text, pictures, sounds, and even movies, as well as links to other Web pages.

Web server   A computer connected to the Internet that can take requests from browsers, such as Mosaic, and return files to the browsers.

Webmaster   The person who maintains a World Wide Web site.

Wide Area Information Server (WAIS)   A network information retrieval system used by many servers on the Internet that allows you to search for information by keyword. A WAIS computer indexes the data it stores not just by file names, but by specific words in each file. When you enter a keyword, the server hunts for files that come closest to matching what you're looking for.

wide-area network (WAN)   Multiple computer systems networked over a large geographic area, such as NSFnet.

World Wide Web (Web or WWW)   The most rapidly growing service on the Internet. It is a network of informational servers that features formatted text, graphics, animated movies, and sound. Some Web sites (or home pages) let you read and post messages, and others let you download files using FTP. The Web features hypertext links, letting you click on a highlighted word to call up more informationeven if its based on another server halfway around the world. To access the Web, you need a software program called a browser.

worm   Originally, a worm was a program that could damage a computer by consuming all the machines memory, causing it to crash. The newer worm is a type of search tool which you can use to find specific information on the Internet.

Bibliography

Andonian, M., D. Steen and D. Wilson. "Effective Uses of the Internet for K-12 Teachers." Unpublished: July 1994.

Barlow, John Perry. "Is There a There in Cyberspace?" *Utne Reader* (March-April 1995), pp. 53-56.

Collis, Betty, and Elske Heeren. "Tele-Collaboration and Groupware." *The Computing Teacher* (August-September 1993), pp. 36-38.

Cyberscope section, *Newsweek* (April 17, 1995), p. 13.

Eisner, Elliot W. *The Educational Imagination: On the Design and Education of School Programs.* Old Tappan, N.J.: Macmillan Publishing Co., 1985.

Elmer-Dewitt, Philip. "On a Screen Near You: CyberPorn." *Time* (July 3, 1995), pp. 38-45.

Engst, A., C. Low and M. Simon, M. *Internet Starter Kit.* Indianapolis, Ind.: Hayden Books, 1994.

Harris, J. "Organizing and facilitating telecollaborative projects." *The Computing Teacher* (February 1995), pp. 66-69.

Harris, Judith B. "An Internet-based graduate telecomputing course: Practicing what we preach." *Technology and Teacher Education Annual* (1993), pp. 641-645.

Grassley, Sen. Charles E. "Cyberporn." *Congressional Record, Senate* (June 26, 1995), pp. S9017-S9023.

Honey, Margaret, and Andres Henríquez. *Telecommunications and K-12 Educators: Findings from a National Survey.* New York, N.Y.: Bank Street College of Education, 1993.

King, Nelson. "i-way@internet.com." *Puget Sound Computer User* (April 1995), pp. 1, 26-28.

Krol, Ed. *The Whole Internet User's Guide.* Sebastapol, Calif.: O'Reilly & Associates, Inc., 1994.

Langford, Glenn. *Teaching as a Profession: An Essay in the Philosophy of Education*. Manchester, U.K.: Manchester University Press, 1978.

Leslie, Jacques. "Connecting Kids: Online technology can reform our schools." *Wired* (November 1993), pp. 90-93.

Levine, Sarah L. *Promoting Adult Growth in Schools*. Needham Heights, Mass.: Allyn and Bacon, 1989.

Little, Judith Warren, and Milbrey Wallin (eds.). *Teachers' Work: Individuals, Colleagues, and Contexts*. New York, N.Y.: Teachers College Press, 1993.

Loucks-Horsley, Susan et al. *Continuing to Learn: A Guidebook for Teacher Development*. Andover, Mass.: Regional Laboratory for Educational Improvement of the Northeast and Islands, 1987.

Marcus, Stephen. "Avoiding Roadkill on the Information Highway." *The Computing Teacher*, v. 22:I (1994), pp. 38-41.

Meizel, Janet. "Impact of Technology on Resource Sharing." *Resource Sharing and Information Networks*. v. 8:1. (1992), pp. 127-141.

Merseth, Katherine K. "Supporting Beginning Teachers with Computer Networks," *Journal of Teacher Education*, v. 42:2, pp.140-147.

Rheingold, Howard. *The Virtual Community*. Reading, Mass.: Addison-Wesley, 1993.

Riel, Margaret. "Approaching the Study of Networks." *The Computing Teacher* (December-January 1992), pp. 5-7, 52.

Riel, M. "Telecommunications: Avoiding the black hole" *The Computing Teacher* (December-January 1992), pp. 16-17.

Rimm, Marty. "Marketing Pornography on the Information Superhighway." *Georgetown Law Journal*, v. 83 (June 1995), pp. 1849-1934.

Rosenberg, Scott. "The Porn Polemic." *The San Francisco Examiner* (July 6, 1995).

Sanderson, David W. (ed.) *Smileys*. Sebastopol, Calif.: O'Reilly & Associates, 1993.

Sivin, J.P. and E.R. Bialo. *Ethical use of information technologies in education: Important issues for America's schools.* National Institute of Justice, U.S. Department of Justice, Grant #0JP-91-C-005, 1992.

Stoll, Clifford. *Silicon Snake-Oil.* New York, NY: Bantam/DoubleDay, 1995.

Strudwick, Karen, John Spilker and Jay Arney. *Internet for Parents.* Bellevue, Wash.: Resolution Business Press, Inc., 1995.

Traw, Rick. "School/University Collaboration Via E-Mail." *Tech Trends* (March 1994), pp. 28-31.

van Weert, Tom. "International Cooperation: What's in it for You?" *The Computing Teacher* (April 1994), pp. 32-34.

Watts, Gary D., and Shari Castle. "Electronic Networking and the Construction of Professional Knowledge." *Phi Delta Kappan* (May 1992), pp. 684-689.

Waugh, Michael L., James Levin and Kathleen Smith. "Network-Based Instructional Interactions, Part 2: Interpersonal Strategies." *The Computing Teacher* (March 1994), pp. 48-50.

Waugh, Michael L., James Levin and Kathleen Smith. "Organizing Electronic Network-Based Instructional Interactions: Successful Strategies and Tactics, Part I." *The Computing Teacher* (February 1994), pp. 21-22.

Wiburg, Kärin. "Teaching Science With Technology: Telecommunications and Multimedia." *The Computing Teacher* (April 1994), pp. 6-8.

Index

A

B

C

D

Q

R

S

T

U

Using the Internet for Education and Recreation

From Resolution Business Press

Teaching with the Internet: Putting Teachers Before Technology™

Written by a team of teachers for other Kindergarten through Grade-12 classroom teachers. Through it, teaching professionals will discover why they should consider using the Internet, how they can do so effectively, and which Internet resources are especially useful to teachers. **Douglas Steen, Mark Roddy PhD, Derek Sheffield and Michael Bryan Stout / $16.95 / ISBN 0-945264-19-4**

Secrets of The Webmasters™

Answers from the experts on how to hang up your shingle in the fastest-growing corner of cyberspace, the World-Wide Web. Several dozen Webmasters of successful home pages share their insights and design strategies with individuals and institutions who are ready to create home pages of their own. **Charles Deemer / $18.95 / ISBN 0-945264-20-8**

The Internet Users' Dictionary

Clear, concise definitions and illustrations of more than 3,000 technical and colloquial terms and concepts that have proliferated in cyberspace. **William H. Holt and Rockie J. Morgan / $18.95 / ISBN 0-945264-16-X**

UNIX: An Open Systems Dictionary

An authoritative reference book filled with jargon-free definitions for nearly 7,000 common and uncommon UNIX terms. Filled with examples, illustrations and diagrams. For anyone who uses UNIX and its look-alike operating systems, from managers to maintenance personnel, novice to advanced users. **William H. Holt and Rockie J. Morgan / $24.95 / ISBN 0-945264-14-3**

Internet for Parents

For busy parents (and grandparents) who aren't sure about the Internet and what's in it for their family. Shows how the Internet is being used at home and at chool—and why it's important to get connected to it. Comes with free software to help you access the hundreds of educational online resources described in the book. **Karen Strudwick, John Spilker and Jay Arney / $24.95 / ISBN 0-945264-17-8**

To Order Our Books

Check local bookstores or order direct with your credit card by calling 1-800-397-4612 (or 206-455-4611 locally). We accept VISA, MasterCard and American Express.

You may also send a check or money order (in U.S. funds) to Resolution Business Press. Please add $3 per order for shipping in the United States and Canada, and $12 per order for other countries.

Booksellers and libraries may order direct or through distribution channels including Baker & Taylor and Pacific Pipeline.

Resolution Business Press, Inc.

11101 N.E. Eighth St., Suite 208

Bellevue, WA 98004

(206) 455-4611 / Fax: (206) 455-9143 / 1-800-397-4612 /

e-mail: rbpress@halcyon.com

World Wide Web: http://www.halcyon.com/ResPress/